The Undercover Scientist

The Undercover Scientist

Investigating the Mishaps of Everyday Life

Peter J. Bentley

BOOKS

Published by Random House Books 2008

10 9 8 7 6 5 4 3 2 1

First published in Great Britain in 2008 by
Random House Books
Random House, 20 Vauxhall Bridge Road,
London SW1V 2SA

www.rbooks.co.uk

Addresses for companies within The Random House Group Limited can be found at:
www.randomhouse.co.uk/offices.htm

The Random House Group Limited Reg. No. 954009

A CIP catalogue record for this book
is available from the British Library

ISBN 9781847945235

The Random House Group Limited supports The Forest Stewardship
Council (FSC), the leading international forest certification organisation. All our
titles that are printed on Greenpeace approved FSC certified paper carry the FSC logo.
Our paper procurement policy can be found at www.rbooks.co.uk/environment

Mixed Sources
Product group from well-managed
forests and other controlled sources
www.fsc.org Cert no. TT-COC-2139
© 1996 Forest Stewardship Council

Typeset in TheAntiqua and Interstate by
SX Composing DTP, Rayleigh, Essex

Printed and bound in the UK by
CPI Mackays, Chatham, ME5 8TD

Who is the Undercover Scientist?

When I watch television I can't help being puzzled. I live in a society built on science, but it is a society filled with contradictions in its attitudes. The painstaking efforts of scientists enable our technology to work, our medicines to be trusted, our criminals to be identified. We know the nature of our world, the life that surrounds us and the universe we share, all because of the work of scientists. Yet opinions have become confused. Science is respected, trusted and largely misunderstood. Fewer and fewer children want to study sciences, thinking that such topics are incomprehensible or boring. Even worse, many adults seem to believe that science might even be the cause of new misfortunes in their lives. If scientists hadn't developed computers, we'd never have to worry about them getting viruses. If they hadn't invented superglue, we'd never accidentally stick our fingers together. If they hadn't created the tiny MP3 player, we'd never be able to drop our entire music collection down the toilet. Perhaps, they think, without science our lives would be so much simpler and we would all be happier. (Ignorant, starving, suffering from many medical conditions, living in caves, but happier.)

In this book I'll try and show that this is entirely the wrong way to think about science. Blaming science for mishaps is like blaming the power of speech for all the arguments in the world. Should we abandon speech or simply learn to exploit its power?

Turning your back on science is closing the door to curiosity. It means you have stopped wondering *why*. Science is nothing more or less than our best way of understanding the world around us. It's not a machine or technology. It's just a simple, cynical process followed by a human being: I will believe something is true only when I have enough evidence to support that belief. If I think a new medicine works better, I've got to prove it. If I think a certain material interacts with heat in a specific way,

I have to perform tests to show that it really does. Like a detective gathering evidence to prove the guilt or innocence of a suspect, scientists gather evidence to support or refute an idea. The more evidence that supports it, the more likely it is to be true. But when the evidence does not quite support the idea, that idea is modified, updated and improved, and then the testing begins again.

So if something goes wrong – if my car skids on the road, or my engine is damaged by fuelling with diesel instead of petrol – science is not to blame, but the results of science provide me with explanations of what happened. What I do with that understanding is my own responsibility. In this book I give you that responsibility. I shall open the door to curiosity and help you wonder again, by questioning those sometimes frustrating events that happen to you every day and explaining the best understandings science gives us to date. In the process I'll show that science can be exciting, fascinating – sometimes a little revolting – and makes it easy to understand the true nature of your world.

What do I know about it? I rarely wear a white coat but am often found in the laboratories and offices of computer scientists, biologists, chemists, physicists and many other 'ists'. I also collaborate with artists, musicians, architects, engineers, astronomers, economists and roboticists. I'm a specialist in complex systems with all the complicated-sounding degrees you could wish for (like a doctorate in genetic algorithms and a degree in artificial intelligence). I'm an active scientist, running a research group and training new scientists. I'm also an ordinary person who drives a car, goes to the movies and enjoys a nice meal like everyone else.

I'm the *undercover scientist*. In this book I'll help you become one too.

Contents

Prologue

There are no sirens or flashing lights. No police cordons. No undercover scientists arriving in discreet vans with tinted windows and no clunk of the doors as they step out, wearing sunglasses and carrying impressive black bags full of anonymous equipment. You are on your own. You will have to try and solve the mess in front of you all by yourself. Whether it's a new stain on the expensive rug, your favourite MP3 player rattling around inside the washing machine or chewing gum dangling from your hair, this is your problem. So what are you going to do about it?

You could move a chair over the stain, sorrowfully throw the soggy MP3 player in the kitchen drawer with all the other non-functioning junk or snip out a chunk of your hair. You could tell yourself that it was Murphy's Law (if it can go wrong, it probably will). You could buy some chocolate ice cream and try to tell yourself that it didn't matter anyway.

Or you could become an undercover scientist yourself. You could look through a magnifying glass and discover the science behind your mishaps. You could understand exactly what went wrong and why. Soon a mishap won't spoil your day any more than a crime spoils the day of a policeman, for you will know exactly what to do to clear up the mess. Get your sunglasses and black bag – are you ready to be an undercover scientist?

Your first step is to understand what a mishap is. We're not talking about accidents that the police, fire brigade or ambulance services have to deal with. No, our mishaps are much more common, everyday occurrences. Even if it's not happening to you, somewhere nearby, someone is suffering a mishap as you read these words. Each mishap is caused by technology going wrong, or, more commonly, by us going wrong with our technology.

Our world is full of the most astonishing inventions, from MP3 players to stain-eating soaps. Each of these is the product of centuries of scientific and technological effort, resulting in an artefact that is designed to improve our lives in some small but significant way. But the technology that surrounds us is based on a set of assumptions about how it will be used. Shampoo works just fine in your hair, but when it is spilled on the floor it suddenly becomes a slippery mishap waiting to happen. The objects that we use every day are designed to operate only in the right context. Put that object out of context – metal in a microwave, chewing gum in your hair, wine on a rug – and suddenly the science works against you. Now the dirt-removing soap acts like a lubricant on your feet – exactly the worst place for it. The metal in the microwave causes alarming sparks to zap and crackle inside. The chewing gum becomes an appalling adhesive impossible to untangle from your hair. The spilled wine is transformed into a dye that seems more permanent than the original pattern in the rug.

Mishaps will always happen, and now you will know exactly *why*. Enter, if you dare, the world of everyday disasters. Imagine that a series of mishaps is happening to you. It is the most accident-filled day of your life ...

Oblivious Beginnings

A little snore emerges from the pile of bedclothes. You're fast asleep, dreaming about being lost in a busy city. You stop to cross the street and a car pulls up in front of you. Without a pause it becomes a truck backing towards you, making a reversing *beep, beep,* warning noise. You wait for it to stop and turn, thinking how familiar it sounds. Of course it sounds familiar, you realise – it's your father's truck that he uses to pick up the groceries with. But he seems to be having trouble turning it, going forwards then backing up again. Finally he moves off, and you see that it wasn't a truck at all. Why would he use a truck for a packet of cornflakes? It was a bicycle. You find yourself riding the bicycle with him, whizzing down a hill, the wind in your hair. There are lovely fields of flowers rushing by, faster and faster. You look down and see you're on roller skates. Surely this is a bit fast to be travelling on roller skates?

You groan and turn over, looking up at the ceiling. That was a weird dream, you begin to think, as it fades from your memory. You rub your eyes and look at the clock. You frown. The hands seem to be in the wrong places. You reach over and pick it up. That can't be right. You look at your watch, also on the bedside table. It is right. You're late! You've managed to sleep straight through the loudest alarm clock ever invented! And you're such a light sleeper as well. How could this possibly happen?

Sleep is not a simple activity. You may like to think of it as a bit of shut-eye or a little snooze, but your body and brain undergo some remarkable changes during sleep. If they didn't, you would literally lose your mind in a matter of days. We're all seven days from madness.

Going to sleep is not an on or off activity. We don't just 'fall asleep' or 'wake up' – it's actually much more complicated than that. We're also never 'half asleep', as the common expression suggests, but we do slowly sink into different depths of sleep. These are called stages, and there are five different stages of sleep that we cycle through, several times every night.

When you settle down into bed and close your eyes, your first task is to move from wakefulness to stage 1 sleep. It's a gradual process, your muscles relaxing, your brain slowing down, your eyes becoming more static. Your breathing becomes shallow and regular. If the electrical activity of your brain was being measured, we would see you moving from alpha waves to theta waves – your neurons are changing from a relaxed, pulsing state to a slower, more synchronised state. But if you're disturbed during this stage, you probably wouldn't even be aware that you'd been asleep. Stage 1 sleep lasts for 5 or 10 minutes, before you start to sink into stage 2.

Now your heart rate slows and your body temperature decreases. You may begin to snore, if you have a suitably floppy throat. Your muscles may occasionally twitch. Taking a look at the electrical activity of your brain, we see there are spiky interruptions to your slow, pulsing theta waves, corresponding to those twitches. Your body is preparing for the deeper sleep of stages 3 and 4. Now your brain slows down even further, the neurons firing in relaxed pulses that become longer, slower delta waves. You're in stage 3 sleep and snoring at full volume. Stage 3 slowly becomes stage 4, when your brain produces the slower delta waves more than half of the time. This behaviour of the brain is very different from the fast-changing, chaotic and unsynchronised behaviour during wakefulness. Not surprisingly, if you're woken when in deep sleep, you are the most disorientated.

Strangely, stage 4 is the stage at which sleep-talking and -walking occur. These behaviours have little to do with dreaming, for you are not dreaming yet. Movement and activity during deep sleep are driven more by primitive instinctive emotions, such as fear or anger. Astonishingly, people are capable of amazingly complex behaviour while in this state. Those with the more severe sleep disorders might jump out of their bedroom window or go to the kitchen and prepare and eat a meal or even drive a car. Somehow all the necessary parts of your brain are hijacked by this deeper, instinctive part of you, without your conscious mind ever waking up. Thankfully, severe sleeping disorders are rare. Many of us may mumble a few words during deep sleep, but most are oblivious to the world, our brains in the most relaxed state they can be in.

The different stages of sleep initially each last around 10 minutes and then go into reverse. Having descended into the depths of stage 4 sleep, your brain now slowly awakens again, moving back to stage 3, then to stage 2 sleep. About 90 minutes after first falling asleep our brain has almost risen back to wakefulness, but instead of moving to stage 1 and waking up, we move from stage 2 into a different kind of brain activity – dreaming. This is known as REM sleep, which stands for rapid eye movement. It's a very easy type of sleep to detect because the brain and body undergo many changes. Your heart rate and breathing will speed up, your body will suddenly relax, yet your eyes will start to dart about behind your closed eyelids. Measuring your brain activity at this point will show that your brain is closer to its state when awake, with a complicated mixture of asynchronous neuron firing. You are now in a dream world, unaware that you are dreaming. You act out different roles in a virtual world made up by your own brain. Your moving eyes are following dream-events as though they are real. To stop your other muscles from doing the same, your brain has cut its own phone lines by blocking all messages from motor neurons to your major skeletal muscles. It can no longer move any muscles except the ones controlling your eyes and your involuntary muscles involved with your breathing and heart.

Dreaming is the best form of virtual reality there is. You genuinely believe you are experiencing the bizarre and often contradictory world unfolding around you. You may be exhilarated, saddened, angered or even frightened by these experiences. They may be heavily influenced by recent events in your waking life, or they may seem to have no clear relation to anything you've experienced. But they are all figments of your own imagination.

It may seem like a lost opportunity – each night we create entire worlds, memories and experiences for ourselves, yet we have no control over them and little memory of them afterwards. If only we could control our dreams, we would be gods of our own virtual universes every night, able to dream whatever we wanted. Fascinatingly, there is a form of dreaming where this is possible. Known as lucid dreaming, it happens when you are in REM sleep and suddenly realise that something just doesn't make sense. Perhaps you've pinched your nose and found you can still breathe through it, or you keep trying to read some text and every time you look at it, it says something different, or perhaps you realise that there are no such things as cartoon monsters in the real world. Whatever the trigger, you realise you are asleep, and suddenly your conscious mind is able to control the dream. More than 50 per cent of us have had moments of lucidity during dreaming. Frequently, the realisation will simply make us wake up and the moment is lost. But sometimes we really are able to control our own dreams. For some, this becomes such a fun experience that they try to improve their ability to have lucid dreams, using practice or even gadgets that slightly disturb them during REM sleep.

Initially, dreaming lasts only about 10 minutes. Then you may briefly wake and turn over, or you may just sink back down through the stages of sleep again. This cycle of descending into deep sleep, then rising up to dream, then descending again will happen several times every night. In each cycle you spend less time in deep sleep and more time in REM sleep, until by the end of the night you may have dreams lasting as long as an hour. A typical person may have about five cycles of deep sleep and REM sleep every night. These cycles are heavily affected by age. Babies and young children spend much more time in REM sleep than adults do. As we get older we also sleep less deeply, so adults spend less time in the deeper stages of sleep. Adults are also more likely to enter REM sleep sooner and for longer in the first cycle of sleep.

We're still not sure why the brain sleeps in the way it does. We don't know why we dream, and we don't know why we yo-yo between deeper and lighter stages of sleep every night. Perhaps it's an old evolutionary trick to make sure we are able to become alert to danger during the night. Perhaps it's a way to enable us to sort through the experiences of the previous day and understand them better. It seems likely that we're not the only ones who use this trick though: most mammals and birds also sleep and dream as we do.

By the end of the night, most of us are spending little time in deep sleep and most of the time in REM sleep. This is why we often wake with a dream fresh in our minds, for we have just stepped from our dreams into reality. But it also means that should we hear any familiar noises that we've heard many times before, we are more likely to incorporate them into our dreams than wake. Even if we do briefly wake (and hit the snooze button), because we're mostly in REM sleep by the morning, we're able to roll over and start dreaming again almost immediately.

Oversleeping often becomes a problem if you have not had enough sleep (you went to bed too late), or if you're depressed, or if you haven't been sleeping normally. People who snore badly (enough to affect their breathing or enough for their partners to wake them) or who suffer from insomnia may have interrupted sleep cycles, making them tired and irritable during the day. But if you are unfortunate enough to be deprived of all sleep (requiring constant and probably life-threatening disturbances to you), it only takes three days before you start to hallucinate and lose the ability to think normally. Prolonged lack of sleep also has a dramatic and serious effect on the immune system, to such an extent that you may die if you have no sleep at all for more than eleven days. But if you are an insomniac, don't worry. During those long hours that you may lie in bed, wishing for sleep, you will slip into stages 1 and 2 sleep regularly without being aware of it. It's enormously hard to stop someone from sleeping, just as it's enormously hard to stop someone from going to the toilet. There are some things we just have to do.

Ironically, waking up at the right time in the morning is a real problem for those who suffer from insomnia, but sleeping late happens to all of us now and again. Oversleeping is so common that there are a huge number of clever alarm clocks for sale. Some try to stop you from getting used to their alarms by making a different noise each day. Others actually jump off your bedside table while making the noise, forcing you to get out of bed and find them.

In the end, the best solution is simply to have a good routine: make sure you go to bed at a similar time each night and make sure you have enough sleep (eight hours is the recommended amount). Then, whether the alarm clock has gone off or not, you'll find you naturally wake up at the right time.

① Bathroom Skating

Steam rises from the hot water. It fills the bathroom with a swirling haze made golden by the morning sun. Standing with your eyes shut, face towards the water, the remnants of last night's dreams flit through your mind like the shadows of birds flying past the bathroom window. You grope blindly for the shampoo. Popping open the top, you pour the shampoo into a wet hand. It feels cold against your skin. As you try to put the bottle back, it slips from your grasp and bounces to the middle of the bathroom floor, the noise echoing around the small space. A quick peek around the shower screen reveals that the bottle is on its side and oozing shampoo onto the tiled floor. You sigh and, leaving the water running, step out to pick up the bottle before its contents are lost. Leaving a trail of steaming water, you grab the bottle and turn, your foot squelching into something cold. Suddenly the world spins upside down. The next thing you know you're staring at the dusty underside of your basin, freezing cold tiles against your back, head throbbing painfully.

We've all had times when a shower or bath seems more like an assault course than a relaxing wash. Surely in our modern world such bathroom danger is unnecessary. Why don't we have non-slippery shampoo? It's not as if we're choosing to wash our hair in a lubricant like car oil ... is it?

Washing your hair with gloopy oil does not sound like a sensible way to clean it. Massaging a nice dollop of pig fat into your scalp has surely got to be a horribly messy experience. Yet the Ancient Greeks and Romans mostly preferred oils when bathing – they massaged the oils onto their bodies and then scraped off the excess along with (at least some of) the dirt, like cleaning a window with a squeegee.

Oil and soap may seem very different, but shampoos and soaps rely on lots of fatty oils to make them. Some of the earliest recorded uses of soap date back nearly 5,000 years, and the Sapindus trees (often called soapberry or soapnuts) have been used even longer. We don't know who first discovered the recipe for soap, but because of the way it is made some suggest that the gooey remains of animal sacrifices may have been involved. Thankfully, this is probably nothing more than a myth.

The recipe for soap is very simple. Find some ashes and run water through them until the water becomes 'lye water' (made alkaline by potassium hydroxide). One old trick to know when it was ready was apparently to see if an egg floated in the solution; if it did, the lye water was good enough. Next get some fat or oil. Animal fats were often used, but olive oil is perhaps a bit nicer. Then you mix the two, making sure you put just the right amount of oil into the mixture. You can boil it or mix it cold – either way, the same chemical reaction will occur. It's called saponification, and although a similar reaction can happen with other ingredients, in making soap it involves an alkali (the lye water) interacting with fats or oils. If we were to zoom in a few million times we'd see what was going on. The oil is made from triplets of similar molecules, stuck together. The alkali breaks down those molecules, breaking bonds between some atoms, which chops off chunks of them. The pieces recombine in a different way, and what's left is no longer oil and alkali – it has transformed into a form of sugar alcohol, called glycerol, and soap.

Because this chemical reaction needs only a couple of ingredients, there have been a few rare cases where it happens naturally to corpses buried in the ground. If the soil happens to be very alkaline and few worms and bacteria are present, saponification can turn the fat in the body into adipocere, or 'grave wax', as it is often called. One of the most extreme cases happened to a woman buried sometime in the 19th century, whose entire body slowly turned to soap. The Soap Woman is now on display in the Mütter Museum in Philadelphia. She wasn't alone – a Soap Man buried with her was also found, and he is sometimes displayed in the Smithsonian Institute.

Thankfully, the soap we use today has nothing to do with dead bodies of any type. It often uses plant oils, such as palm or olive oil, with a few extra ingredients to make it smell nice. The soap is carefully purified to remove unwanted compounds, such as glycerol, and sometimes some fine scouring powder, such as pumice, is added to help the soap scrub away the dead cells on our skin.

Hopefully you are aware that soap is good at removing dirt (if not, go have a wash – you stink!). Soap has this property because of another chemical reaction. Soap molecules are like tiny snakes made of sodium or potassium fatty acid salts. When water comes into contact with these long salt molecules, the head of the snake becomes negatively charged. This results in the head falling in love with the water around it (becoming hydrophilic) and the tail hating the water (being hydrophobic). When it is dropped into water, it's a bit of a dilemma for each soap molecule – one end wants to be in contact with the water, and the other wants to get as far away from the water as possible. Their clever solution is to join forces with their friends and form themselves into little spheres, with all the heads pointing outwards and all the tails tucked inside away from the water. But drop soap into oil, and suddenly the tables are turned. Now the tails love the oil, and the heads want to hide away. So this time the little globules are inside out, with heads buried away from the oil and tails on the outside.

The strange behaviour of soap molecules makes them a surface active agent, or surfactant – they are able to break down the normal resistance between liquids such as water and oil and allow the two to mix in an emulsion. Soap does not allow oil to dissolve in water – it can't do that because the two liquids hate each other so much that they are unmixable (or, to use the right word, immiscible). Instead, it does the next best thing. When you put soap on your skin the oil-loving tails of the soap molecules attach themselves to the natural oils and grease. Then, when you rinse off the soap, it forms itself into those little globules with the heads on the outside and the tails – still holding onto the oils – on the inside. So the soap has wrapped the oil from your skin in little parcels that like oil on the inside and like water on the outside, allowing the oil to be dispersed in the water and washed away. Most dirt is soluble in either water or oil, so if you are removing oil and using water at the same time, then you're going to take away most of the dirt.

Although we have had soaps for thousands of years, soap-based shampoos are much newer inventions. Originally, primitive shampoos of various types were usually made from mixtures of herbs, water or sometimes oils. More recently, the success of modern soap led to the first soap-based shampoos. These were liquid soaps designed to clean and remove oils from the hair, made from soap flakes dissolved in water. Unfortunately, soap works too well – it removes all of your natural hair oil (sebum), making the hair brittle and prone to damage. For this reason, in the 1930s the first synthetic shampoo made from synthesised detergent rather than soap was invented. Since then all shampoos have been made synthetically, carefully designed to strip away some, but not all, of the natural oils of the hair. They use slightly different compounds from those in ordinary soap to make the detergent a little less effective, but the underlying principles are identical – shampoo is a surfactant and its molecules grab the oils and dirt and wrap them in water-loving parcels, allowing you to wash the water–oil emulsion away.

Shampoos also have another thing in common with soaps. They are slippery. This property helps us to apply the soap or shampoo, so it is useful. But we did not choose to make them slippery – it is a property that all soaps, shampoos and, indeed, surfactants have. Even if we wanted a non-slippery shampoo, we would find it extremely hard to make one. Soaps and shampoos are made from oils, meaning that their molecular structure is similar enough to give them many of the same properties as oils. They also like to grab hold of oils and hold them in suspension, adding yet more slipperiness.

A substance is slippery because of friction, or the lack of it. Friction is the force that slows down the motion of two surfaces rubbing together. Even two surfaces that may seem perfectly smooth and shiny will have countless little bumps on them when they are examined under a microscope. Sliding one past the other is like grinding them past each other, all those rough bumps slowing down the motion and heating up the surfaces. (In fact, a lot of friction is caused by temporary chemical bonds forming between two surfaces, so they don't have to be rough to be high in friction.) Friction is great when you are moving around – tyres wouldn't stick to the road without it, nor would our feet stick to the ground. But for anything that has moving parts (and that's most of our machines in the world), friction is a problem. Unwanted friction inside an engine will make it heat up, wear out or seize up altogether, which is why we need a lot of oil in a car. Oil is a lubricant – a gloopy substance that gets between the two surfaces and stops them from rubbing together. Most lubricants are based on oils because they are good at coating surfaces and forming stable layers or films rather than being squeezed away as water would be.

But the latest research in tribology (nothing to do with tribes – it's the study of interacting surfaces, friction and lubrication) is pointing to a new type of lubricant, surfactants. Not traditionally considered suitable for lubrication (who wants an 'oil' that is washed away by water), it is only in the last few years that the compounds in shampoos and soaps have been investigated seriously. It turns out that they also have the same properties as oils – they are good at coating surfaces and forming films between surfaces. Although you and everyone you know may have been slipping on soap for decades, it is only now that scientists and engineers are realising that these compounds would make great lubricants, perhaps in machines that already use water, such as hydraulic systems or drilling platforms that use water for cooling the drills.

So the next time you slip on some shampoo, remember: it's not your fault. The stuff is literally as slippery as the oil that was used to make it in the first place.

Sword Fighting

You stand in front of the mirror, razor in hand. It's an old one, and you know you should replace the blades in it, but you're in a hurry, your head hurts and you've still got to make the early meeting at work. After a squeaky wipe of the mirror to clear the fog, you apply some shaving foam and begin using the razor. It feels smooth as you hurriedly pull it along your skin. Nice. You wash off the remaining foam and admire your handiwork. Just one little bit you missed, but that is easily remedied – ow! You stare in disbelief as a line of red blood pushes its way through a perfectly straight cut in your skin. You haven't got time for this, so you wet a tissue and wipe away the blood. But the line of blood keeps reappearing, every time you wipe it. It doesn't hurt, but it's going to make a mess on your clothes if it keeps bleeding like this. Why doesn't it stop?

For more than 7,000 years unwanted hair has been plucked, shaved, dissolved and even burned from our bodies. In Ancient Egypt the upper classes shaved their faces and heads with razors, but pharaohs had carefully trimmed beards. A thousand years later in Greece Alexander the Great shaved himself so that his enemies could not grab his beard in battle (or so he told his generals) and influenced fashion around the world. Greek women would burn off leg hair with a lamp (don't try this at home unless you want a trip to the hospital). Before long the Romans were influenced by these new styles. A daily visit to the *tonsor* (barber) became part of normal life and a good place to chat to friends. Beards would be trimmed, hair styled and faces shaved using iron razors. This was often a painful process as the razors did not stay sharp for long and no soap or cream was used. Eventually, the first shave for young Roman men even became a rite of passage into manhood, celebrated by a ceremony. Among women, unwanted hair was more likely to be plucked than shaved. For many centuries a high forehead and thin eyebrows were seen as a sign of aristocracy, so women would pluck their hairlines back an inch or two and remove their eyelashes and all of their eyebrows. They painted thin brows on afterwards.

The first safety razor was not invented and sold until the 20th century. A salesman called King Camp Gillette noticed that the traditional cut-throat razors became blunt and needed to be sharpened all the time. They were also dangerous and had a habit of cutting your skin. Gillette thought that a disposable razor could solve both problems. He teamed up with an engineer from the Massachusetts Institute of Technology and together they created the first razor with a wire in front of the blade to help prevent the skin from being cut. Gillette also created what is now known as the 'razor and blades business model' when he decided to sell the razors at a loss but then make a profit by selling replacement blades that would fit into the holder. It was a cunning plan that launched a highly successful company. Gillette (and its other brands, including Braun and Duracell) was eventually sold to Proctor & Gamble in 2005 for $57 billion and continues to be a market leader today.

Modern razors are safer than they have ever been, but they are not infallible. They always contain some of the sharpest blades we can make, so they are dangerous. Use one incorrectly – press too hard, use without proper lubrication or shave across a bump, wrinkle or spot – and you won't just slice the hair, you will slice your skin.

Cutting hair is no problem. Hair is the extrusion of a kind of protein in a tubular shape, like a slow squirt of toothpaste solidifying from a tube. The toothpaste tube is a hair follicle, a group of cells that grow very rapidly, deep within the skin. These are fed by our blood supply to keep them alive. Nerves are wrapped around the follicle to allow us to feel the movement of each hair, and a tiny muscle allows the hair to be raised up (and cause a goose bump). Closer to the surface a tiny gland produces sebum, the oil that coats the growing shaft of hair and keeps it supple. There's also sometimes another little gland to produce scent. The shaft of hair (the toothpaste) is made from keratin, and so the part of the shaft visible above the skin is not alive. When we cut it we feel nothing, for all the nerves are deep within the skin and the hair follicle itself is unharmed. But plucking or waxing is another matter – you are ripping out the hair and taking some of the deep-seated follicle with it, ripping away the nerve-endings. So it hurts!

Fascinatingly, we have every hair follicle we'll ever use in our skins by the time we are a 22-week-old foetus. The follicles may become more or less active depending on our age and hormones, but we will never lose them, even if we might hurt them now and again through plucking. (Even those of us who go bald on our heads still have all our follicles there; they just work less well.)

Our skin is another matter altogether. Hair follicles, nerves, sebaceous glands, muscles and scent glands are just a few of the extraordinarily diverse components of this organ (which is the largest and heaviest organ of the human body). The skin also helps us maintain our body temperature by excreting water from pores in the form of sweat and even excreting a very dilute form of urea (the stuff you pee into the toilet). That's why if you eat something particularly smelly, you may smell of it for a while. It's not only your breath that has the odour, it's your skin as well. Your skin is also packed full of sensory cells, allowing you to feel temperature, pressure, surface contact and pain. It has cells called melanocytes that create the melanin that gives your skin its pigment and helps protect you from the sun. It even has special enzymes that help cells repair damage caused by the sun to the DNA within skin cells and prevent them from becoming cancerous.

Your skin has a remarkable blood supply, which not only feeds all of these cells but also allows you to cool down further by dilating vessels close to the surface. It's why you might go a bit red in the face after running and look rather pale on a cold day. When you're hot, moving blood closer to the skin surface helps the heat radiate away; when you're cold it's best to keep the warmth more centrally, away from the chilly air.

One of the primary functions of the skin is to protect our internal organs from the outside world. There are countless viruses, bacteria, fungi and parasites all doing their best to find a new home to raise their young. Our warm, wet bodies make lovely homes for them, if they can only get inside us. This is where our skin comes in. Not only does it form a tough, stretchy barrier, ideal for protecting us against bumps and bashes, it also has its own built-in army ready and waiting to attack potential invaders. Some of the important soldiers in the army are called Langerhans cells. These are a type of immune cell within the skin, designed to gobble up anything nearby and tell their friends what they have found. If one happens to eat something nasty, like a no-good bacterium, it will send out an alert and will quickly attract other immune cells to it, causing swelling and allowing the main force of the immune system to attack any more invaders. It's a good strategy, as most of the nasties like bacteria and viruses reproduce themselves exceedingly quickly. If one is there, the chances are high that another million are also nearby. This process goes on continuously, for bacteria are so small they can squeeze into us through the pores in our skin. The response by the immune system causes a spot or zit to form.

But if they can enter through a pore, which is too small to see, when we cut ourselves shaving we open up a Grand Canyon for them. Although a razor cut is usually not deep enough to cut beyond the dermis (the lowest layer of skin where the hair follicles live), this is still deep enough to hit the tiny blood vessels and so you will see the leaking blood pushing through the cut like a burst water pipe in the ground. It may seem like a disaster for the security forces in the skin – a hole ripped in a wall is not good for keeping unwanted visitors out – but although razors are a relatively new invention, living creatures have been encountering sharp objects throughout their evolutionary history. Sharp rocks, sticks or, more often, sharp teeth have been injuring us for hundreds of millions of years. If we didn't have an effective way of surviving these wounds we would not live very long, so life has evolved some clever mechanisms to cope.

When our skin is punctured and blood oozes out, the best thing that could happen would be for the blood itself to seal up the hole it is escaping from. So that is exactly what it does. As soon as a blood vessel is damaged and blood meets air, a series of chemical reactions takes place. Little cells known as platelets that are present in the blood find themselves in this new chemical environment, and they become activated, getting very excited and activating their friends around them. The platelets immediately become sticky and glue themselves to the edges of the wound, and they even create a net of a protein called fibrin, which is glued across the wound and catches more platelets. Before you know it, the gap has been plugged. It may be a slightly messy plug, but it was done in a hurry and can be cleaned up later. This plug is a blood clot, and when it hardens in place we call it a scab. An army of immune cells gathers in the area just in case anything nasty got through while the defences were down, causing redness and swelling. Over the next few days your cells slowly regrow and repair the damage under the scab until after around a week there is fresh, clean skin again and the scab is discarded.

One advantage of a nick by a razor blade is that it is a clean cut. A blade that is more blunt would rip your skin and create more damage. A shallow, clean incision means less destruction to the skin, and so if you are quick and press on the cut for 20 minutes you may find that the platelets manage to bind your skin together from within quite invisibly. However, one common mistake is to keep touching a bleeding area with wet tissue paper or even to tear a little dry piece of tissue off and stick it to the wound. It's a bad idea for several reasons: you're bringing a foreign object into contact with an open wound, giving a free taxi ride to all of the bacteria and viruses straight to where they want to go. You're also wiping or pulling away the platelets that are doing their best to plug the hole, so you'll only make it bleed for longer. For something as minor as a nick by a razor, your body knows exactly how to repair itself, and keep you healthy and looking good.

⟨7⟩ Dark Clouds

A feeling of relief washes over you: the kitchen clock is saying you have a whole half-hour before you need to leave. Plenty of time for breakfast. You grab a bagel and roughly cut it into two, pushing the uneven bready surface into the toaster. While it toasts, you go back to the bedroom to iron the creased shirt you hurriedly put on, thinking you were late. On the way you turn on the radio. One of your favourite songs is playing and you have a little boogie as you iron. Just three or four minutes later you are done. Turning off the iron, you smell something. Is the iron overheating? It looks fine. Suddenly your smoke alarm starts shrieking, and you realise something is amiss in the kitchen. You run back and are greeted by the sight of black smoke billowing from your toaster. Your bagel is burning!

Toasters are dangerous things. If you take a look at one while it toasts, you'll see a meandering wire on each side of the toast that glows orange and emits heat. This wire is carrying live electricity straight from your socket. If you were unfortunate enough to touch it with a metal knife, you'd be electrocuted as surely as if you'd stuck that knife into a live socket. All a toaster does is push an electric charge through that little wire to make it glow red hot and turn itself off after a certain amount of time. A light bulb makes light and heat in the same way, except the little wire is called a filament and it's held inside a glass bulb filled with gas to make it shine brightly and have a long life. An electric iron also works using the same principle. Electricity is so commonly used to generate heat that it is often taken for granted. Even a computer gets hot and needs little fans to cool itself down. But how exactly does electricity turn into heat?

The electrical current that flows in the wiring of your house or apartment is called alternating current, or AC for short. It's different from direct current (DC), which comes from batteries, because it doesn't exactly flow. Alternating electrical current is a push–pull–push–pull current, a crazy tug-of-war with the rope going back and forth 50 or 60 times per second depending on the country. (This is why electrical appliances say 50 Hertz or 60 Hertz on the back of them.) AC is used because it makes transmitting the energy from the power stations to our homes a little simpler – it can be transformed to different voltages and currents very simply.

If AC is like an oscillating tug-of-war rope, the rope inside the wires is made from little tiny particles called electrons. These naturally orbit atoms like planets orbiting the sun. They orbit a long way from the neutrons and protons in the middle, and they zip around at different distances, just as Pluto orbits our sun much further out compared to the Earth. In metals the outermost electrons are able to hop from one atom to another. The movement of these 'free electrons' is what we call an electric current. The pressure exerted on those electrons in order to move them is the electric voltage (that pressure is like an invisible electric field such as magnetism). So our AC tug-of-war is an in–out–in–out pressure produced by the generators of power stations that moves free electrons back and forth within the wiring of our homes. Power stations don't really make electricity. They are like giant pumps that push–pull–push–pull the electrons that are already there. By doing this they can transmit power, just as a hydraulic system transmits power by pushing water, but does not create the water.

If we then connect something like a toaster, we are attaching to the circuit a little wire that has more resistance to the flow of electrons. Now the free electrons find it harder to move through the metal of the wire, for impurities have been introduced like an obstacle course. The electrons are trying to move in–out–in–out, but there are other atoms in the way that have electrons that are not so free. So some of the moving electrons can't go where they want to – they bounce off the others in their way (actually they are repelled like magnets of the same polarity). The result is that fewer electrons can get through a wire that has higher resistance. The ones that can't get through are left bouncing around and jolting all the other electrons in the metal. Jolting electrons around doesn't sound very interesting, but the effect is surprising. The wire heats up.

Heat is really all about the movement of atoms. Take water: when it is at room temperature, the atoms are all jiggling about freely. Reduce their temperature, and you slow down those jiggles until movement ceases and you're left with solid water, or ice. Increase their temperature and you speed up the jiggles until they float free as a gas, or water vapour. This is true of all materials. To go from solid to liquid to gas, just add heat and watch those atoms dance. Most materials can also conduct heat in the same way: if I heat up one end of a piece of wood, its atoms jiggle about at that end and start to vibrate their neighbours, which vibrate their neighbours and so on, until the other end starts to feel warm. But materials like metal are much, much better at conducting heat. They do it using those free electrons, which chaotically hop from one atom to another, bouncing off their friends and causing everything to jiggle.

So when an electric current tries to flow through a wire that has been designed to give some resistance, those frustrated electrons that can't go where they want to go, bounce around and jolt everything nearby. Every time they bounce off something, they transfer more of the energy of their motion into the surrounding electrons and atoms, and in doing so they create heat.

This is ideal in a toaster. Just use the right kind of wire, make it meander left and right to produce heat over a surface and place some sliced bread in front of it. A little electricity and you have toasted bread. Unfortunately, the machine is sometimes not so reliable. Older toasters often fail because of the way they are switched on and off. Most have a little tray that lowers the bread down inside the machine, operated by a lever at the side. When the lever is pushed down, the tray is at the bottom and the power is activated – the wire is connected to the electrical current. But if the bread is too thick, the tray might become stuck down and the power might be stuck on. Even worse, if the bread is uneven, it might come into contact with that glowing red-hot wire.

There's a certain chemical reaction that likes these conditions. It just requires oxygen, fuel and heat. There's plenty of oxygen in the air, plenty of fuel in bread, and the toaster can provide the heat. If the fuel reaches a high enough temperature, known as the ignition temperature, then suddenly the chemical reaction can begin. The molecules of the fuel are broken apart, releasing volatile gases as smoke. If the gases get hot enough, their molecules are broken apart, and they recombine with the oxygen to make water, carbon dioxide, carbon monoxide, carbon and nitrogen. What's left is known as char, and the carbon in this black stuff can also break down and combine with oxygen in another reaction. As the fuel reacts with oxygen, a large amount of heat is generated, which keeps the fuel and gases above the ignition temperature. Once started, the chemical reaction keeps itself going, making enough heat to enable it to consume all the fuel and oxygen nearby. The region where the gases are undergoing this reaction may be visible as a flickering, hot, bright flame. We call the whole reaction fire.

Fire is scary enough when it's out of control, but a fire that has been caused by electricity is even worse. It is the movement of electrons that is generating heat, and electrons are quite happy to flow through water as well as metal. Put water on an electrical fire and all you are doing is providing new exciting places for the electrical current to flow, such as into you. It's not great to be faced with a burning toaster and to be electrocuted at the same time. If possible, it's always best to turn off the power, either at the socket or at the main fusebox, and then worry about the fire.

Thankfully, modern toasters have built-in protection mechanisms to cut off the power after a certain period of time regardless of the position of the tray, so electrical fires involving toasters are quite rare. In fact, investigations of electrical fires have shown that one of the most common causes is an overloaded extension socket, and one of the most common places for the fire to start is in the bedroom. Nevertheless, the best toaster in the world can't protect you if you force a lumpy bit of bread against its wires. Expect burned food if you do that!

Some people actually prefer their toast a little blackened, of course. Research on what happens when you eat burned food is still a little unclear. Some suggest that burned toast might actually help soak up alcohol and prevent hangovers later, but there is no real evidence that this works. Most of the results are not so optimistic. Benzopyrene is one nasty compound that is known to increase risk of cancer because of its occurrence in coal tar. In the 19th century it caused cancers in chimney sweeps and fuel industry personnel. It occurs in tobacco smoke and diesel exhaust fumes, and it is found in lower levels within chargrilled food and burned toast. Acrylamide is another substance linked to higher cancer rates. It's a substance used by the construction industry in dam foundations and tunnels, and it can be generated in low levels when food is burned. Despite these findings, it's highly likely that a small amount of burned material on food will do us no harm at all. If you really don't like the taste, you can always scrape off the blackened top layer. Or eat cereal instead.

Flash in the Pan

A cup of tea is what you need. You pick up the kettle and fill it.
It's a stylish electric kettle, a cordless design. As you take it back
to its base, you notice a trickle of water coming from the bottom.
Is it leaking or have you just spilled water on it? Either way, you
decide not to risk it. You're getting a bad feeling about today.
Instead you find your shiny new mug, bought the day before, and
fill it with some bottled water. Good, clean healthy water. You
can use the microwave to boil it, you realise, and have your tea
despite the kettle. You carefully place the cup inside and set the
timer for three minutes. Even if it boils for a while, it's only water
so it won't matter. The morning paper passes the time until the
microwave bleeps. Retrieving the cup, you notice with a frown
that it doesn't seem to be boiling. Not much you can do about it,
so you drop a teabag into the liquid. As if you've added some
magic ingredient, the water suddenly explodes like a bubbling
cauldron, tea jumping out of the cup and making a brown stain all
over the paper. You jump back in alarm, barely avoiding being
sprayed by the scalding liquid. How could a teabag make water
do that?

Explosions come in many shapes and sizes. Exploding water may not be
one that seems very likely, but in fact it is perhaps the most common
kind of explosion that happens in the home. It's known as a steam
explosion, and it happens when a liquid becomes superheated beyond
its normal boiling temperature.

Normally when a liquid is heated, the heat soaks through gradually,
and the container has many imperfections in its surface. As the boiling
point of the liquid is reached, the liquid is trying to transform from

liquid to its gaseous form. Because the heat is conducted through the container, tiny bubbles form on the imperfections of the container, which slowly grow, in a process called nucleation and growth. The bubbles soon become larger and larger as the liquid boils and is transformed into gas. (If you heat water in a kettle the bubbles form on the rough surface of the internal heating element, but the mechanism is the same.)

There are, however, some rare circumstances when the liquid cannot behave like this. Put a smooth and shiny container of a pure liquid into a microwave and things are a little different. The microwave heats up the whole liquid at once, so it does not circulate in the container, and the lack of any imperfections in the liquid or on the container walls means that nucleation cannot happen. The liquid wants to become gas, but there is nothing for the initial gas bubbles to cling to. They just can't get going, so the liquid sits there, getting hotter and hotter. When you finally take the superheated water from the microwave and put something into it, the gas bubbles go crazy, immediately forming around the foreign object with such speed that the remaining liquid explodes from the container in a superheated frenzy.

It's why most microwavable drinks, such as hot chocolate, have instructions that suggest you microwave the liquid in short bursts, stirring the contents frequently. If you don't, it is quite possible that the drink will silently explode within the microwave and you'll be left with a cup about one-third full and a lot of mess, or even worse, it will explode in your face and cause serious burns.

Steam explosions can be much more devastating than this, however. On Saturday, 26 April 1986, in the early hours of the morning, a test of the cooling system of reactor 4 of the Chernobyl nuclear power station went horribly wrong. Ordinary water was used to cool and control the temperature of the nuclear core; in the test they attempted to check whether back-up systems could power the pumps that normally circulated the water. They disconnected the turbine that normally powered the pumps and, through a series of errors, the fuel rods were fractured and began a runaway meltdown reaction. The resulting sudden heat caused a devastating steam explosion in the water, which threw radioactive gases and fragments from the core into the sky.

A total of 237 people suffered acute radiation sickness, and fifty-seven died. Four square kilometres of pine forest around the plant turned brown and died, and 135,000 people were evacuated from their homes in the surrounding area, leaving everything behind, never to return. Many of the surrounding countries in Europe were affected by the resulting cloud of radioactive material, which was blown by the variable weather conditions. It is not known how many have died from cancer as a result of the disaster, but some estimate the numbers to be many thousands.

Thankfully, most steam explosions are nothing like as horrible as this. In fact, strange as it sounds, sometimes steam isn't even hot. Not only can water be superheated without it boiling immediately, it can be boiled without heating it. The process of nucleation and growth of little bubbles of vapour in a boiling liquid depends on pressure as well as temperature. Go to the top of a mountain, and the air pressure is much less compared to the pressure at sea level. There is, literally, far less air above you, pushing down on you. Try boiling some water up there and you'll find that it boils at much less than 100°C (212°F). It's actually a big problem for mountain climbers, who can't make the boiling water hot enough to cook food properly. The reason why pressure affects the boiling point of liquids is down to those jiggling molecules again. In a liquid, although the molecules are jiggling about quite freely, they are attracted to each other and so together form a big sloshy mass. When the pressure of the vapour (the gaseous state of the liquid) is enough to overcome that attractive force, a bubble of vapour forms and the liquid starts to boil. The hotter the liquid, the more actively the molecules fly about, and so the easier it is for molecules to start flying free as a gas. Also, the lower the pressure, the less there is pushing the molecules together in the liquid, so the easier it is for them to fly free as a gas. So if you want to boil cold water, just lower the air pressure around it, and eventually it will boil just as if it was in your kettle. This is called Henry's Law, after the English chemist who discovered the principle in 1803.

Some thirty-two years after Henry had figured it out, Charles Darwin encountered the phenomenon when on an expedition to the Andes. He wrote:

At the place where we slept water necessarily boiled, from the diminished pressure of the atmosphere, at a lower temperature than it does in a less lofty country ... Hence the potatoes, after remaining for some hours in the boiling water, were nearly as hard as ever. The pot was left on the fire all night, and next morning it was boiled again, but yet the potatoes were not cooked. I found out this by overhearing my two companions discussing the cause, they had come to the simple conclusion 'that the cursed pot (which was a new one) did not choose to boil potatoes'.

Darwin's potato problems are no more. The common trick used by mountaineers today is to use a pressure cooker. The very first pressure cooker was invented over 300 years ago, but the idea became popular only in the 20th century. It is really nothing more than a sealed pot that doesn't let much escape while cooking. As the water inside becomes hot, it turns to vapour. There is still the same number of atoms in the pot, but now they are no longer sloshing about together as a liquid – they are flying around as a gas. At the same pressure, a gas needs more space than a liquid (and a liquid needs more space than a solid). If there is no more space, then, as the liquid turns to a gas, the pressure inside the container rises. But if the pressure is going up, this means that the boiling point of the remaining liquid is now higher, so the liquid must get hotter before more of it can turn into gas.

The result is that a pressure cooker that cooks at 15 pounds per square inch or PSI (the normal pressure for most pressure cookers) will allow water to reach 120°C (248°F) and so food cooks much faster, and more harmful bacteria are destroyed. Take a pressure cooker up on a mountain, and you can use it to increase the boiling temperature back to what it is at sea level and cook potatoes properly. The whole process of pressurised cooking is so effective that it has been used to cook food during the canning process (to prevent it from spoiling once canned) for nearly a hundred years.

It's not just mountain climbers who have problems with Henry's Law. Divers and pilots can suffer serious health problems or even die because of it. The illness is called decompression sickness, and one of the first groups of people to show symptoms were miners. In 1841 pressurised air was pumped down into coalmines to stop them from filling up with water – it was easier than pumping water up and away all the time. But when they came back to the surface, the miners started complaining of sore muscles and cramps. When the first deep-sea diving began, things were even worse. Divers would complain of sore joints and itchy skin; they would become confused, have headaches and might even have seizures, fall unconscious and die.

The problem is caused by the pressure. It's more of a problem in water, because water is heavy. You only need to dive 10 metres (33 feet) to double the pressure around you. If you want to be able to breathe, the air in your air tank has to be pressurised to the same degree (otherwise your lungs will collapse as the pressure squishes them). Dive to 30 metres (100 feet), and you need to breathe air pressurised to around 60 PSI – that's more pressure than many car tyres are pumped to.

At that pressure, some of the gases in the air start to turn to liquids in your blood. Levels of nitrogen and helium increase. This is not a problem until the pressure is reduced again. Now all that dissolved gas starts to form bubbles in the blood, like the bubbles of carbon dioxide in fizzy drinks that escape when you release the pressure by opening the bottle. If the diver rises too quickly, the pressure change will be so sudden that bubbles will form in the muscles, joints and brain, causing many nasty symptoms. The same thing can happen when a pilot in an unpressurised aircraft gains altitude too quickly – the sudden drop in air pressure will make the normal levels of nitrogen fizz in their blood. The cure for divers is to use a hyperbaric chamber, which compresses the air to push those nitrogen bubbles back into the blood. It then slowly, slowly lowers the pressure, allowing the excess nitrogen to be released through the lungs without bubbles forming. Today the principles are well understood and divers are trained to take 'decompression stops' on the way back to the surface. It is also important that they do not fly at high altitude shortly after a deep dive, so don't dive while on holiday and fly home immediately afterwards. The cabins of passenger aircraft are pressurised, but often at an air pressure equivalent to 2,440 metres (8,000 feet) above sea level so that unnecessary strain is not placed on the structure of the planes. It's why your ears pop when taking off and landing – you are feeling the pressure drop and increase. A rapid change from a high-pressure underwater environment to a low-pressure cabin environment can cause decompression sickness, or 'the bends', to occur, even when the diver made his decompression stops coming to the surface.

People are made from a lot of water, so it's not surprising we are affected just as a cup of water is affected. Babies are around 78 per cent water, adult men are about 60 per cent, and adult women about 55 per cent. Thin people are made of more water than fat people. Whether you're a person or a cup of water, it's best not to have sudden and large temperature changes or sudden and large pressure changes. Take your time, keep stirring and there should be no fizzes or bangs.

Cheesy Grimace

The kitchen clock leers at you. Only five minutes before you need to leave and you've had nothing to eat or drink yet. If a hot drink is no good, what's left? You leave the soggy mess on the kitchen table and walk to the fridge. The radio continues to broadcast its happy tunes, oblivious of your darkening mood. You open the fridge door, but all you see is its skeleton of mostly bare shelves. Right. You need to get some food. No juice left, no eggs. But there is milk. You grab the carton and fill a clean glass with the cold, creamy liquid. As you bring it to your lips, you anticipate the refreshing cold drink. A nice glass of milk – that's surely a great way to start the day. But instead of chilled refreshment, your mouth is filled with a lumpy sour porridge. Trying not to vomit, you run to the sink and spit it out, looking at the glass in disgust.

Milk is the source of many products: butter, cream, cheese, yogurt and even soured milk. A lot of these are just milk with things growing in it and they're not only edible, they're tasty too. And yet spoiled milk tastes awful, could give you food poisoning and could even kill you. It doesn't just turn into cheese – as you may have noticed, there is a big difference between dairy products such as milk and mouldy cheese. But why is spoiled milk foul and cheese nice?

The origins of cheese predate recorded history, but we can have a pretty good guess about how the process of cheese-making was first discovered. In the stomach of mammals there is a naturally occurring complex of enzymes (proteins that help begin chemical reactions) that enable us to digest the milk from our mothers. Rennet, as they are collectively known, breaks down milk, causing it to separate into solids, which we call curds, and liquids, which we call whey. We can then digest the results more easily. It seems likely that in ancient times the stomachs of cattle were used as handy waterproof skin bags for carrying milk. The enzyme present in the stomach lining then curdled the milk, and by pressing together the curds and draining off the whey, the first cheeses were made.

It may sound nasty, but the traditional method of extracting the rennet to make cheese was worse: dried and cleaned stomachs from young calves (which were still at the age when they needed to digest their mothers' milk) were chopped up, soaked in wine or vinegar, filtered and then used to curdle milk. This process is still used today in central Europe, but the rest of the world has moved on. Alternative sources for rennet have been found naturally occurring in plants, such as fig tree bark or thistles, or in moulds and fungi. Remarkably, however, today a large percentage of cheeses (60 per cent of all hard cheeses in the USA in 1999) are made using rennin (the active ingredient in rennet) from genetically engineered fungus. The genes from calves that produced the appropriate proteins were transplanted into the DNA of the fungus and then huge quantities were grown.

Modern cheeses are generally first coagulated by adding bacteria to change milk sugars into lactic acid. Then rennet or rennin is used to curdle the liquid into curds and whey. The curds are dried, salted to preserve them and treated in a variety of manners, depending on the type of cheese. Some are dried, some heated, some washed, some stored for long periods, or pressed into moulds or stretched or milled, and others even have special varieties of mould added. The leftover whey is also used in various foods, to make ricotta cheese, and as an ingredient in many bakery products and confectionery.

Clearly, cheese and spoiled milk are very different animals, but what of butter? Butter is made by churning milk until butterfat starts to form. All full-fat milk is full of tiny little globules of fat to help the nursing infant grow quickly. But fat does not naturally like to dissolve in water, so each little globule is surrounded by special proteins that act as emulsifiers (just like the method used by soap to let oil and water form an emulsion). When the milk is churned, the emulsifiers coating each globule of fat are broken away, and the fat clumps together. Churn for long enough, and drain away the water, and you have butter.

Yogurt is different yet again. To make yogurt, bacteria are added to the milk. These little single-celled bugs feed on the sugars in the milk, turning them into lactic acid. This acid then affects the proteins naturally floating about in the milk, making it coagulate and turn into a gloopy, lumpy mixture. It's likely that the first yogurts were discovered in a similar way to the first cheeses – milk was carried in goatskin bags and the natural bacteria turned the milk into a mixture that they did not want to waste. Today sugars and jams are added to give flavour.

Spoiled milk is clearly not like yogurt, butter or cheese, even though it begins life as the same stuff. So what's the difference? There are a lot of useful things in milk, but the main constituents are butterfat, lactose (milk sugar) and proteins, all suspended in 85 to 90 per cent water. Naturally occurring bacteria find it all extremely tasty, especially when it's at a nice warm temperature. When they encounter the milk, the first part of it they eat is the lactose, and so the first thing that happens is the same process as used in yogurt- and cheese-making: the sugars are turned to acids, and the milk proteins start to clump together and turn the milk lumpy. The milk is now sour, but not spoiled. But there are other types of bacteria that also like milk, this time the proteins in the milk. These bacteria (called pseudomonads) break down the proteins in a process called putrefaction. Now the milk smells bad, and if you drank it the pseudomonads might just decide to try living in your warm, cosy gut for a while and make you very ill. Yet more nasty microbes may find the butterfat and break it down in a process called rancidification. Now the milk is really smelling bad, and there is little left in it that is good for you. Leave the milk longer, and moulds may discover the acids and remaining proteins and fats, and start feasting. None of these is good for you if you're stupid enough to drink the foul, evil-smelling liquid that's left. And the same processes of natural decay will also happen to yogurt, soured milk and cheese if you wait a bit longer.

One advantage we have over all these nasty bacteria is that they are intolerant of low or high temperatures. This is why food and milk keep for a long time in the fridge, for the bacteria have a lot of trouble growing when it's cold. When the temperature is several degrees below freezing, the bacteria can't grow at all, so food lasts even longer. Things can't go putrid or rancid when it's very cold. We know this is true, for scientists have found almost perfectly preserved woolly mammoths, frozen in the Siberian ice for 10,000 years.

The other thing that bacteria hate is high temperatures. In 1862 a French chemist called Louis Pasteur proved that heating milk would kill most of the germs present and dramatically slow the subsequent spoilage. The process became known as pasteurisation, and today, almost without exception, all milk (including the milk that is used to make products such as butters, yogurts and many cheeses) is pasteurised by heating it to 72°C (162°F) for 15–20 seconds. This does not sterilise the milk – it does not kill all the bacteria, which is why the milk and products derived from it still need to be refrigerated and will eventually spoil. But pasteurisation kills those bacteria that might just decide to kill us if they made their way into our guts. There's a more extreme form of pasteurisation known as UHT processing, which heats milk to 138°C (280°F) for a fraction of a second. This does kill all the bacteria, and so UHT milk has a much longer life and needs no refrigeration (like canned foods). But the more you heat milk, the more the proteins, vitamins and friendly bacteria are affected and its taste changes, so most of us prefer 'ordinary pasteurised' milk if we can buy it.

Some countries, such as the USA and Australia, actively prohibit unpasteurised 'raw milk cheeses' or require them to be aged for at least sixty days in the hope that harmful bacteria will not survive for this amount of time. Many well-known and popular cheeses are still made from 'raw milk', such as Swiss Gruyère, Emmental and French Roquefort. It turns out that very few people ever fall ill from eating properly made cheeses, whether made from raw or pasteurised milks. Because pasteurisation does not kill all bacteria and because cheese tends to be aged for some time, some argue that pasteurisation makes little difference for cheese, except that raw milk cheeses retain more vitamins and flavours. But the argument is not true for milk and other 'wet' products, such as yogurt and butter. These dairy foods can and will go putrid and rancid very quickly without pasteurisation. Those 'use by' dates are on the food for a reason.

Your own nose and taste buds are also there for a reason. It's no coincidence that we find decaying foods revolting. The reflex to vomit immediately after consuming something that we realise is rancid is also no coincidence. It's much better to get it out of our stomachs before it has a chance to infect us. But surprisingly, many of our responses to different smells and tastes are learned as we grow. There are plenty of cultures that happily eat evil-smelling cheeses or fermented fish or vegetables that we might consider to be worse than spoiled milk. They know these foods are safe because of the long history of preparing them in the right way to prevent harmful germs from being present, and so they appreciate the flavours we might find repugnant. We are programmed to associate feelings of health or illness with the flavours of the foods. Grow up in a culture like South Korea where *kimchi* (spicy fermented cabbage) is one of the main dishes, and you will associate its smell with good food. Grow up in the UK where eating something like rotten cabbage may have made you ill as a child, and you may find the smell of *kimchi* is enough to make you run in the other direction. We tend to stick to the flavours and foods we are familiar with and avoid foods with radically different flavours. It's a strategy that makes sense: as humans evolved we almost never experienced the foods of other cultures, so anything different from our norm meant it would probably make us ill. Luckily, the smell of rotting food is generally sufficiently distinctive and different that we can almost always distinguish it, and we quickly learn to avoid anything that smells unpleasant – 'if in doubt, throw it out'.

Drowning Out Noise

Stomach growling, you put the washing in the washer-dryer and then figure that you had better leave. Who knows what the traffic will be like this morning. On the way out, bag swinging from your arm, you decide on the spur of the moment to bring your MP3 player with you. You can plug it into the car stereo and listen to some favourite tunes. Now, where did you put it? A strange banging noise is coming from inside the washing machine. You frown. The MP3 player was clipped to your jogging pants. You put the jogging pants in the dirty washing pile. You put the dirty washing into the ... You run to the machine and look inside. There is your expensive digital music player, banging and sloshing its way round and round with your shirts. You can see that its screen is already looking strangely discoloured. The earphones are wrapping themselves around the jogging pants. You hit the drain button on the washing machine and anxiously wait as the water gurgles away, then turn it off. It seems like an eternity before the machine allows you to open the door. Finally a click releases the catch, you rip it open and grab the soggy electronic device. You dry it with some kitchen towel but you know it's too late when you try to switch it on. The MP3 player is dead. It's so infuriating – why does water ruin electronic gadgets? And can you ever make them work again?

Water and electronics are not a good mixture. Without batteries, the plastic and metal components of the electronic device may well survive immersion for many hours or even days with no harmful effects. But if there are internal batteries producing electricity (whether the gadget is switched on or not) everything becomes less certain. Immerse certain kinds of batteries in water and the result may be dead batteries. With some kinds of battery, you might even produce a small explosion. Yet other types of battery will survive a washing machine and keep going without much problem.

An Italian physicist called Alessandro Volta invented the first battery in around 1800. A contemporary of his, Luigi Galvani, had discovered that placing certain metals next to each other and then touching a disembodied frog's leg would make that leg twitch as though still attached to a living frog – although his explanation that the cause was 'animal electricity' was incorrect. To find a better explanation, Volta refined the ideas and discovered that alternating layers of silver and zinc separated by blotting paper and placed in salty water would create electricity, although he did not understand why. What was happening was a Faradaic reaction – a chemical reaction that made electrons flow from one metal to another. Metals and chemicals made electricity.

The same kind of reaction happens in all batteries, although the chemicals and metals are different in each type. For example, in a car battery lead and lead dioxide are placed in sulphuric acid. When sulphuric acid meets the lead it reacts with the metal, forming a new compound called lead sulphate, which has a spare electron for each new molecule. If you connect the lead plate and lead oxide plate into a circuit (perhaps connect one to each terminal of a light bulb) the spare electrons will flow from the lead, through the circuit (through the bulb) and combine with the lead dioxide. This causes another reaction, which transforms the lead dioxide into lead sulphate as well and produces molecules of water. The 'push' given to the electrons by the chemical reaction, or the voltage of the electricity, is about 2 volts. So in a car battery six of these lead and lead dioxide 'cells' are joined together to increase the total 'push' to 12 volts. Not all such chemical reactions are reversible, but in a car battery it is. This means that when too much of the lead and lead dioxide plates have been turned to lead sulphate and the power is low, we just need to apply electricity at a higher voltage to the metal plates and the reaction reverses, giving us lead and lead dioxide again and recharging the battery.

Because batteries push electrons out of one battery terminal and back into the other, it is possible to short-circuit them. Instead of connecting them to a circuit that gives some resistance to the flow of electrons, like a light bulb or electronic gadget, if a piece of metal or wire accidentally connects the two terminals directly, the flow of electrons will have little to slow them down. Huge numbers will flow very quickly (a high current), which may generate so much heat that either the metal connected to the battery becomes red hot and melts, or the battery itself becomes too hot. Because batteries often have chemicals in them (such as sulphuric acid in a car battery), it's not nice to get them very hot. In the worst case, the chemicals inside might boil, turn into rapidly expanding gases and explode the battery casing with a bang. Typically, the larger the battery, the more power it can produce, and so the more dangerous it is to short-circuit.

Car batteries are large, high-power batteries and are actually particularly prone to exploding. Not only can you make them go bang by short-circuiting them, but as a side-effect of its normal chemical reaction, highly flammable hydrogen gas can be produced. If the battery is not well maintained and a naked flame or spark ignites a build-up of hydrogen gas, the explosion may ruin your whole engine. If you are working on the car at the time, you will be seriously hurt. People have lost their hearing from the bang or been blinded by the acid spraying out.

It's not a good idea to immerse batteries in water because water conducts electricity. The water shouldn't get inside the battery, because the metals and chemicals are sealed inside casings to protect them. But it will create a short circuit, a wet path from one terminal of the battery directly to the other. What happens next depends on the water, the power and the type of the battery.

The conductivity of water is dependent on what's in it. Pure water is actually a poor conductor of electricity, but add lots of salt (like seawater) and water is able to conduct electricity much more effectively. It does this because salty water contains a lot of ions, or electrically charged atoms or molecules that have lost or gained electrons so that they have fewer or more than the normal number that fly around them. A positively charged particle missing an electron is attracted to negatively charged particles, just as magnets are attracted to other magnets of opposite polarities. So the more salty the water is, the more free ions it contains, and the more those ions enable the solution to conduct the flow of electrons via their movement. Substances that have this effect are known as electrolytes, and they are used through our bodies to allow us to maintain the right balance of fluids within our cells.

Even the saltiest water is still a million times worse at conducting electricity than metals, however, and pure drinking water can be 10,000 times worse than that. Bring water into contact with a low-voltage electrical supply and not much happens. But spill water on a household supply of 240V (or 120V) and it will find its way through, just as it will find its way through you if you touch it (so don't). If you have enough voltage, electricity can even jump through the air. Lightning does exactly this because its voltage is more than a billion volts. The air molecules are exploded apart into free electrons and ions, making them much more conductive than normal air.

Batteries are a long way from lightning. Take a low-power, low-voltage watch battery and drop it into drinking water and not very much happens. The battery may discharge quicker than usual, but the poor conductivity of water means that you'll probably be able to fish it out, dry it off and still have a usable battery. Children sometimes swallow these batteries and have them pass through their systems without harm to child or battery. But take a modern lithium-ion battery designed to provide lots of power to a portable computer and dunk it in water, and something else happens.

Modern batteries like these are not just simple combinations of metals and chemicals. Many now also have little electronic brains that monitor the current state of the batteries. The little circuits inside the battery casing keep a close eye on the batteries as they are being charged, to stop them from becoming overcharged and becoming too hot. They also check to see how much current is being drawn from the battery. If you were stupid enough to try and short-circuit this kind of battery, the electronic brain would sense the excessive drain and would cut out the power. There's also a fail-safe internal fuse that is triggered by heat. If the battery somehow became overcharged or was short-circuited or indeed was put in a fire, this fuse would blow, cutting all power from the battery permanently. When that fuse has gone, your battery will never work again, so all you can do is buy a replacement and recycle the old one.

So when a lithium-ion (or similar modern battery) is accidentally put in water, in the worst case (if the water is very salty), the short circuit may cause enough heating of the battery for its fuse to blow. In the best case (if it is fairly pure water), the battery may just cut its own power for a while, until it dries off and its terminals are no longer being connected by the water.

Older batteries (such as AA- or AAA-sized batteries, whether rechargeable or not) and some of the smaller modern batteries do not have these safety features. Get them wet, and the short circuit may make them hot enough to burst and contaminate whatever gadget they are sitting in with their corrosive contents. Even worse, because there is no safety cut-out and they might be powering the gadget at the time it gets wet, the short circuit may happen in the electronics first, forcing a large amount of current through one of the chips and destroying it, rendering your gadget dead for evermore. (And if you're very unlucky, this might happen even if your device is powered by a modern battery with a built-in fuse.)

Dropping electronics into water is actually very common. The top ways to get your gadget wet are in puddles, the washing machine and the toilet. If your electronic gadget has explored new underwater worlds, the first thing you should do is take out the batteries and dry everything off. If the batteries have leaked inside, then carefully clean everything. Do not attempt to charge it, power it from an adapter or use it at all until it is completely dry. An expert will quickly dismantle the device and dry it by hand. If you don't want to do that, a warm spot in the sun (or airing cupboard) for a couple of days should do the trick. The longer you wait, the better. If you can, replace the battery. Then, when all is dry again, when you insert the battery and press the 'on' button, your gadget might just work again.

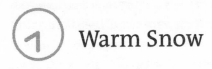

Warm Snow

You're now slightly late. You step out of the house and slam the front door with barely enough time to make the 10-mile drive to work. You press the remote to unlock the car, half expecting it not to work. The locks make their reassuring clunk, accompanied by the usual flash of the lights. It's a new car, shiny black, kept clean with a wash each week, and your parking space is sheltered under a lovely old tree, so it never gets much rain on it. As you open the door you feel a few drops land on your jacket and hear a little pattering on the car. Is it raining? The sky is blue. Brushing the water from your jacket, you climb into the driver's seat, placing your bag on the seat next to you, and close the door. Hand on the steering wheel you insert the key in the ignition ... and then stop. Your hand is white. Your car has a splattering of white all over its bonnet. Your jacket has a big streak of white down the sleeve, which has deposited yet more white into the fabric seat of the car. Everywhere you look you see bird poo.

If you must have a creature defecate on you, then perhaps a bird is not a bad choice. Birds' droppings don't smell very much, you can see them very clearly, and they're not usually that large. Imagine a dog turd falling from the sky. And what a good thing pigs can't fly!

What use is bird poo to anyone? It's easy enough to dismiss as just another of life's daily annoyances, but in fact birds' droppings are very valuable. Amazingly, bird poo business is worth over a billion dollars, and there's not enough of it to meet demand. Countries have even gone to war over who can keep the most bird poo. That white gloop contains something extremely useful.

Birds, like marsupials and lizards, do not have separate openings for urine and faeces. Instead they do it all out of one opening, known as the cloaca. This is why the result is rather runny. There are three elements to any dropping: the urine, the urate and the faeces. The watery bit around the edge is the urine. It should be clear; if it's green the bird may be suffering from liver disease; if it's red, the bird might have eaten a lot of red fruits or it might be suffering from lead poisoning. The white stuff is the urate; it's a useful adaptation evolved to enable birds to continue to remove waste in arid environments without losing too much water. If the urate is white, the bird is stressed; if it looks yellow the bird is malnourished or starving. Birds produce more urate than urine, for most birds have no bladders – it's another useful adaptation to keep them light and able to fly more easily. (The exception is the ostrich, which, being a large, flightless bird, loses nothing by having a bladder – but its bladder works slightly differently from mammalian bladders.) Finally, the dark blobs in the middle of the urate are the faeces. Their colour really depends on what the bird just ate.

It's the urate that people are interested in as it contains ammonia, and uric, phosphoric, oxalic and carbonic acids. From large quantities of bird poo you can extract phosphorus, nitrogen and potassium nitrate. These just happen to form some of the important ingredients for fertilisers and gunpowder. Plants are fertilised by these substances, for the fertiliser provides many of the raw materials needed for the plants to make themselves. Plant cell membranes are made from phospholipids (which derive from phosphorus), their internal chemical energy supplies also make use of phosphorus, and the amino acids used to build proteins all contain nitrogen. Gunpowder (black powder) relies on potassium nitrate for the explosion, for it releases oxygen, which causes everything else to burn quickly.

You need a lot of bird poo to make a bang or a flower. Luckily, birds like to poo a lot. A little bird, the size of a budgerigar, will generally poo every 30 minutes or more. A larger bird, the size of a magpie, may only poo every hour. (They can't help it: they have efficient little intestines and no bladders so their food may be digested and out the other end in anything from 10 to 45 minutes. Flightless birds are able to take their time and may take several hours digesting.) Because of the constant need to poop, birds aren't so picky about where they go to the toilet.

They'd never get anything done in the day if they always went to a certain place to relieve themselves. However, inevitably, wherever a lot of birds roost for the night or nest to rear young does become somewhat covered in droppings. Park your car under a tree and you're almost asking for it to be pooped on. But there are places in the world where birds do more than a few droppings.

In some remote islands, originally undisturbed by humans or any other predators, millions of seabirds made their homes. There are many examples, such as Nauru (in the south Pacific), Juan de Nova Island (near Madagascar) and Navassa (in the Caribbean). Over hundreds of thousands of years millions of birds each year would live, rear young and poop many times a day on the islands. These were dry places with not much rain to wash it all away. The result was unimaginably huge deposits of dried droppings, or guano as it became known. Deposits about 45 metres (150 feet) deep are quite common on some islands. The island of Navassa is 3 kilometres long, 1.6 kilometres wide (2 by 1 mile), and is solid guano.

The ingredients in guano are so useful for gunpowder and fertiliser that they were extensively mined. By 1879 the business in mining guano and other minerals from the Atacama Desert was so good for Chile that Bolivia decided to increase the taxes on Chilean companies in the area. This led to a dispute between Chile and Bolivia that quickly deteriorated into a territorial dispute and then a full-scale war. Bolivia demanded the assistance of Peru, which resulted in fierce fighting at sea and the eventual occupation of Peru by Chile. The War of the Pacific lasted four years and resulted in Chile gaining new territory and leaving Bolivia cut off from the coast as a land-locked country. Even to this day, tension remains high between the countries.

Similar sad stories exist about other guano islands. In Navassa black slaves were forced to mine guano for very little pay and were tortured or killed if they complained. (Surprisingly, this was after the American Civil War, when Navassa was owned by the USA.) Eventually the slaves revolted and had their revenge on the whites, chopping off their arms, legs and heads, killing fifteen and injuring many others. The island became known as 'Devil's Island'.

Amazingly, bird poo does more than create islands. Guano plays a significant role in the world's ecosystems. It has been estimated that seabird droppings transfer somewhere between 10,000 and 100,000 tons of phosphorus from the sea to the land each year. Waterfowl may transfer as much as 40 per cent of the nitrogen and 75 per cent of all phosphorus in wetland environments. Without these birds fertilising the land, many environments might have remained too nutrient-poor and so may not have been colonised by plants. Without the plants, there would be no insects, no animals and no ecosystem. Indeed, about a hundred years ago, when arctic foxes were accidentally introduced to the Aleutian archipelago (volcanic islands extending westward from Alaska), the resulting reduction in seabird numbers dramatically affected the nutrients in the soils, which transformed the landscape from lush grasslands to sparse dwarf shrubs.

But what is valuable in one place, is a nuisance in another. Bird droppings aren't going to fertilise anything if they land on our clothes or our cars. In fact, they're more likely to do harm than good, as they're slightly acidic. Leave a dropping for a while on a shiny car and it will leave a mark even when you do clean it off. The acid in the dropping actually eats away a layer of paint, leaving a tiny dimple in the surface where the dropping landed. It's the result of another chemical reaction, the molecules of the substance reacting with water and the surface of the car, resulting in bonds being broken between molecules and their hydrogen ions (protons) or electrons from atoms, and then the formation of new substances instead. Both the acid (within the bird poo) and the base (the car paint) are slowly transformed and used in the reaction, leaving a non-acidic poo and a spoiled area of paint.

The effects of the acid are very noticeable on cars because their surfaces are so carefully maintained to give them a perfect shine. Often the only way to restore the shine of your car after this kind of mishap is to use a slightly abrasive polish, which removes a tiny layer of the surface of the paint and allows you to even out the damage and make it less noticeable. The best way to avoid damage from droppings is to wax your car. A layer of wax between any droppings and the paint will prevent the acid from reaching the paint and will also make it easier to clean nasty substances from the bodywork. But take care when wiping it away: birds often eat small particles of grit to help break down and digest food in their stomachs – they have no teeth to perform this role in their mouths as we do – so most bird poo has enough grit in it to scratch your car if you carelessly brush it or wipe with a dry cloth.

Bird droppings can cause serious problems for many other manmade structures. Apart from nuisance and damage to statues and buildings caused by the acids, sometimes droppings can cause serious safety problems. For example, the landing pads for helicopters (helidecks) are often the only way to reach normally unmanned structures out at sea. The droppings of sea birds can cover markings and lights used by the pilots for guidance, making landing hazardous.

It pays to be careful around bird poo because it contains many kinds of bacteria that can cause infection and illness. Limping pigeons with swollen and deformed feet are actually suffering from a poo-borne infection. These birds commonly injure their feet on sharp edges and 'anti-pigeon' spikes on buildings. The injuries frequently become infected from the droppings at their roosting sites, leading to swelling and deformity known as 'bumble foot'. Humans can't catch bumble foot, but we can be affected in other ways because dried bird poo becomes quite powdery when it is disturbed, and the chalky cloud may contain several nasty varieties of fungus, some of which can cause serious respiratory illnesses in humans. It may be great as a fertiliser, but you don't want to breathe that stuff in.

Losing Track

You slam the front door and hurriedly climb back into the car.
Your jacket is now in the washing machine, and you're just hoping
it doesn't rain. You've wiped the marks off the car, and at last
you're ready to go. As you begin driving, you start to relax. The
music on the car radio is calming you down and the traffic is
blissfully light. You've left your troubles behind you. You pull up
at a red light, and frown. That reminded you of something ... The
light turns green and you continue. Only about 10 minutes before
you reach the office now, which will give you just enough time to
prepare the papers you have in your bag. You glance to your left,
where you'd put the bag. It's not there.

Your eyes widen in disbelief. How can it not be there? You
remember putting it there! Was it stolen? No, you'd used tissues
from the bag to wipe at the bird poo, so the bag was definitely in
the car. But you'd put the bag on the roof of the car to open it
and retrieve the tissues. Then you'd thrown away the tissues
inside the house and put the jacket in the washing machine. And
then you'd hurried back to the car with its door still open, got in
and shut the door and backed out and ... driven off with the bag
on the roof. You pull over and jump out of the car. The bag is no
longer there.

Think of a number between 10 and 100. (No pens or paper – this is a
memory test.) Without forgetting that number, think of the age of one
of your parents or siblings. Without forgetting both those numbers,
think of your height in centimetres or inches. Keeping those three
numbers in your mind, think of the number of a house or flat you grew
up in. Now add a fifth number to your mental list: the sum of the last

two numbers multiplied by two (use a calculator if you need to, but clear it after getting the answer). Now add a sixth: the last two digits of your phone number. Finally, one more: the approximate number of minutes past the hour that you woke up this morning. Without re-reading this text, write down your seven numbers.

How did you do? (You can judge your score by reading through the text again.) If you got four or fewer correct, don't worry, that's quite normal. If you managed to remember all seven, then you have a superb short-term memory. The average person can remember only about four or five different things at a time (and the memory test above was full of distractions to make you less likely to remember them all). Some research suggests that the more you remember, the higher your IQ, but there are plenty of extremely bright people who have very poor short-term memories.

What is a short-term memory, anyway? Memory, like everything else that the brain does, is not a straightforward process. Much of what our brain chooses to store depends on the time it happens and its significance to us. For example, sensory memory is nothing more than a split-second snapshot of our perceptions. It's what happens when you glance at something and then recall what you saw less than a second later. Those things that we find more relevant may then be pushed through to our short-term memories, which last no more than a minute. And a few details (but really not that many) that are important may then be pushed further into our long-term memories, which can sometimes, through a process of recall and refreshing, last for the rest of our lives.

Short-term memory is different from the shorter sensory memory because you're not actually remembering what your senses detected. Instead, you're remembering what other parts of your brain thought about the things you saw or heard. Glance at a giant M on a billboard and a half-second later you can recall the shape that made up the letter. Thirty seconds later you remember that you saw a big letter M, but not necessarily what it looked like. Long-term memory becomes even more vague – a week later you might remember that you saw a big letter of the alphabet, but not what the letter was. An awful lot of information is simply discarded; in fact, many of our sensory experiences never even make it to our short-term memories. If you perform the same action every day (putting sugar in your tea, washing your hair, cleaning your teeth) you can often perform the action without bothering to remember that you've done it, and find yourself checking later: has my tea got sugar in it, did I put the shampoo on already, did I clean my teeth earlier?

Because we only remember useful information that our brain has already processed, we are able to store much more in our heads. It's the difference between storing a continuous movie of everything we see and hear and a set of textual notes about our experiences – the notes need far less space to store them. But our brains are also designed to fool us about our memories. Whenever we recall something, we use the notes to reconstruct imaginary movies, pushing the information back through the vision centres of our brains as though we're really seeing what happened. Like our dreams, it makes our memories seem vivid and real, but most of it is simply reconstructed out of our imaginations. (This is why we can enjoy novels so much – our brains are very good at extrapolating entire worlds from just a few pieces of information.) Every time we recall something we see a slightly different movie, and over time we may make new mental notes about that experience or change the original notes. So our memories are fluid, changing slightly each time we access them and sometimes becoming corrupted and wholly incorrect. It's a phenomenon well known to the police when they ask witnesses what they saw at the time of a crime. Even when someone has paid attention, they can misremember significant details, such as height, hair colour and clothing; and ask the same witness what they remember two months later and you may hear a substantially different description.

It's also very easy to produce false memories in people, especially when relaxation states such as those used by hypnosis are employed. It has been known for people to be 'regressed' under the suggestive state of hypnosis and then, with the help of prompting from the therapist, construct entirely fictional past experiences (or even past lives). As you dwell in the fictional past, often acting out roles for the therapist, your brain follows its normal method of making notes of the experiences and storing them as memories. When you wake after such a session, you remember the experiences just as clearly as you remember any real experiences, and indeed you may firmly believe that your hypnosis-induced dream is real and you have 'reawakened' a previously lost memory.

Memories rely on various regions of the brain. The temporal lobes on each side of the brain, about the level of your ears, help you remember things that you see (on the right hand side) and things you hear (on the left hand side). The hippocampus (a pair of little regions shaped like seahorses that form part of the temporal lobes) also has something to do with memory, helping us retain memories as longer term memories and providing us with spatial memory. Indeed, some studies have shown that London taxi drivers, who are obliged to learn the whole street map of London, have hippocampuses that are larger than normal.

The movie *Memento* provides an excellent portrayal of what happens when an individual suffers damage to these areas of the brain and can no longer convert short-term memories into long-term ones. Those with this condition (known as anterograde amnesia) may recall everything before the accident, but are unable to lay down new memories. When anterograde amnesia combines with retrograde amnesia (the loss of all memories before the accident) the person may have a perpetual feeling of just awakening, of never having existed or been conscious before that instant – and yet older skills, such as playing the piano, may be retained.

But our knowledge and understanding of exactly how the brain creates, stores and manipulates memories is extremely limited. We look at many brains of different mammals, but most of what we know comes from three sources. We know what separate neurons look like and what they do on their own. We can see which parts of the brain seem to have the most active neurons when performing certain tasks (as measured by machines such as electroencephalograms, which measure electrical activity, and functional magnetic resonance imaging, which measures blood flow). We know what happens when chunks of brains are damaged because of an accident. But that's about it. It's equivalent to trying to understand how a country works by watching one person, and also identifying the areas in the landscape that use the most power and examining countries that may have had a power cut in some places. You can identify the major towns and cities, but you have no idea how the people work together to keep a country healthy. So we can identify the major regions of the brain, but with a hundred billion neurons involved, each connected on average to 20,000 neighbours, we don't really understand how the separate neurons work together to do everything the brain does.

While neuroscientists, neurologists and neurobiologists continue to work on the problem, we do know a few useful things. We know that our brains get better at certain tasks with practice – the more you use it, the better it becomes. We know that old age does not mean an impaired ability to think – if you are still active mentally you should be just as good as ever (there are many professors who continue to do groundbreaking research in their seventies and eighties). And we know that short-term memory can be improved or, at least, used more effectively. One simple way to change your ability to recall something is to change how the information is presented to you. Sound is a linear input: we have to listen to one word after another or we would not understand them. Sight is a parallel input: we see many things at once. Research has shown that people are better at remembering a list of numbers when hearing the list, compared to when they see it. The parts of our brain designed to cope with linear sound are good at coping with the linear, one-at-a-time items in a list. This is especially true with music – the highly complex linear arrangement of notes in melodies are often remembered with ease, even by those people who think they have terrible memories.

Another way to improve the short-term memory, beyond simple repetition of what you've seen, is to develop skills or memory techniques. There are many variations, but most rely on the fact that your short-term memory is not a perfect record of your senses but a collection of meaningful aspects of your perception. So if you need to remember a list that may seem quite uninteresting to you, the trick is to give it some meaning. The sequence of letters BSCFBIBAABBC may seem very hard to remember, but chunk it into triplets – BSC FBI BAA BBC – and it becomes much easier. Make it into a story (I was awarded my BSc degree and joined the FBI, my current case involved the British airports owned by BAA and was being reported on BBC television) and it's even easier to recall. Other techniques involve mnemonics – for example, to spell 'arithmetic': A Rat In The House May Eat The Ice Cream. Or you might learn to associate numbers and symbols with familiar objects in your life and then make up a story. For example, if 1 is banana, 2 is a pair of shoes, 3 is Tricksy the cat, and the number was 322133, the story could be: Tricksy (3) chewed one pair of shoes (2), peed in another pair (2), slipped on a banana skin (1) and came face to face with himself in the mirror (33). Remember the story and you've remembered the number.

If you do have a problem remembering to do something or to take something, just use one of these tricks. Acronyms are used universally for exactly this reason. For example, when travelling in Europe don't forget your BIKE: Bag, ID card, Keys, Euros. A little effort spent on making something relevant and memorable may save an hour of running around screaming, 'What the hell have I done with it?'

Losing Grip

You check your watch. You're going to be late. Despite retracing the drive from home to the spot where you pulled over, there is no sign of your bag. It must have come off and landed in a ditch at the side of the road somewhere. Without spending several hours checking, you'll never find it. All you can do now is try not to be too late and perhaps print out the crucial papers in your office before running to the meeting. You reach an empty stretch of road, press the 'sport' button on the car and put your foot down. This stretch is a windy country road, just a few miles from the office. You know it well, and despite the corners being a little wet because of run-off from the banks on each side, you're confident your car can take the corners at this speed. Anyway, you're not above the speed limit, you try to justify to yourself. A particularly sharp bend approaches and you suddenly realise there's a cyclist in the way. Time seems to slow down as you wrestle with the steering wheel, swerve around the bicycle and then cut sharp left to take the corner, but you can feel that you're going too fast. The rear of the car loses grip, and the world spins sickeningly to the right. After what seems an eternity, the car slides to a halt and you look around, dazed. You're now facing in the other direction but you're still on the road. The cyclist pulls up and asks if you're OK. Thankfully you're fine, just feeling foolish.

It's actually very difficult to spin a modern car, but you can do it if you try hard enough. More than a hundred years of tyre technology and eighty years of safety systems development mean that today's vehicles are designed to stay on the road and pointing in the direction you steer them. Some will even override the driver and reduce power or apply brakes to make sure you are safe. But if you drive in a car with worn tyres, on a very slippery road, or with the anti-lock brakes and traction control disabled by a 'sport' setting (or not there) it's quite possible to spin the car on a wet corner (and end up in a heap of trouble if you're unlucky). So what do all these components and gadgets in your car really do? How can they keep the car wheels from slipping and sliding?

The most effective way to make sure your car stays on the road is to have decent tyres. Modern tyres are made of vulcanised rubber. Ordinary rubber just oozes out in the sap of a tree called *Hevea brasiliensis* when you cut it. Rubber can also be derived from by-products of petroleum refinement; today 70 per cent of rubber is synthetically made in this way. But untreated rubber is not very useful for tyres. It goes extremely soft and may completely melt in the sun, while in winter it becomes hard and brittle. This was good enough if all you wanted was an eraser – which, indeed, was one early use of rubber – but not much good on a wheel.

The key lay in heating the stuff in the presence of sulphur. Rubber is made from a latex, a bunch of long, spaghetti-like molecules called polymers that give it the oozing, stretchy quality. When heated with sulphur, the sulphur molecules act like glue, sticking the long polymers together at different points to form a springy, spongy structure. Once vulcanised, rubber becomes deformable and much more stable at different temperatures.

The American businessman and inventor Charles Goodyear invented the process of vulcanisation in 1839. Sadly, Goodyear struggled with debt for most of his life, and despite being honoured by the French Emperor Napoleon III for his work towards the end of his life he never made any real money from his invention. The Goodyear company, formed several decades after his death, was named after him but was nothing to do with Charles or his family.

Early rubber tyres were used on bicycles, but although the solid rubber produced good traction on the ground, it was uncomfortable. A Scotsman called John Boyd Dunlop came up with the solution – an air-filled or pneumatic rubber tyre. These weren't just good at making the ride more comfortable on wheeled vehicles, they also had much less rolling resistance. A solid rubber tyre would hit each bump and be slowed down by the collision, but a pneumatic tyre allowed rough bumps to push into its surface without a collision, smoothing out the ride and creating a much more efficient motion. It turned out that Robert William Thompson (another Scotsman) had patented the idea before Dunlop, but nevertheless the Dunlop tyre company soon grew to become one of the most important companies in the industry. Pneumatic tyre technology quickly developed, with tyres being reinforced with fabric and wire to prevent tearing and reduce the number of punctures. Today tyres are ubiquitous for all road vehicles, with thousands of different types designed for different conditions and clever patterns of tread designed to pump away surface water and keep the tyre in contact with the road.

Even the best tyre cannot always provide enough friction to avoid skidding. If the surface of the road is too slippery or an excessive amount of acceleration (from an over-enthusiastic engine) or deceleration (from braking too hard) overcomes the friction, the tyre will skid over the road instead of gripping it. These conditions happen rarely, but so many people use our roads today that you don't have to drive far on a motorway before you see the tell-tale black skid marks left behind from somebody's frightening skid.

Cars were not the first type of vehicle to suffer from this problem. Aircraft travel at much greater speeds than cars, and when they land their brakes have to cope with far more weight and pressure. Aircraft also use their main engines to power all movement, and the main form of steering they have on the ground is braking a left wheel to turn left or a right wheel to turn right. When a plane lands, the pilot has to apply the brakes hard to slow from several hundred miles an hour before the plane reaches the end of the runway. If the wheels of an aeroplane locked up and skidded when slowing, the whole aircraft could slew to the left or the right and destroy itself in a fiery rollover. The problem is as old as the aircraft themselves, and so a braking system had to be invented to prevent such disasters. One of the pioneers of aviation, the Frenchman Gabriel Voisin, developed a hydraulic system that helped prevent the wheels from locking in 1920.

It was many years before our technology became good enough for anti-lock brakes to be reliable and small enough to use on cars. Early systems were mechanical, detecting the too-sudden slowing of a wheel and releasing the pressure on brakes momentarily to allow it to roll and find more grip on the road. By the early 1970s electronics and motion sensors were small enough for the first modern-style anti-lock braking system (ABS) to be placed in production cars. These systems use computers to monitor the speed of rotation of each wheel continuously. If brakes are applied and the speed of the wheels slows dramatically, the brake pressure is momentarily released. It's a very noticeable effect for the driver: brake hard when travelling over slippery or gravelled surfaces and you will feel the judder of the anti-lock braking system as the brakes are applied–released–applied–released to give the tyres more chance to find grip instead of just locking up and skidding out of control. Cars with ABS can still be steered even when braking hard. A car without ABS will skid and slide in the direction you were travelling, whether you move the steering wheel or not. But you must always continue to steer in the direction you want to go, whichever way your car is pointing, for you never know when your tyres might start to grip the road again. Get it right and after a minor slide you will just carry on along the road under perfect control. Steer the wrong way and you may end your skid by simply driving into a ditch. The 'racing driver' skill of controlling a sliding car is very hard to learn, which is why most modern cars use ABS to save you the trouble.

ABS has some significant effects on the performance of the car. Brake hard on a gravelled or icy surface, and the ABS will stop you more quickly than a car without ABS. But brake hard on a clean and dry road, and the ABS will actually bring you to a halt more slowly than a car without it, for the ABS is lifting the pressure from the brakes in a series of judders and letting the wheels roll to stop them from spinning. Some drivers find the juddering brake pedal frightening and lift off, which is the worst thing you could do. The more they judder, the more you know they're working. Pumping conventional brakes produces a similar (slower) effect. You can always tell the cars that had ABS from those that didn't by the black skid marks on the roads: the ABS produces pairs of dotted lines, - - - -, while the older cars just leave big black stripes.

Sometimes even ABS is not enough. If you're going round a bend, brake and lose grip on the road, you may still end up spinning round in a circle and end up facing the wrong way. If your car has a habit of 'oversteering' (the rear of the car stepping out and rotating the car around) a spin may not be hard to produce. Again, an expert driver would be able to correct the car under these conditions, while an inexperienced driver might over-correct, steer too far in the opposite direction and cause the car to 'fishtail', sliding left and right before spinning. This can be very dangerous if the spin happens on a busy road full of fast-moving vehicles. To overcome this problem, many newer cars have electronic stability control (ESC, sometimes called dynamic stability control or something similar). This is integrated with the ABS system, but may also have sensors connected to the steering. When you go round a corner and brake at the same time, the ESC will alter the pressure on the brakes, using the brakes to help you get round the bend just as a pilot uses his brakes to steer his aircraft. The cleverer systems will also adjust the power to the wheels at the same time. The result is that such cars almost never experience oversteer (or understeer) and remain fully controllable. Many studies have shown that ABS and ESC have dramatically reduced the number of serious accidents since their introduction.

Even if you've got new tyres with decent treads on them, they can lose grip when under acceleration (if you've ever heard the screech of a wheel spin when pulling off you'll know what this feels like). Having ABS is no help when you've got your foot on the accelerator pedal – it works only when you brake. If you're cruising along a motorway on a cold day and hit a patch of black ice (invisible to the naked eye) your tyres may well lose all grip, and you may start to slide out of control again. Alternatively, if you've got a car with a huge amount of power, it's possible for the engine to be so strong that the wheels just slip and slide rather than grip the road. One of the first solutions to this problem was invented for such performance cars. The limited slip differential is a clever system for applying power from the engine to the wheels. All modern cars need a differential – this is a clever set of gears that allow the wheels to turn at different speeds. (When a car goes round a corner, the inner wheels have less far to travel than the outer ones, so the inner ones need to travel more slowly than the outer ones.) But if one wheel loses traction altogether, the differential transfers all the power to that wheel and it spins, with the result that the car goes nowhere or goes out of control. A limited slip differential prevents one wheel from going substantially faster than any other and avoids the whole problem.

Modern electronics now provide an even more advanced method. It's called traction control and often integrates with all the other electronic systems, such as ABS and ESC. Traction control senses the movement of the wheels when under acceleration, and if one wheel suddenly starts to spin too quickly the power to that wheel is reduced. It's a remarkable system that allows a car to drive on pure ice – the electronics feeding power to whichever wheel has the best grip and making adjustments hundreds of times a second.

Cars that have good tyres and are full of modern safety systems such as these are amazingly reliable and safe to drive. Some suggest that because modern cars almost 'drive themselves' they encourage greater speed and careless driving, but there is no clear evidence for this. Nevertheless, there are drivers who still like to enjoy the feeling of oversteer and learn the skills of handling their cars in extreme conditions. For this reason certain cars have settings (such as a 'sport' button) that makes the suspension firmer and the steering more responsive and that may reduce the effectiveness of or actively turn off the electronic support. If you have such a car (or if you have an older vehicle without these clever electronics) then take care. The electronic support systems are there to keep you safe. If the road conditions are not optimal or your tyres are old then you may be disabling the electronic brain that will keep you alive.

Mixing Your Drinks

The car starts immediately; you turn in the road and continue your journey. You're still feeling shaken by the spin. Up ahead there's a petrol station, so you decide to pull in and take five minutes to calm down, check the car and maybe have a cup of sweet coffee. You walk around the car and see nothing wrong – no dents or scrapes, and the tyres are fine. Deciding that you may as well fill up with petrol while you're there, you drive up to a pump and realise in your flustered state that you've parked on the wrong side of it. Luckily, the hose seems to reach around the car. You insert the nozzle and fill the tank, trying not to breathe the unpleasant fumes, which somehow seem worse than usual. It's an older pump that doesn't let you pay by card so you go to the kiosk and pay, buying your coffee at the same time and taking it back to the car. The rich, nutty smell of the coffee relaxes you. But time is moving on. You can drink the coffee when you get to work. You start the engine and begin to drive away. Before you've even left the forecourt, a horrible thought hits you like a sledgehammer. The petrol had smelled wrong when you put it into the car. It was also the wrong price. You hit the brakes and fumble for the fuel receipt. Diesel? You've just put diesel into your petrol car!

Diesel and petrol engines may often power identical-looking cars, but they are dissimilar in many ways. Their history, and more importantly, the way that they work, is very different. One clue to the difference is that petrol engines have spark plugs, but diesel engines do not. Another clue is that putting the wrong kind of fuel in an engine may cause it serious damage. But why would two engines that both burn fuel to make vehicles move, work so differently?

Engines have been around since about 1700, but in those days steam was the main source of power. Coal-powered furnaces would be used to heat water into steam. The steam required much more space than the water, so it produced a high pressure. This pressure was the key to making the wheels turn, for the pressure forced pistons to move, and the pistons pushed the wheels around. An ordinary bicycle pump can give you an idea of how a piston works. If you were to pump a tyre until its air was at a very high pressure, the pressure would naturally push the handle of the pump open. It's exactly how a piston works – the pressure of the gas forces the internal piston out of the cylinder. The resulting linear (straight-line) movement is converted into a rotary (circular) movement in just the same way that hoops are rolled along by children. Each push on the rim is a linear motion, and that is converted into a rotary motion by the hoop. Connect a piston to a cam (often attached to a camshaft) and the piston rotates the cam, pushing it round and round.

The origins of internal combustion engines lie in a modification to the steam engine. Instead of heating water to make the pressure, why not create a little explosion inside the cylinder of the piston and produce pressure that way? Perhaps injecting some flammable liquid, such as oil, and then adding a spark would provide the pressure needed to move the piston and rotate the wheels. By 1863 Frenchman Jean-Joseph-Etienne Lenoir had invented the first petroleum-powered internal combustion engine and managed an 80 kilometre (50 mile) round trip in his three-wheeled vehicle. His engine used a simple carburettor to mix air with the fuel to allow it to ignite in the enclosed space of the pistons. It employed electrical sparks to explode the fuel inside the cylinders. The design was refined considerably by other pioneers, such as Germans Gottlieb Daimler and Wilhelm Maybach, who manufactured the first four-wheeled automobile, and Karl Benz, who patented one of the earliest forms of petroleum-powered cars and also founded a successful automobile factory.

The designs of petroleum-powered engines have improved and become much more efficient in the hundred years of development since then. Today, for example, computers are commonly used to inject fuel (in fuel-injection systems) instead of relying on carburettors.

Nevertheless, the principles of the engine remain exactly the same: fuel and air are injected into the cylinders and are ignited by sparks (produced by the spark plugs); the resulting pressure from the explosion moves the pistons, which push cams around and, through a series of gears, make the wheels turn.

Diesel engines are slightly different. At around the time that Benz and Daimler were creating their spark-ignited petroleum engines, other engineers were investigating alternative ways to move pistons. One idea was to use combustible vapour or gas (as opposed to liquid fuel) mixed with air. Another was to use coal dust or oil. But all of these ideas used the same trick to ignite the mixture in the cylinders – compression. Take any gas or liquid and increase its pressure, and that substance becomes hot. It's a simple principle – when you increase the pressure, you're packing more molecules of that substance into a smaller space. Like a crowd of people pushed into a smaller room, the molecules jostle against each other more. The more molecules jiggle about, the hotter the substance is. (Use an old-style bicycle pump for a while, and it gets warm for exactly this reason.) If you have a very hot substance in the presence of oxygen and that substance is flammable, once the ignition temperature is reached the substance will catch fire and burn. If the fuel is rich enough, the burning will occur so rapidly that an explosion will take place, creating a large amount of gas. So if your engine relies on the burning of fuel, there is no need to create a spark to ignite it. You just need to compress the fuel (or the air) until it heats up enough to ignite by itself. This is how diesel engines work, and it's why a diesel engine has no spark plugs.

The first reliable engines that used compression to trigger ignition were developed in the 1890s: German refrigerator engineer Rudolf Diesel obtained his patent in 1892, and this type of engine has borne his name ever since. (It's no coincidence that a refrigeration engineer should think of compression to heat a substance, for the external compression and internal depressurisation of a liquid is how refrigerators and air conditioners transfer heat outside.) Modern diesel engines draw air into the pistons, which compress it as much as 25:1, then fuel is injected into the hot gas to ignite it. Modern diesels also have 'glow plugs', which help warm up a cold car to enable the compression of air to reach the right temperature (they have nothing to do with spark plugs).

Diesel engines have many advantages over their petrol cousins. The lack of extra ignition sources mean that they tend to be more reliable and less fussy over types of fuel, and also more economical with fuel. They run at slower speeds and have better torque at lower speeds (they exert more force in order to move), making them ideal for trains, ships, buses and trucks. But because their power is limited to a small band of low speeds, a truck may need sixteen gears in order to allow it to travel faster. Diesel engines can also be rather noisy and may produce blue sooty smoke when they are cold and not all the fuel is being burned. This, combined with their small power band, led to an image problem that prevented them from being used in cars until quite recently. Today, the performance of modern diesel engines is almost identical to that of petrol engines, and this, combined with their cheaper running costs, has led to a dramatic increase in the number of diesel engines in cars. In Europe diesels are now just as popular as petrol engines (and in some countries more popular). In the USA the image problem persists, and diesels are still uncommon in private vehicles. The increase in the use of diesel engines means that mistakenly putting diesel fuel in a petrol engine, or petrol in a diesel engine, is one of the most common errors made by drivers today. In 2005 120,000 drivers made this mistake in the UK alone.

Diesel engines are surprising in the range of fuels they can handle (especially the older engines that did not use carefully timed electronic fuel injection). A diesel can happily run on vegetable oil, peanut oil or bio-diesel, a plant-derived oil that may become increasingly popular as natural oil reserves dwindle and become expensive. The normal fuel for diesel engines is a product similar to kerosene derived from crude oil. This is rather different from petrol. Diesel is oily and needs to be so to provide lubrication; petrol actively strips away oil. Because older diesel engines (earlier than about 1996) are very forgiving, they would probably cope with a small amount of petrol if you were accidentally to add it to your tank. But put too much petrol in a diesel engine and run it and you are likely to destroy the injectors and the seals on the fuel pump. On modern cars even unlocking the doors may activate the fuel pump, spreading the petrol through the system. The solution is usually to drain the fuel from the car and bleed the fuel up to the pump, then refill with fresh diesel. If you've just filled an empty tank with petrol then whatever you do, don't try to drive anywhere, or the resulting bill from the garage may be very big.

If you managed to put diesel in a petrol engine, then again you are likely to be in trouble. More than 10 per cent diesel and the engine probably won't run at all, or if it does you will really hear, see and smell the difference. There will be a strange plinking or pinging noise and lots of smelly black smoke, and you'll be lucky to get far. Too much diesel and the spark plugs simply can't ignite the fuel, so once the nasty mixture is drawn into the engine it will probably just stall. The solution is not to try and drive anywhere, to drain the tank and fuel lines and to refill with petrol, and hopefully all will be well. If you do manage to run the car for a little while on this unfortunate mix, you will probably ruin your catalytic converter from the sooty mix coming from the exhaust, and you might even damage the pistons within the engine. (Putting leaded petrol into a car designed for unleaded will also ruin the catalytic converter just as effectively.)

In the UK some (but not all) fuelling pump nozzles are different sizes: diesel large and petrol smaller, preventing you from putting diesel into a petrol engine. For those driving cars with diesel engines, this does not prevent you from putting in petrol and ruining your engine. There's also no coherent colour coding system, and the accident is so common that insurance companies usually refuse to pay out. Unfortunately, car companies, garages and even the petrol stations only gain more sales when we make these mistakes, so no automatic 'wrong fuel' detectors exist in cars or pumps (although scientists have published and patented solutions to the problem). The only option is to check and double check each time you fill your vehicle that you've got the right fuel for the right engine.

An Unpleasant Trip

You're not happy about leaving the car, but the friendly staff at the petrol station said they'd handled the situation before, and you're now in a real hurry. Clouds are starting to blow in from the west, hiding the sun and turning the bright morning into gloom. You walk briskly along the road you should have driven down 20 minutes ago. It's a good 4-mile walk, but you're in the outskirts of the town now and you think there are buses that go in the right direction. In fact, you see a bus stop just ahead – and there's a bus coming! You put on a burst of speed you didn't know you had. At least you don't have a bag to slow you down. Each foot hits the ground solidly, powering you along like an athlete in formal shoes. There's no way you're going to miss the bus. Without warning your foot slips on the edge of a kerb and twists. The ground reaches up and hits you in the face. You land heavily, bruised and out of breath, feeling stupid. How hard can it be just to run?

Walking, running and even standing still may not seem like very impressive feats, but all such actions actually require a surprising amount of computation by your brain. When you consider exactly how many joints there are between your head and your feet, it becomes easier to see why it's such a tricky task. Ankles, knees, hips, more than twenty joints of your spine and your neck, not to mention the joints in your arms to help you balance. All have to be at the right angles at the right times to stop you from falling. It's like balancing thirty pens on top of each other end-to-end (with elastic threaded through them) and then somehow being able to move the wobbly tower without it toppling over.

In engineering, computer and rocket science a highly simplified version of the problem is known as the pole-balancing, or inverted pendulum, problem. Imagine a pole on its end, standing on a moveable platform. The problem is to keep the pole balanced vertically by only moving the platform. The problem is equivalent to keeping a rocket pointing upwards as its engine fires beneath it. If the rocket starts to topple, its engine may make it spiral into the ground – not an ideal way to launch a satellite into space. We can solve the pole-balancing problem using fast and clever controllers, which sense the direction of the topple and move the base in the same direction to halt it. But moving from the pole-balancing problem to the double pole-balancing problem (another pole balancing on the end of the first) or triple pole-balancing problem, and we have enormous trouble in making computer controllers that are fast enough and precise enough to keep them balancing end-to-end. It's one reason why our robots never quite move with the grace of living organisms. We have the technology to build the bodies and make all the same joints, and have motors to move all of the joints in the right ways. We just haven't managed to create electronic brains that are flexible and responsive enough to use the robot bodies effectively. In a very real sense, we solve problems harder than those in rocket science every time we stand up.

There are many good reasons why organisms are good at moving themselves around without tripping over all the time. It was so crucial for animals to get this right that early on in our evolutionary history the primitive brains of our ancestors mainly concentrated on coordinating muscles and senses. Any creature that fell over too much was eaten by predators pretty quickly, creating a strong evolutionary pressure towards animals that could move reliably. Only the creatures able to sense where their limbs were and where the ground was, and how to use this knowledge to move, would survive long enough to have children. So generation after generation of better moving animals resulted in animal brains that could instinctively move over rough ground. We still have this primitive brain buried deep inside our own. In the millions of years of evolution since then, we've added layers of new brain material around this brain stem. But we have an instinctive ability to stand on our limbs, walk and cope with rough ground that is given to us by the unconscious reptilian brain inside us. Without it, we would be much like one of our robots – stumbling, clumsy and prone to falling over.

Another reason why our robots move 'robotically' and not smoothly as we do, is feedback. We have a huge number of very precise built-in sensors. Without all the senses, even the best brains in the world would never be able to keep themselves standing up. These senses are nothing to do with sight, sound, touch, taste, smell, heat, pain, pleasure and all the other diverse senses we have. In order to move we need proprioception senses (known as kinaesthesia) and balance.

Close your eyes and raise your left hand above your head. How do you know it's above your head? You can feel it is there, but how? It's not touching anything. If you're thinking that perhaps it's the feeling of weight changing on the joints in your arm as you reposition it, then try moving while floating in the bath or a swimming pool. You will still instinctively 'know' where your limbs are.

This sense is called kinaesthesia – the sense of our own movement and position. It works through specialised stretch sensors in our muscles that tell the brain that muscles are in use. It also uses sensors linked to tendons and joints, telling us that a joint is being repositioned. Our brains also integrate feelings of skin stretching and touch to help us fine-tune our awareness of where all our joints, muscles and limbs are. The myriad tiny senses are all correlated to individual muscle and joint movements, enabling us to make microscopic adjustments to every muscle and joint, giving us extraordinary control and precision in our movements.

Of course, like all senses, there are times when they can be a little confused. Drinking a lot of alcohol impairs our ability to make use of the information from these senses and so a simple test of touching our noses with eyes shut or walking along a straight line becomes a real challenge. There are also simple sensory illusions that demonstrate the senses of kinaesthesia. One example used to study how the brain processes these senses is the Pinocchio Illusion. Close your eyes, touch your nose and apply a vibrating device (perhaps the handle of an electric toothbrush or razor) to the triceps (the outer) muscle of that arm. The vibration will fool your brain into thinking that the muscle is contracting more than the biceps, pulling your hand further from your nose. But because your brain can also feel that the hand is still touching your nose, it assumes that your nose must be growing longer and longer.

In addition to these internal senses, we also have another hugely important sense: balance or equilibrioception. In mammals this sense is found in the inner ears in a maze-like network of tubes known as the labyrinth. The vestibular system is a set of circular tubes and little sacs filled with fluid. The circular tubes are called canals, and we have three inside each ear: the horizontal, anterior and posterior canals. Imagine taking a tractor tyre inner tube, somehow coating its inner surface with fur and then pumping it full of a viscous, gloopy fluid. Rotate the tube and the fluid takes a little while to catch up. Because the tube moves faster than the fluid, the fur lining the inside is swept against the motion. Shrink the whole thing a few thousand times and that's how the canals work. Whenever the fur (hairs) are moved, nerves in the hairs tell our brain that a rotation is taking place. To make sure we can sense rotation in all directions, we have one for turning in a circle, one for forwards and one for sideways rotation. But we can do more than this. When we go up or down in a lift we *feel* the motion – and that's not a rotation. Or when we accelerate in a car, we can feel the change in speed. To enable this kind of linear (straight line) sense, we have two other little tubes, filled with fluid and tiny particles called otoliths. One detects any change in vertical movement, and the other detects a change in horizontal movement. They are also sensitive enough to detect that we're tilted at an angle. Fascinatingly, because these sensory organs work in a similar way to the way our inner ears detect sound (little hairs are disturbed by sound waves), some research has suggested that one of these tubes – the saccule – may even enable some people to hear ultrasonic speech (which is too high to hear using our normal hearing).

Our sense of balance is wired directly to the muscles of our eyes through just a few neurons. Every time our heads or bodies move, the change in balance makes our eyes move to compensate. It's exactly like the anti-shake mechanisms used in modern digital cameras (which move their internal light-sensitive chips to counter the effects of a shaking hand), and because the compensating eye movements happen so quickly, our vision is kept sharp and in focus. But the direct wiring from balance to eyes has another side effect. If we spin round and round for a while, the fluid in those canals eventually catches up and starts spinning with us. Then when we stop spinning, the fluid takes a little while to slow down. So for a few seconds, there's a flow of fluid moving the little hairs, telling our brains that we are spinning in the other direction. Our automatic eye movements then constantly adjust to compensate for the imaginary motion, and we become very disoriented. We call this effect dizziness.

Despite the occasional false readings from our senses, the detailed and precise information that they provide to our brains enables us to propel ourselves around with amazing proficiency. Standing upright by balancing on two legs is impressive enough, but walking is an extraordinary balancing act. We have to initiate a controlled topple, but before we fall flat on our face, we must move a leg to support us, shift our entire weight onto that leg, continue the topple, move the other leg to support us, and so on. Make a single mistake and we could be badly injured. Running is even more amazing – we actually make little jumps, pushing off the ground with one leg, landing on the other, transferring our weight to that leg, absorbing the impact and pushing off for another little jump to land on the first leg again. Look at our best humanoid robots walking and you'll see a careful, clumsy and extremely slow zombie shuffle. We can't make robots that can run like us – they just fall over.

With our stabilised, anti-shake eyes and large mammalian brains with impressive vision-processing centres, we are also able to look ahead as we move and predict the height and texture of the ground before we reach it. This clever automatic computation compensates for unexpected circumstances, falls, trips and shoves, without any conscious thought. Once we've had some practice, we can even look at the movement of other creatures around us and effortlessly predict where they will be in the future. The information from these higher layers of the brain is then fed down to the brain stem, which automatically adjusts the different muscles to change our pattern of foot placements. Watch any four-legged animals run together and you'll see constant split-second adjustments to their gaits to ensure each foot is placed on safe, steady ground, and no collisions take place. We all have this ability. It's so automatic that consciously controlling where we place our feet takes quite a lot of concentration. And while we don't have four legs or a tail to worry about, we do use our arms as aids to balance. Again, the swinging, counterbalancing movements of our arms is entirely unconscious, and actively trying to control it while walking can be a real mental challenge.

Amazing brains and senses are no use if we don't use them. Run for a bus without looking where you are going and you will be unaware of any rough terrain ahead. Your brain stem will assume that the ground continues without change, and so when a foot encounters an unseen hazard your gait will be wrong – too much weight will be placed on a leg that has nothing to support it, and you will stumble and fall. It's best to pay attention to where you're heading, especially if you're in a hurry.

Coming Unstuck

You reach the bus stop just as the bus arrives. Thankfully the fall did nothing except hurt your pride. You step aboard, squeeze past the standing passengers and collapse into the only free seat with a grateful sigh. Before long, the passenger seated next to you rises to leave and you stand to let her out. As you get to your feet, you feel something strange on the back of your head. Your searching fingers find a blob of something warm and sticky in your hair. As you touch it, you smell a sugary, minty fragrance. Your nose wrinkles in disgust. It's chewing gum! And worse, as you stood up, it must have stretched into a long sticky snake that has glued itself to the back of your head and onto your collar. You try to pull it off and bring nothing more than a string of minty-fresh sticky glue before your eyes, which is now also sticking fast to your fingers. You sit back down and obsessively try to pull away the horrible substance, but all you seem to do is make it stick more. Why does the stupid stuff not come off?

The problem of sticky chewing gum is an unpleasant one, not least because it involves a substance that has spent a while inside somebody's mouth. In fact, the problem is so severe that Singapore banned gum from the country in 1992. This may seem a little extreme, but in the 1980s vandals were habitually disposing of gum in mailboxes, on lift buttons, inside keyholes, on the door sensors of trains, on floors, walls and the seats of buses. The whole transport system of the country was suffering because of chewing gum. The ban solved the problem, but Singapore was not allowed to keep its prohibition for long. American chewing gum giant Wrigley managed to have gum listed on the Singapore–America Free Trade Agreement, and lobbied the country to accept gum. In 2004 the country was forced to allow chewing gum (but only for health reasons) once again. Whether this means a return to chewing gum nightmares for the inhabitants of Singapore remains to be seen.

The problem is that chewing gum doesn't degrade or get broken down by bacteria and insects as most of our food waste does. It behaves like tar, coating whatever surface it is left on with its sticky, stretchy goo. So when it ends up somewhere undesirable, that's exactly where it will stay, until it is removed. How many times have you sat at a desk or a chair and found your fingers squelching in somebody's gum? There's a lot of old gum out there, and more is being thoughtlessly left every minute.

Chewing gum is not a new invention, despite its modern use for vandalism. Archaeologists recently found three wads of chewed birch resin in the remains of the floor of a hunter-gatherer hut, on a Swedish island called Orust. The teeth imprints in the gum were those of a teenager. The gum was 9,000 years old.

Many of the original gums were formed from resins extracted from the mastic tree, which grew in Greece and Turkey. The Ancient Greeks used the gum to clean their teeth and sweeten their breath. This is also the source of the English word 'masticate', meaning 'chew'. The Greeks were not unique. Native Americans in New England used the resin from spruce trees, and early settlers learned to copy this practice and substituted other substances, such as sweetened paraffin wax, rubber or the milky juice of the chicle tree. All these sticky resins are natural latexes or rubbers, but today most gums use a manmade latex, mixed with oils to keep in moisture. Sweeteners and mint oils give it flavour, and it is coated with sugar powder (for stick gums) or a sweet candy shell (for pellet-style gums) to stop the pieces from sticking to the packaging. Once you begin chewing, your mouth dissolves and removes the sugars, while also mixing the ingredients and warming them to optimal stretchy, sticky temperature.

Gum has its stretchy property because of the composition of latex. Whether manmade or oozing from a cut in a tree, latex is a mixture of water and polymer molecules. A polymer is a long string of smaller molecules called monomers, all chained together in a long molecular conga line. When you pull a piece of ABC (already been chewed) gum, it's like pulling a fork through a bowl of spaghetti – all the long spaghetti molecules are pulled out into strings. The result is that the gum is pulled out into strings, instead of simply breaking. Although these polymers are closely related to the rubbers used in car tyres, balloons and other products, in chewing gum they are not elastic. So when you stretch out a piece of gum, it stays stretched. (As we saw in an earlier chapter, rubber is made elastic by heating the long polymer molecules with sulphur until the separate spaghetti-like molecules join to each other where they touch. Then when you pull them, they stretch out a little way and bounce back into their bowl-of-spaghetti shape again.)

Gum sticks to surfaces like hair for a similar reason. You may notice that when gum is wet, it is less sticky. That's because your saliva provides a thin barrier of liquid between the long polymer chains and the surface it's on. But leave gum outside for a few minutes and the water will dry up, leaving the bowl-of-spaghetti molecules ready to hook onto anything that catches them. Unfortunately, hair happens to be the ideal surface for gum to stick to.

Despite appearances, hair is not silky smooth. Look at a strand of hair under a microscope and you'll see it's as scaly as alligator skin. Hair conditioner will glue down some of the scales and make the hair smoother, and oils and moisturisers will coat the hair and make it more flexible, but all hair is naturally scaly – it's the way it grows from the hair follicles. These scales are jagged and rough, forming countless little rough edges. So at a molecular scale your hair is like a collection of trillions of little hooks, and the polymer molecules have been chewed into a nice messy ball of loops. Bring the two together and it's just like Velcro – they stick beautifully. But because gum stretches rather than breaks, when you try to pull it off, the molecules stay stuck, and all the others stretch out into a sticky string.

If you're not careful, things will get worse. The warmth of your hands and oil on your fingers will keep the gum nice and supple. All those long molecules will be eagerly waiting to catch on anything nearby – especially your clothing. Cloth has many of the same properties as hair: whether it is made from cotton or wool, it's just a bunch of tiny hair-like fibres, woven into threads that are woven into cloth. So the molecules of the gum will grab onto the scales of wool (sheep hair) just as nicely as they will to your own hair. It will even stick to the cells on your fingers if they are too dry.

The stickiness and long life of gum is not always a disadvantage. Over the years, many emergency repairs have been made using ordinary chewing gum. Gas pipes have been repaired, as have radiators, musical instruments, car tyres and on one occasion even the landing gear of a bomber! But none of this is much help if you're angrily reading this with a big lump of chewing gum dangling in front of your face.

So what should you do? First, stop pulling at it – you'll only make it more likely to stretch, exposing more polymer molecules ready to glue themselves to more things. If you must touch it at all, make sure your fingers are wet, so you form a liquid barrier between the cells of your skin and the long molecules. Second, don't cut your hair out – there's no need for that. Instead, a little knowledge about the composition of gum will tell you the answer. Remember that gum is composed of latex and oil to make it supple. Like any mixture, if you change its composition, you will change its properties. Because ABC gum has had its ingredients mixed by chewing to form a very viscous (thick and gloopy) liquid state you can mix in other ingredients. If oil makes it more supple, then mixing in more oil will make it thinner and will help those long molecules to slide around more. This is why people have a lot of success removing gum using oil, or products containing oil such as peanut butter, mayonnaise or even perfume. By mixing in this oily substance, you are changing the composition of the gum and helping the long molecules to slide off your hair or clothes.

There's also a second alternative. Like any liquid, if you heat it up, it will become more runny (the heat provides more energy, making the molecules jiggle about more). If you cool it down, it will turn into a solid (the energy will be so low that the molecules just lock themselves together). Since gum is already very gloopy (not very liquid), it doesn't take much cooling to turn it into a solid. Just take a piece of ice and hold it against the gum, and you will find that the gum sets into a solid. Before it warms up again, you can then smash that solid, like breaking ice. Instead of sliding the long polymer molecules off, you're simply smashing them apart.

Once you know the chemistry of gum it's easier to get rid of it. If you have a blob of chewing gum in long hair, cooling it and smashing it may be the simplest approach. If it's too close to your skin or you can't reach it, perhaps because it's stuck to the back of your head, or if you've sat on the gum and embedded it into your clothes, then oil or an oil-based product will liquefy the gum and get rid of it in no time.

Coming Unstuck

⑦ Staying Afloat

You suddenly realise that the bus has gone past your office. The sticky distraction has made you miss the right stop. You jump off at the next stop and discover you're in a part of town you don't recognise. Hopefully, if you walk back in the direction the bus came from you'll see something familiar soon. The light is now ominously dark. Large black clouds have gathered overhead, and you feel a cold breeze blowing. Suddenly the wind drops, and there is a moment of stillness before the air is filled with torrential rain. You run for the nearest shelter – a nearby bookshop. But it's on the other side of the street. By the time you've found a gap in the traffic and crossed you're already soaked, cold water running down your neck, feet squelching in their shoes. You enter the air-conditioned shop, dripping and bedraggled. There you stand, miserably looking out at the rain, shivering with cold.

Despite our national obsession with the weather here in the UK and despite the fact we may be soaked by rain several times each year, we take the rain, rivers and the oceans for granted. Water covers 70 per cent of the surface of our planet, so it's perhaps not surprising that we might become a little wet now and again, wherever we live. But there's a deeper question that is often overlooked except by space scientists or astrobiologists: where did all that water come from in the first place? Why is the Earth not as dry as its neighbour, Mars? Or if the Earth had been colder, would we have seas of methane or ethane (as recently discovered on Titan, one of the moons of Saturn)?

Considerable research has gone into finding the answer to this tricky question. The Earth, like the other planets and our sun, formed out of the swirling clouds of debris left over from the death of previous stars and solar systems. Gravity caused clumps to form, which attracted more and more material to them until hot spheres were rotating around each other. (A giant mass of molten rock held together by its own gravity naturally forms a sphere, just as a single drop of water held together by its surface tension also forms a sphere.) Most of the remains of the debris were then blown away by the solar winds as the sun ignited its hydrogen-bomb fires and began its current hot, fiery existence.

Because the birth of our planet was so hot, it was believed that water could not have formed among its aggregating particles. In contrast, in the further out, colder regions where the giant planets formed, a great deal of ice was able to solidify (some of the moons of Jupiter are almost solid ice). So one solution to the mystery of Earth's water was that chunks of ice from this region hit the young Earth as comets. We know that there was a period of time called the heavy bombardment period (4.5 to 3.8 billion years ago) when comets did rain down on us – just look at the craters on the Moon to see what happened there. But when our space probes analysed the mixture of compounds in the ice of comets, their composition was quite different. Earth didn't receive its water from comets. So another source of ice was proposed, this time from meteorites (which come from the much-closer asteroid belt, circling between the orbits of Mars and Jupiter). But there is still controversy over the issue. We do not know whether the ice combined with the Earth as it formed from its swirling mass of debris or whether the ice rained down in meteorites. We'd like to know, because water is hugely important for life on Earth, and if we can figure out just how lucky we were to receive our water, we could figure out how likely it would be for other planets to resemble ours, and maybe have life like ours. It may be that all solar systems like ours have huge amounts of ice floating around, just waiting to hit the right kind of planet that has the right temperature and atmosphere to hold onto it.

The Earth turns out to be just perfect for holding onto water. It has colder regions at the poles that receive such diluted sunlight that water remains in its solid state as ice. On most of its surface it is warm enough for water to pool in the lower areas in its liquid form, as seas. In the tropical regions the sun's heat is strong enough to cause evaporation from the sea: without actually boiling, now and again the molecules in the water manage to move vigorously enough to leave their neighbours in the sloshy liquid and fly free into the air. Just 0.001 per cent of the water makes it into the atmosphere, but this is still ten times the amount of water in all the rivers and streams of the world.

The process of evaporation causes a cooling effect as the most energetically moving (hotter) molecules fly free from the liquid, leaving the slower (cooler) ones behind. It's why you feel cold when wet – your skin temperature helps to evaporate the water, but those escaping water molecules are stealing your heat as they go. Without evaporation, the temperature of the Earth might be as hot at 67°C (152°F). Evaporation is also affected by the moisture content of the air, or the humidity. The warmer the air is, the more water vapour it can support (warm air means more energetically moving molecules, making it easier for water to stay in its gaseous state). If the humidity is too high then no more evaporation can take place. So you'll find that water will evaporate quickly in front of the dry air produced by an air-conditioner, but in a steamy, tropical country the water just doesn't want to evaporate.

When the humidity is so high that the air is saturated (the 'dew point') all those water molecules start gluing themselves back together to form a liquid again, and you have precipitation (rain or dew). In cold air the dew point is lower, meaning a lower humidity, which is why after a warm day has sucked up moisture into the air, a cool night may create dew on the ground. It's also why, when rising hot air takes water vapour high into the thin, cold air, lots of droplets of liquid water form, often seeded by tiny particles of dust. Clouds are just droplets of dew forming on dust in the air. When the droplets become large enough they eventually fall as rain, hail or snow depending on the temperature. (In fact, water vapour is lighter than air so will always tend to rise high into the cold heights until it has little choice but to fall down again as a liquid or solid.)

Water vapour cannot escape from Earth's atmosphere as it has from the Moon and other planets like Mars because Earth is massive enough to keep its cloak of gases wrapped around it by the pull of its gravity. The Moon has no atmosphere at all – anything it may once have had just evaporated into space. Its gravity is too weak to hold onto those gas molecules. Mars has a thin layer of carbon dioxide but not much else. Venus is massive enough to keep all its atmosphere like Earth, but Venus is much too hot to allow water to exist as it does on Earth.

So it's really no coincidence that the Earth has kept all of its water, unlike the other planets in the solar system. Earth is the only planet to be the right mass and the right distance from the sun to allow the water to stay. All the other planets may have originally had water, but lost most of it. In a similar way, Titan is exactly the right size and temperature for seas of methane and ethane to exist, producing weather and shorelines resembling those of the Earth. Some scientists suggest a different form of life, perhaps based on silicon, could exist there, relying on the methane just as we rely on water.

But if life on Earth relies on water so much, perhaps we should be singing in the rain every time it falls. One important reason we don't like to be soaked is the loss of heat. It's very easy for us to become chilled and weakened, allowing infections to take hold and make us ill. Humans are particularly susceptible to heat loss through evaporation because we have a habit of wearing cloth over most of our skin. When the cloth becomes saturated in water, which then slowly evaporates over many hours, we suffer tremendously more heat loss than an animal with no clothes. The solution is either to go naked in the rain, which might cause a few comments from other people, or to wear waterproof clothes.

Most cloth is not waterproof. In fact, most cloth is the opposite – it actively attracts water to its surface and sucks it inside. One reason this happens is called 'capillary action'. The molecules of water are some-times more attracted to another surface than they are to themselves. Put water into an ordinary glass and instead of lying perfectly flat, you'll see the water creeps up slightly at the edges forming a concave surface, or 'meniscus'. The water likes the glass so much that all the molecules are doing their best to touch it, but the surface tension and mass of the bulk of the water prevents it from climbing the walls. Make the glass much, much smaller – in fact, use a tiny little glass tube – and the water will climb up inside. Propelled only by the desire of the water molecules to touch the glass, water can climb tiny vertical tubes. It's a principle exploited by plants, which grow tiny little tubes (roots) that suck water from the soil through capillary action and, in the case of trees, pump gallons of water many metres into the sky. Most cloth is just as attractive to water, but instead of forming little tubes to suck water, cloth has trillions of little fibres all woven together. Just as the wick of an oil lamp sucks the oil into its fibres, so the fibres of our clothes suck the water along their surfaces. Spill some water on fabric (or other fibrous materials such as paper) and you can watch it being sucked into the material before your eyes. The wick effect, using the capillary action of fibres, will happily pump all the water from rain into your clothes until they are nicely saturated or soaked with water.

The solution is to prevent this attractive force between water and fibres from taking place. Water may be attracted to some substances, but it is positively repelled from others. Look at water on a waxy surface and you'll see it forms into a convex droplet – the water is trying to keep away from the surface as much as possible. So all you need to do in order to prevent water from soaking into clothes is to wear something waxy or oily (or perhaps oil-derived like rubber or artificial rubbers, such as neoprene).

Nature discovered this principle a long time ago. We have oily skin for a good reason – the oil makes our skin waterproof. If you want to know what happens when the oil is washed off, then stay in a bath for half an hour or more. Because much of the oil has been washed away by the soapy water, the outer layers of your skin start to attract the water and let it soak in. Your skin becomes wrinkled as the upper surface is swollen by the water, but the layers of skin and tissue beneath remain the same size. (Take a dry sponge, draw around it, then soak it in water and try to fit the swollen shape in the smaller outline – the only way to do it is by wrinkling it up.) Our skin quickly returns to normal as the excess water evaporates once we leave the bath.

Today these principles are well understood, and so fabrics with special water-repellent coatings are common. Some are so clever that they use the wick effect to draw perspiration away from our skin on the inside, but have a water-repellent layer on the outside to stop water soaking in. And if you'd rather not wear waterproof clothing, the fabric of umbrellas works in exactly the same way. If you do get wet through, then try to change into dry clothes as soon as possible and stay warm. Leaving wet clothes on is like stepping into a giant refrigerator on a cold day.

Knowing Your Place

As suddenly as the rain began it's over. Barely believing your eyes, you look up at a blue sky again. Already steam is beginning to rise from the wet pavements as the sun heats them. You leave the bookshop and start walking briskly back the way the bus had come. Perhaps it's the bright reflections or the spray from the cars, but nothing seems familiar. You keep walking for ten more minutes, becoming increasingly nervous. The shops have gone and you now realise that you've entered a quiet, tree-lined residential street. There's no one around to ask for directions, and you feel too foolish to knock on somebody's door. Somehow the trees seem menacing, their branches looming over you. You look back the way you came. It looks much the same as the direction you were walking. You're lost. Completely lost.

We've all experienced a few minutes of panic in our lives, caused by the simple realisation that we don't know where we are. Nothing seems familiar. We feel a mixture of danger, alertness and confusion as we anticipate unknown perils, try to understand our surroundings and attempt to link what we're currently seeing with any kind of memory that might aid us. Why can't we figure out where we are?

Compared to other creatures, humans have traditionally not travelled long distances. While many of us may travel daily to work or holiday abroad, we rarely have to navigate the route ourselves. Today we are pampered by luxuries of electronic gadgets that tell us where to go, maps that describe where everything is, and tarmac paths that have signs all along their lengths to inform us where we are. Imagine making a journey of several thousand kilometres with no gadgets, maps, roads or signs to guide you, and no vehicle to propel you. Yet such journeys are successfully undertaken by an incredible variety of creatures. Mammals such as wildebeest migrate hundreds of kilometres across America to find seasonal water and food. Turtles swim thousands of kilometres across entire oceans to return to the exact beaches they hatched on, laying eggs in the same safe place they were born. Salmon fight their way against the currents for hundreds of kilometres through the ocean and back up the rivers they came down after spawning. Birds regularly migrate thousands of kilometres, sometimes from one end of the planet to the other, to find warmer homes for the winter and longer days in the summer (in the northern hemisphere). Even butterflies are able to migrate across countries to find food, their journey so long that it takes several generations to complete. All these different creatures travel staggering distances and somehow safely find their way, perhaps to the same beach or even the same nest, each time. When the average human can easily become lost in just a couple of square kilometres of unfamiliar landscape, these creatures put our large, supposedly intelligent brains to shame.

All migratory creatures share the same problem: navigation. They need to know where they are and where they want to be. The methods they use are generally fairly similar. One basic trick is simply to follow everyone else and learn the route from them. Many species of birds rely on being taught which way to go, for they must often pick complex and tortuous paths through mountain ranges and around oceans to reach their destinations. The trick they use is to memorise important landmarks: a mountain here, a lake there, and to use them as road signs, pointing the way ahead. Remarkably, honeybees don't even have to lead their companions to show them the way. Instead they communicate with their companions in the hive by performing a 'waggle dance'. The orientation of the bee performing the dance provides the direction relative to the sun, and the amount of time spent waggling indicates the distance to fly. The smell of the nectar on the bee also helps them follow the instructions and find the flowers and the new source of nectar. Different species of honeybees use slight variations on the dance, as though each has its own accent or dialect.

Creatures don't only use their eyes when migrating. Salmon imprint on the chemical content of the rivers they were born in, and use this 'smell' to guide them as they get closer to the source. Ants lay down pheromone trails from the nest to useful food sources, guiding their companions along their smelly paths. Turtles and many mammals may also rely on smell to help them recognise the places they were born. Because their olfactory senses are so much better than ours, they create mental maps of smells using specific scents as landmarks just as other creatures use sights. Humpback whales migrate to the warm Hawaiian waters to rear their young, and return to Arctic waters for the rich food in the summer. In addition to sight and smell, they use their sonar to hear the underwater landscapes and also learn to recognise the feel of the oceanic currents.

But while these conventional senses provide the detailed information for creatures to fine-tune their routes, sight, hearing and smell are not enough to enable them to travel thousands of kilometres. There's a big difference between finding the right house in a town and finding the right house in a continent. No bird could ever remember 500 landmarks, nor could a salmon remember a thousand smells to follow. Instead, a more general sense of direction is needed by migratory creatures. They need to know which overall direction they should fly, swim or walk, and then use their more precise senses to keep themselves on track.

One obvious solution is to use the position of the sun, and many organisms do exactly this. By automatically adjusting for the movement of the sun, birds, bees and fish are able to figure out where north or south is, and keep flying in the right direction. Some night-time migratory birds (for example, the Indigo Bunting) use the patterns of stars to help them navigate. Bees and ants are even able to cope when it's cloudy by having eyes that can detect and analyse the polarisation (direction) of sunlight.

But sunlight (or starlight) is not always visible enough to be a reliable navigation aid, and when crossing the equator, having the sun directly overhead provides little information about direction. What migratory creatures need is a compass that tells them where north is, and then they can figure out where to go relative to that. Astonishingly, that's exactly what they have, built into their brains.

A compass works because the centre of the Earth acts like a giant magnet, producing a large magnetic field that sweeps around and beyond the planet for some distance. The cause of this field is not fully understood, but the current theory is that the molten iron outer core within the planet is swirled around by Earth's rotation, which produces huge electric currents. The electricity generates a magnetic field, which is thought to reinforce itself again and again, resulting in a reasonably stable polarity with a north pole of the magnet at one end of the planet and the south pole at the other end. The magnetic field is not entirely stable, however, and the magnetic poles constantly move around, somewhere between 10 and 40 kilometres a year. Scientists have also discovered that lava from volcanoes can 'trap' the direction of the Earth's magnetic field when it cools, preserving a record of its changes. According to this evidence, the magnetic field may sometimes completely reverse itself (about every 300,000 years), north becoming south and south becoming north.

Luckily, the magnetic fields are constant for such prolonged periods that they make excellent navigation aids. We use them by watching a little magnetic needle become attracted towards the north pole in a compass. Some mobile phones, watches or cars contain solid-state compasses, which use two or three tiny magnetic field sensors in a chip to detect the strength of the field at that point and trigonometry to calculate the current orientation of the device they are within.

Birds, fish, some insects, amphibians, mammals such as whales, and reptiles such as turtles also use the same trick. Somehow they are all able to sense the direction of the Earth's magnetic field. Scientists are still trying to figure out exactly how they do it – whether there are minute particles of iron in the brain that affect the firing of some neurons, or whether the receptors in the eyes contain some kind of chemical mixture that makes them slightly receptive to magnetic fields in addition to light. Many birds are known to have a well-defined sense of magnetic fields (indeed, migrating birds that fly over iron deposits in the ground that disturb the Earth's magnetic field can become very confused and disoriented). Research has shown that the areas of the brain that birds use for vision are also active when they are subjected to different magnetic fields, so perhaps birds can actually 'see' the Earth's magnetism.

Some of the most controversial research also suggests that humans may have some very basic form of magnetic sense. Experiments have shown that some blindfolded people can remain aware of their orientation after travelling some distance, but this awareness can be disrupted by placing magnets near their heads. More compellingly, neuroscientists have measured changes in our brain activity that correspond to the presence of magnetic fields, suggesting that something in our brains is being affected by the fields whether we are aware of it or not.

Sadly, even if we do have some kind of 'magnetic sense', we surround ourselves with so many metal and electrical devices, and transmit so many radio waves and microwaves for communication and entertainment, that it is probably hopelessly muddled up most of the time. We also do the same with odour, temperature, sound and sights, filling our towns and cities with so many repeated experiences that all our other senses become overloaded and confused. Architects try to counter these effects with different ideas. One popular method in the USA is the simple solution of turning cities into regular 'grids' with numbers for each street, to make navigation more a process of plotting coordinates. Other architects try to turn understandability into a science, by measuring lines-of-sight in different street and building layouts, and showing that the more we can see from any given point, the more we can understand the space we're in.

Most of the towns and cities we inhabit have not been designed in a very sensible way (and many almost seem designed to confuse us). Becoming lost is all too easy, so the best thing to do is copy migratory creatures: learn landmarks along the route so that you'll be able to find your way back – consciously point out unusual buildings or trees to yourself. Try to understand the general direction you need to be heading, either from signs, the shadows cast by the sun or even a compass in your mobile phone. Remember, you have a brain considerably bigger than the peanut-sized brain of a salmon or the grain-of-rice-sized brain of a bee, so if you're really lost, ask for directions!

Pain in the Neck

Having retraced your steps back to the bookshop, your mistake is obvious: you'd turned right instead of turning left when you walked out of the door. On track once more, you walk briskly, swatting a bee as it hovers annoyingly around your face. Things are looking much more familiar and – that bee won't leave you alone. It's attracted to your hair or something. Perhaps it likes your shampoo. You walk more quickly, waving your hands around to persuade the bee that you're not a flower. It follows you like some miniature evil demon, intent on mischief. Now your flailing hand hits the bee, sending it into a high-pitched buzzing frenzy, darting around you like a miniature dive bomber. You continue to try and swipe the insect away, connecting with it again and again, until suddenly you hear a loud buzzing by your ear and feel a sharp pain. You've been stung just below your ear, you can feel the sting embedded in your flesh. The intensity of the sharp pain keeps increasing as though someone is pushing the sting deeper and deeper. How can one little insect cause so much pain?

There are between 1.5 and 1.8 million named species of living organisms on our planet, with estimates of the total number of species somewhere between 5 and 20 million. Half of all species known are insects. (There are 300,000 different species of beetle alone.) Of this vast number, very few insects use poisons or venoms to protect themselves. Some rely on poisonous hollow or glass-like hairs (as in the case of some caterpillars) or may use compounds injected during a bite to numb the skin of their prey and prevent the blood from clotting (as used by mosquitoes). Some ants will squirt formic acid at attacking predators to drive them away, or they may inject acid from their jaws as they bite. (Spiders also use venom to paralyse their prey, but they are not insects – they're arachnids and belong to the same family as scorpions, mites, ticks and harvestmen.) Thankfully, the vast majority of insects do not sting or bite us in any way.

Insects belonging to the family (or more properly, the order) known as Hymenoptera are best known for their venom. Ants, sawflies, wasps and bees all belong to the order, and we all learn from an early age that there is something special about wasps and bees. They sting!

The sting of bees and wasps is for defence only. These insects live on nectar from flowers and gain no advantage from attacking mammals such as ourselves. They're not carnivorous like some ants and so have no interest in eating us. Most of the time, stings are used against other bees or wasps trying to enter a hive and steal food. So most stings (for example, those of the bumble bee and wasps) are smooth little hollow spikes at the rear of the insect, designed to act like hypodermic needles to inject painful venom into the victim and then be withdrawn. Invaders are either killed outright or are so badly hurt that they just fly away as fast as possible.

Unfortunately for honeybees, their personal food storage system is very tasty. Field bees gather nectar and store it in a special pouch separate from their stomachs. They regurgitate it into the mouths of house bees, which then chew it for a while, adding enzymes and transforming the mixture into a sticky, oily, sweet and slightly acidic gloop that resists fungi and bacteria for years. They store the fluid in special waxy boxes, fan it with their wings to remove most of the water and prevent it from fermenting, and then seal it away for later, to feed to their larvae. The result is a hive full of honey, a super-sweet fluid that is always fresh and tasty. It's so good that large mammals such as bears find it irresistible and happily smash their way into hives to lick out the sweet food.

Bears (and humans) have been stealing honey for so long that there are even species of birds known as honeyguides. Some seventeen species of these birds exist, all with a fondness for eating the wax and larvae of the bees. These remarkable birds deliberately lead humans or large mammals to the hives of honeybees, feeding on the remains once the honey has been removed.

Under such concerted attack, the honeybee was forced to improve its defences. It already had a good sting for keeping other insects away, so its sting was improved further. In the life or death situation of the hive being potentially destroyed, it became acceptable for bees to act as kamikazes – sacrificing their lives for the good of the hive. So the sting of the honeybee evolved to become a very nasty weapon. Instead of being a smooth spike, it developed barbs to make it harder to remove from the skin. When stinging another insect, the bee can still sting more than once. But the skin of a mammal or bird is more elastic, so once the barbed sting is forced through, it cannot be retracted and the bee is trapped. In its fight to escape, it tears the sting from its own body. The dying bee then flies away, releasing pheromones (smelling a little like old socks) that turn all the other bees into angry attacking machines. Its sting is left in the skin, along with the venom sac, muscles and a nerve cell. Although the bee is now gone, the nerve cell continues to activate the muscles, pumping more and more of the venom from the sac into the skin to cause the maximum possible pain to the mammal. If the honey thief is stupid enough to stay near the hive, then more and more bees will sting and release attack pheromones, until the whole hive is an angry swarming mass of attacking insects. This is more than enough to make most creatures run away as fast as they can.

The reason bee stings hurt is because of their chemical composition. Bee venom, or apitoxin, contains a complex and acidic mixture of different proteins and compounds. The main constituent is melittin, a mixture of venom proteins. One of the most damaging of these is called phospholipase, which breaks down the cell walls, decreases blood pressure and slows clotting. Another, called hyaluronidase, makes tissues more permeable and easier for bacteria to spread. The one that causes much of the pain is called apamin, a nerve toxin that interacts with our pain receptors, making them react violently and sending their own equivalent of a siren wailing to our brains.

Our bodies react immediately to this nasty cocktail of chemicals, producing swelling in an attempt to flush away the toxins. If the sting stays in place for more than about 30 seconds the large amount of venom may remain in the tissue for two or three days, causing pain and discomfort. Bee stings are generally not fatal, unless the person is weak and receives a large number of stings. Recent statistics show that deaths from bee stings have mainly occurred when the victim is over seventy years old and has been stung between 50 and 150 times. The bees are also typically Africanised bees in Central and South America, descended from aggressive Tanzanian bees, which were artificially bred for honey production and are now loose in the wild.

Despite the occasional rare death from a swarm, there are far more cases of fatalities caused because the victim was allergic to the venom. Often triggered by just a single sting, the body enters anaphylactic shock. In these people the venom interferes with special immune cells in tissues called mast cells, causing the cells to release too much histamine and other normally useful chemicals. Fluid from the blood then starts to leak into the surrounding tissues, causing a variety of symptoms, including low blood pressure, swelling, pain and difficulty in breathing. In a small number of cases the symptoms are so severe that they lead to death if untreated. But the treatment is very straightforward: an injection of adrenalin reverses the symptoms almost immediately. Those who know they have this allergy may have to carry adrenalin with them at all times, just in case.

Bee venom is supposed to be nasty, but a surprising result has emerged in recent years. For centuries people with arthritis had noticed that their symptoms were improved after a bee sting. It turns out that melittin (the main constituent in the venom) works as a potent anti-inflammatory drug and also kills off many harmful bacteria and yeasts (including the bacteria that cause Lyme disease). The first scientific studies took place only in 2004, so researchers have not fully uncovered the mechanisms behind the effect. However, patients suffering from rheumatoid arthritis saw noticeable improvements when treated with bee venom, so this may be the beginning of a new treatment. In the meantime, there are plenty of 'holistic' treatments that use the idea in perhaps one of the most painful kinds of alternative medicine you could imagine: combining acupuncture with bee venom. Ouch.

Bees die when they sting us, so they have to be provoked until it literally becomes a matter of life or death to them before they will sting. If you do accidentally provoke a bee or disturb a hive without meaning to then the best advice is to stay away from them until they calm down.

If necessary, run! If you are stung, then you must try and remove the sting as soon as you can. It doesn't matter how you do it (pinching it out with thumb and forefinger will not inject any more venom compared to scraping it out, for the sting needs to pump its own venom through little one-way valves). Just try and remove the sting within 5 seconds of being stung to minimise the amount of venom injected. If anyone in your family has an allergy to stings, or if you have experienced symptoms such as shortness of breath after a sting, get yourself tested to see if you have the allergy. Luckily, being allergic to bee stings is easier than being allergic to certain foods, such as nuts. Bees are very clearly 'labelled' with black and yellow warning stripes and they'll give you plenty of chances to go away before they attack. They don't want to sting you any more then you want to be stung.

Lost Underfoot

The sun is now warm overhead; the wet pavements mostly dry again. Even your squelching shoes seem to be drying out. Ignoring the throbbing pain by your ear, you make your way back towards the part of town where you should be attending this morning's meeting. The sunshine is turning your feeling of hopelessness into optimism, as though the rain has washed away this morning's disasters. Perhaps you can persuade your colleagues to wait for 15 minutes. You take out your mobile phone, standing to one side as you try and find the right number. As you search, you notice your right foot feeling colder than usual. You wiggle your toes in irritation. They only feel colder. Glancing down at your shoes you see to your dismay that the right shoe is now gaping open at the front like a mouth, exposing your toes to the world. The sole has come away, unpeeling like the lid of a yogurt pot. You can't go to the meeting like this. However, this is a problem you can fix – you're outside a news-agent's, so you quickly enter and purchase some superglue. Back outside, you place a couple of drops on the damaged shoe, press down for 30 seconds and let go. At last, you are fighting back!

Or at least you try to let go. Your hand doesn't move. You've just glued your thumb to your shoe.

Shoes need to be made from several different materials. We prefer them to be waterproof and comfortable on the foot, so the 'upper' is usually made from soft leather or a manmade leather substitute. But most leather is not hardwearing enough to be used for the sole, so we usually use something that is tough, flexible and gives us good traction, such as rubber. We also prefer to have a fairly good thickness of rubber so that the shoe won't wear out too quickly. Shoe manufacturers and designers are thus faced with a dilemma: how to fix the rubber sole to the leather upper. Stitching the two together is a good, secure method, but often expensive and slow. Even if they are stitched, there's still the problem of keeping the inner sole (the part that your foot rests on) in contact with the outer sole. The solution, used in the majority of shoes today, is to use that strangely sticky substance: glue. But what makes glues so sticky? And why do some glues, like superglue, stick so quickly?

Glues have been in use for millennia. Early glues, or adhesives, were based on naturally occurring sticky substances, such as the sticky resins or gums from trees, or tar from the ground. But one of the most commonly used early glues was produced from animal products. We discovered a long time ago that boiling bones, skins or fish leftovers would produce a sticky jelly. This could be diluted with water to make it spread more easily, and it could be left to dry, when it would become a sticky glue.

The sticky ooze is called gelatin, and it's made from collagen or connective tissue. When it's still part of an animal such as you or me, collagen is a mass of fibrous protein molecules that are woven together to form a strong connective tissue. We use a lot of it in our bodies to keep everything attached to everything else; a quarter of all protein within us is collagen. When the collagen starts to fail in our skin we develop sags and wrinkles. Boiling the remains of animals melts and separates the protein fibres. They are torn apart like rope being unwoven, leaving lots of curly, spring-like proteins, all tangled up together. These springy molecules are what gives gelatin its bouncy, jelly-like behaviour. (It is the same stuff as used in jelly or Jell-o.) When it dries out, the springs lock themselves together more tightly and so become more solid and less wobbly. If you put a layer of gelatin or 'animal glue' between, say, two pieces of leather and let it dry, the molecules will work their way into all the little rough gaps and holes of the leather before locking solid. The result is a mechanical join just like the pieces of a jigsaw puzzle, and the leather becomes stuck together.

Today we rarely use animal glues. Many modern glues are based on polymers (the stuff we make plastics from) – long chains of molecules that are in a solvent such as water to make them move around. When the solvent dries out, the molecules are locked in place and the glue is set. The trouble with drying adhesives is that they can be dissolved by their solvents again. In humid countries water-based glues simply don't stick. One solution invented to overcome this was hot glue. Typically using an electric 'glue gun', which heats sticks of thermoplastic, hot glue simply relies on melting this special kind of plastic. When melted, the molecules form random coils and little crystals, which together form flexibility and hardness as the plastic cools and solidifies, locking itself to the surface.

Often it is not practical to use drying or hot glues on complicated shapes – like shoes, for example. The drying might take too long, meaning that clamps would be required to hold the pieces in place for many hours, or the heat of the glue might melt the surface being stuck. A good solution to these problems was created in the form of contact adhesive. Two substances are used, one placed on each surface separately and allowed to dry. When the surfaces are brought together, the two substances interact, chemically locking together very quickly to form a secure bond. It's a clever idea, combining the easy application of solvent-based glues with the fast sticking of a hot glue. Because of this, many manufacturers of shoes use contact adhesives to stick the soles of shoes to the leather uppers.

The origins of many glues were accidental, as new substances were discovered or developed and found to be surprisingly sticky. One notable example was superglue. In 1942 a scientist called Dr Harry Coover of Kodak Laboratories was trying to develop a new kind of clear plastic, based on a new compound called cyanoacrylate. He wanted to make a super-clear, yet tough new substance to replace the glass in gun sights. It wasn't good enough so he put it aside for several years. Later he had a new project – making canopies for aircraft – and again he looked at the substance, this time putting it between two optical prisms to check its optical characteristics. To his surprise (and probable dismay), he found that one drop had glued the expensive prisms together with an enormously strong bond. This was the beginning of superglue.

Superglue is so effective at sticking, even in extremely small quantities, that it's clear that it must have some really clever way of doing it. Other glues rely on mechanical interlocking, or even chemically melting into the surfaces, like some plastic glues. But we rarely use enough superglue to allow it to provide much interlocking, and it doesn't melt into most surfaces it sticks. Just a one square inch of superglue can support a ton – how can one drop of this glue stick so well?

The short answer is that we're not entirely sure how it works. A popular theory is that the glue exploits a type of intermolecular force known as the Van der Waals force. Unlike chemical bonds (which work because electrons or protons may be moved or shared across molecules, transforming the substances and locking them together), Van der Waals forces are more general forces between molecules, caused by the interaction of their polarities. Just as magnets attract each other, the 'north' polarity attracting the 'south' polarity, so do molecules. There are a lot of complicated forces when you look closely enough. One type is the electrostatic force (which enables clingfilm to cling). Another is polarisation (caused by the separate atoms in a molecule sharing electrons unequally and producing slight differences in polarity). Yet another is called 'London dispersion' forces (which allow certain gases to condense at low temperatures and are caused by some very complicated interactions between different molecules that can induce temporary polarities).

We're fairly sure that some or all of these forces are involved with superglue, and indeed many of the other types of glue. But because the molecules are so small and the forces occur over such tiny distances, it's extremely hard to measure them, so the scientists will be working on the problem for some time to come.

However the superglue molecules stick surfaces together, we do know what happens to them when they come into contact with water. It turns out that the molecules of superglue (or cyanoacrylate) work in the opposite way to water-based glues. When cyanoacrylate meets water molecules, its molecules all join up to form long chains that coil around each other and bond together to form a hard resin. Since most surfaces on Earth typically do have some water molecules on them, the glue works very well on a wide range of materials. Superglue is so reactive to water that it has another use, as discovered by forensic scientists. Put an open tube of superglue in an airtight container with any object that might have fingerprints on it and the vapour from the glue will react with the moisture (and other organic compounds) of the fingerprints, gluing itself to their patterns and making them more visible. It's another reason why these glues say 'use in well ventilated areas' – cyanoacrylate will happily do the same thing inside your lungs if you breathe it in. While it won't kill you, and your body will produce mucus to help you cough it all out, the idea of having superglue setting inside you is not very nice.

Skin also contains lots of water, which is why superglue is so effective at sticking fingers together if you're not careful. Indeed, it's so good at sticking to skin that it was used by US soldiers during the Vietnam War to close wounds and help prevent bleeding, saving many lives. It's not a good idea to use ordinary superglue for this purpose for it can irritate the skin, and if a lot is used (especially on materials like cotton), it can become sufficiently hot as it reacts that it can burn. Today there are less toxic versions designed for this purpose that can be used instead.

Superglue reacts with water, becoming a resin. This means that if you leave a tube of superglue for too long, the water in the air will make the whole tube solidify. It also means that the resin is waterproof, so you won't unstick fingers with water, you'll only help make the resin harden. Luckily, there is a solvent for superglue. Acetone (often found in nail varnish remover) will dissolve the resin away nicely. Another good solvent is nitromethane, an explosive, high performance fuel used by drag car racers, often known as 'nitro' (but this is not recommended for your skin). Instead you can buy solvents designed to unstick you. If you don't have a solvent available and the accidental gluing is only minor then you'll find you'll naturally become unstuck in time. The glue sticks only the outer layer of your skin, which is always in the process of shedding away. As the cells naturally detach, so will the glue. If you've managed to stick something a little more delicate or inconvenient, then a trip to the hospital A&E department may be necessary so that they can apply the solvent and free you again. Superglue has its name for a reason!

Crossed Connections

You walk past a police car, parked by the kerb. The right shoe flaps annoyingly as you continue towards the office. It's even worse than before, and now you have a piece of leather stuck to your thumb. It makes operating your mobile a little more tricky, but you finally locate the number for your boss, who'll have been at the meeting for over half an hour by now. Almost exactly as you press 'dial', the siren of the police car behind you goes off, scaring you with its screaming wail. You cancel the call, giving the idiots inside an annoyed glance. The siren stops just as you press 'cancel'. But there is no one inside the car. You look around, wondering if this is a joke. Seeing nobody, you select the number again and press 'dial'. Instantly the police siren wails again. As soon as your finger jabs the 'cancel' button, the siren stops. You stare at the car. How can this be happening? You choose the number for the third time and press 'dial', finger on the 'cancel' button just in case. Again the siren wails, and falls quiet as soon as you cancel the call. Suddenly, two policemen burst out of the nearby shop and run towards you. What in the world is going on?

Mobile phones are sophisticated radio transmitters and receivers. They broadcast our voices to receivers, which pass on the signal to other receivers and move it to the right recipient. They also listen to the signal from transmitters and decode it, so that we can hear the voice of the person we are calling.

Mobile phones do not talk to each other directly. The range of a normal phone is not much more than 50 or 60 kilometres (30–40 miles) in completely flat terrain or 8 to 12 kilometres (5–8 miles) in a hilly landscape, so we'd never be able to call anyone very far away if our phones worked like walkie-talkies. One solution would be to put enormously powerful transmitters into each phone and boost their ranges, but this is not a great idea for many reasons. The phones would need huge antennae and giant batteries, and would probably heat our heads like microwave ovens. Even if we could solve these problems, the billions of phones we use today would interfere with each other so much that no one would ever hear anything. We'd fry our brains for white noise.

The solution used in mobile phones is to make every call a local call. Radio masts are placed in 'cells', each covering its own small area. Neighbouring masts use slightly different frequencies so that their signals do not interfere with each other, just as radio stations use different frequencies for the same reason. Every mobile phone, wherever it is in the world, talks only to its nearby radio mast, and listens only to that mast. The signal is then transferred to the telephone exchange 'switches' (which are really computers designed to do the job very quickly), which then pass it on to other switches in the mobile exchange or into the public telephone network. So if you call my mobile phone using your mobile phone, your call will really be made to your local 'cell site', and the voice I hear will come from my local cell site. The transmission in between is routed using the switching computers, often through other transmitters or down optical cables.

It's a neat idea, and it works brilliantly. Perhaps surprisingly, it continues to work even when we're travelling on the train. The size of each cell may have a radius of less than 1.6 kilometres (1 mile) in our cities (because of limitations of capacity), and up to 40 kilometres (25 miles) in the countryside. Travel 160 kilometres (100 miles) on a train and you may pass through ten or more cells, and yet somehow the phones keep working (at least most of the time). This is achieved because each cell overlaps with its neighbours. At the boundaries of two cells, your phone's transmissions will be visible to two cell sites at once. The switching computer works out which signal is the stronger, and if necessary tells your phone to switch to the new frequency of the neighbouring cell without a break in the transmission and reception. The transmission from the new cell is then pushed through to the same destination without the slightest pause.

Because modern communication is digital, phones often share

frequencies, sending pulses of coded information and leaving time for other phones to use the same frequency. (Some use another method where each uses a unique code and transmits in its own distinct 'language' to prevent confusions with other phones using the same frequency.) The switches, cell sites and phones always know who is talking to whom because they don't just send and receive our voices (and text messages and other data). Every phone sends and receives regular little messages to and from the nearby cell sites, identifying itself and being told which frequency and code it should use to transmit with. These little messages are sent every few seconds while your phone is on. In each message, the phone is saying, 'Hello, I'm still here,' giving its name (a bunch of codes), and explaining which carrier network it prefers to use. The cell site responds, telling your phone which frequency it should use and whether your phone might need to switch to the frequency of a neighbouring cell site. Each company uses a slightly different frequency; if your phone cannot see its home carrier signal then it will report 'no signal' (even though there may be signals from other carriers). If you're in another country and your network has agreements with the foreign providers you may well be able to roam onto their networks, your phone registering itself onto the new networks and using them as though you were at home.

Wherever you are, your phone needs to keep on chatting to the local cell sites so that it always knows which frequency to use, and it can always make or receive calls at any time. These little 'chats' are so important that more power is used for them compared to ordinary voice and data transmission. So use a radio microphone, or put your phone too close to audio electronics (perhaps the amplified speakers of your computer or your MP3 player) and once in a while you will hear the communication: *dit dit di-dit, dit di-dit, dit di-dit, dit di-dit*. The reason you hear this noise is the same reason antennae can pick up radio waves.

Radio waves are electromagnetic waves – the same as light and heat, except that radio waves have a longer wavelength. The length of each wave (the wavelength) of the light we see is much, much smaller than one millimetre. The wavelength of a radio station broadcasting at 100 MHz is about 3 metres (10 feet). The wavelength of a phone using a 900 MHz band is 30 cm (12 inches). Electromagnetic waves have this name because they are composed of two parts: they have an electric field and a magnetic field. The electric field is produced by the charges of particles – for example, electrons are negatively charged. The magnetic field is produced when charges move – for example, in an electric current. These fields are as fundamental to our universe as gravitation.

Because electric fields and magnetic fields are aspects of the same thing, we can generate magnetic fields using electricity, and we can generate electricity using magnetic fields. We do this all the time: an electric motor spins because the electricity creates a series of little magnetic fields that are repelled from internal fixed magnets and push the shaft round and round. An electricity generator spins a shaft that passes coils of wire through magnetic fields, generating electricity in the coils.

An antenna works in much the same way. When an antenna of the right size is placed in a radio wave of the right frequency, its electrons are vibrated by that wave and so the electromagnetic energy is converted into tiny amounts of electricity. It's a little like the effect sound can have on glass. Take a crystal glass and flick it with your fingernail. The *ding* noise is the sound of the glass resonating. Produce a pure noise at the same pitch (a sound wave of the same frequency) and the glass may resonate so much that it smashes. Just as a glass will resonate at a particular frequency of sound – the sound waves matching the resonant frequency of the glass – so an antenna resonates at particular frequencies of electromagnetic waves. Instead of making a noise, its vibrating electrons produce electricity. That's why antennae all have to be designed very carefully to make sure their lengths match the wavelengths of the radio waves they need to receive.

But radio waves don't just affect audio electronics, they affect all electronic devices that happen to have wire or metal in them of the same length as (or some multiple of) their wavelength. Parts of metal casings or wires that are designed to perform a different function will accidentally behave as antennae. It may not be anything more than a nuisance in your MP3 player, but if the signal is picked up by the metal in your car's ABS electronics, then it's a bit more serious. Interference introduces an electric current where it's not supposed to be, and that might cause an electronic circuit to do almost anything. In the early days of electronics this is exactly what used to happen. The clever new anti-lock braking systems of cars would fail regularly when exposed to radio transmissions, causing many accidents. There was one curved stretch of autobahn in Germany near to a radio transmitter that caused so many problems that a wire mesh fence had to be erected to absorb the radio waves and prevent them from causing cars to spin out of control.

Some vehicles rely on relatively high-powered radio transmitters within them for communication, such as those used by the police or taxi drivers. A huge variety of problems have occurred over the years caused by the interference from these internal radios. As well as numerous reports of ABS electronics failing, other examples included a fire officer's car having its sunroof constantly open, a police car having its siren sound 'strangled', a police motorcycle slowing down and the courtesy lamp of a customs and excise car flickering.

Modern vehicles are extensively tested and shielded to make sure that our mobile phones do not affect their electronics, and there are many stringent regulations that limit the amount of electromagnetic radiation any device can produce. Nevertheless, computers are used extensively in our vehicles, from engine management systems that control the timing of the spark plugs, to ABS and other safety equipment. Some major car manufacturers have warned that mobile phones could accidentally trigger a car's airbags. Just as airlines tell us to switch off our mobile phones for the duration of flights, so some car manufacturers and motoring organisations are now suggesting that we switch off the phones while driving. Remember that phones constantly chat to their local cell sites every few seconds, so the only way to stop them from transmitting their signals is to turn them off (or put them into 'airplane mode').

Thankfully, these kinds of interference by mobile phones are relatively rare and usually occur when the car has become faulty or its electronics are improperly installed. If you're nervous about it, just turn your phone off when driving. Nevertheless, one form of interference is still common. The 'radar detector' gadgets that some people use to detect speed traps happen to have internal electronics that resonate at very high frequencies. These gadgets produce so much interference that they scramble the signal being received by satellite television dishes or GPS gadgets. So if you notice your TV loses its picture just as a certain car drives by or your GPS gadget becomes very confused at certain times, that's why.

Hissy Fits

Leaving the bemused police officers to play with your phone, you decide that the best solution is to abandon your disintegrating formal shoes and quickly purchase some running shoes. You enter a sports shop and grab the nearest pair your size. Three minutes later you're jogging your way to work, carrying one of your old shoes in each hand. You've bought some bouncy, 'air-filled' trainers, making you feel as though each step is powering you forwards more than usual – you're flying with each stride. The road curves to the left and suddenly you see your office. You're going to make it! But something is uneven about the new shoes: the left one is making a strange hissing noise each time you bring it down, and it no longer has the same bounce. Running has become a lopsided *thud-hiss, thud-hiss, thud-hiss*. You stop and look at the left shoe. It's got a large drawing pin embedded in its sole. You have a puncture in one of your expensive new shoes.

The spring in our steps always used to be entirely natural. The combination of the fleshy pads under our feet and the yielding, deformable nature of most natural surfaces (soil, sand or foliage) gave us organic cushioning when we walked or ran. But we no longer run around on natural surfaces – we now surround ourselves with hard stone or concrete. To protect our feet from such unkind floors we wear shoes. And to replace the natural cushioning of our feet and the soils we once ran on, most shoes designed for serious walking or running have springy soles. Run around barefoot on a concrete floor (or even worse, in solid wooden clogs on a concrete floor) and you'll notice the difference – the hard, jarring impacts on your feet and legs will quickly cause you discomfort and prevent you from going any further. Springy cushioning in shoes is an essential part of modern life.

Springy shoes are just the latest example of cushioning, often called suspension, that protects us from the unwanted jolts caused by moving around. Perhaps the first use of bouncy suspension was in early passenger vehicles. Back in the days of horse-drawn carriages, the roads weren't particularly smooth. Riding in a wheeled carriage, if your solid wood-and-metal wheels were connected to an axle, and the axle was slotted directly into the chassis of the carriage, then every bump on the ground would be transmitted directly to your backside. Ouch! Ouch! Ouch! Padded seats might cushion the ride a little, but a much more sensible idea is to put some kind of spring between the wheels and chassis of the carriage. Then if the wheel judders over bumpy ground, the spring will absorb much of the violent moment, cushioning and smoothing the motion of the carriage. It's exactly the same idea as having a bouncy sole in a shoe to protect your feet and legs against the jolts of your own footsteps.

Springy suspension systems may seem like an obvious solution to the problem of being jolted around. But bouncy springs are not obvious devices at all. Why should a solid lump of metal ever be bouncy like rubber? Their molecules certainly don't have the same springy, spaghetti-like structures. Even more mysteriously, why should a gas be bouncy? Clearly some shoes use pockets of gas to provide an extra bounce, but how can a bunch of loose air molecules act like a better bouncy spring than rubber?

The springy properties of metal and gases are caused by tiny but strong forces between their atoms. Take a piece of common household metal – perhaps a stainless steel spoon or knife from the cutlery drawer. You will find that if you try bending it the piece of metal will flex slightly. If you apply too much force it will suddenly bend and you've just ruined it. The metal flexes because its atoms are all clinging on tightly to each other with very strong bonds, but the metal is thin enough that you are able to pull and compress the individual bonds between them without actually breaking them. Like a crowd of commuters stuck in a train carriage, they can be pushed and moved a little, but they're stuck together too tightly to be able to move far, and they prefer to maintain a certain distance from each other, so once you've stopped pushing them they'll settle back to their comfortable pattern. The metal becomes bent when so much force is applied that the bonds are broken between the atoms, forcing them to move around and heat up. (The doors of the commuter carriage are forced open and the commuters are free to move in that area, changing their relative positions.) So when you flex a piece of metal, you are effectively storing energy in it, often called 'potential energy'. (In the commuter train analogy we'd measure the energy in terms of grumpiness of commuters as they are pushed where they don't want to be.) But when you bend the metal, the energy is transformed into heat as the molecules all move around, so the energy is lost.

The trick in making a metal spring is to make sure that the metal is allowed to flex, but never bend. The original carriage springs used in early vehicle suspension systems were designed to do exactly that. They were made by laying strips of thin metal, one on top of each other, each smaller than the last. Imagine a pile of metal rulers, each shorter than the last, placed on top of each other to make a little pyramid and loosely joined so they are free to flex against each other. The ends of this spring are fixed to the chassis and the middle part is fixed to the wheel axle. The result is a pile of flexing metal. The longer strips have more leverage so will flex more compared to the smaller strips. So flexibility is provided by the longer strips, and stiffness and support is provided by the smaller ones, so that none is ever flexed so much that it becomes bent. Such carriage springs, or leaf springs, were enormously successful and used for many years, even in quite recent automobiles. But before long, somebody spotted that the same properties of a leaf spring could be obtained using much less metal, formed in a different shape. The result was a coil spring.

Coil springs are almost everywhere you look. Take a ballpoint pen and look inside: the chances are that you'll see a coil spring inside, enabling the click-top to spring in and out. They work using exactly the same principles as the leaf spring. Imagine a stiff piece of wire, perhaps a straightened paperclip. The wire flexes a little before bending, just like the strips of metal in the leaf spring. Bend the straight wire into a coil (wind your straightened paperclip around a pen) and compress (or stretch) the coil, and you see exactly the same flexing, only now because of the way the metal is wound round and round, the flexing is added together to provide a much greater movement. You can still bend the metal in a coiled spring by stretching it too much or bending against the direction of the coils, but the shape of the coiled spring protects it from most types of damage. Try to compress it too much and the separate coils just touch, preventing you from bending the metal out of shape. Even the circular shape of the coil helps give it strength and resistance to bending.

Coil springs provide tough, lightweight and extremely springy solutions wherever they are needed. Most modern vehicles use coil springs in their suspensions. But coil springs are actually too good at being bouncy to be used on their own. Fit four big springs between the wheels of a car and its chassis and it would be like driving a pogo stick on wheels. Hit a bump and the car would bounce all over the road. The solution, as used by all vehicles, is to dampen down the springiness using shock absorbers.

Some shock absorbers – those in hydraulic systems – make use of the movement of fluids. Imagine a pipe filled with water and a valve inside that controls how much water can flow through. If the valve allows only some of the water to get through, when you use a piston to push or pull at the water, it will flow, but it will resist any effort you make to force it to flow fast. If we connect that piston in parallel to a spring, whenever the spring tries to bounce too quickly, it will try to move the piston too quickly and the water will slow down and dampen its motion. That's exactly how a hydraulic-based shock absorber works.

Other types of shock absorbers use pneumatics or compressed air. Instead of water being pushed and pulled by a piston, air is compressed by a piston. Compress the gas and its molecules heat up, moving more quickly and placing more pressure on everything around it, including the piston. So the more you compress a gas, the more it pushes back at you, rather like a spring, except that the pressure from the gas is an even, smooth force, not like the sudden jolting *sproing* of a spring. Pneumatic shock absorbers are common in vehicles, and so are their related cousins, air springs. Open the rear door (the boot or trunk) of your car and you may well see an air spring in action, looking like a black bicycle pump as it smoothly raises the door. Just the carefully balanced pressure of air, exerting its smooth, even force, powers the door-lifting mechanism. Every time you shut the door, you repressurise the air, compressing the air spring ready for next time.

The smooth properties of liquid movement and gas compression were noticed by Citroën in the mid-1950s, and the company broke with convention and took away all metal springs from their cars, using hydropneumatics (liquid and gas) for the complete suspension of their vehicles. Today many vehicles use pneumatic suspensions, for by adjusting the pressure of the air, the ride height and firmness of the vehicle can be altered.

Vehicles weren't the only things to benefit from air suspension. In 1977 a former aerospace engineer teamed up with a certain shoe manufacturer and invented the idea of an 'air-filled' sole that would use the smooth force produced by compressed gases to give a comfortable but not too springy bounce to trainers. Nike air cushioning hit the shelves in 1979 and has been a hit ever since.

Ironically, many 'air-filled' soles are not filled with air. Each shoe has a capsule made of polyurethane plastic (or a polyester polyol-urethane composite) to hold the pressurised gas in its sole, and they are filled with a very dense gas, probably sulphur hexafluoride (which was listed in the patent for the technology). More recent designs may be able to use nitrogen. Dense gases are needed because otherwise the molecules slowly seep through the polyurethane capsules, making the sole go flat. With the use of these gases and capsule materials, it is possible for gases such as oxygen and nitrogen to seep into the capsule, so the pressure inside can actually increase as they slowly inflate themselves!

Some of the early patents for the technology expired in 1997, so other companies are now free to use air cushioning in their shoes. One more recent concern has been that the fluorinated gases that are used within some shoes are major contributors to global warming. In 2004 the European Union drafted legislation that would make the sale of shoes containing these gases illegal in all twenty-five member nations. Perhaps because of these issues, most other manufacturers continue to use foam as the easy solution for providing cushioning and bounce in their trainers. Foam is nothing more than millions of bubbles of air, each trapped inside a type of plastic, so although the plastic removes some of the bounce, it makes the shoes much easier to manufacture.

The other problem with air cushioning is, of course, that it can be punctured. Accidentally step on a sharp drawing pin and you may well pierce the internal capsule holding all that pressurised gas. Because the capsules are completely sealed within the soles, once punctured there's no way to repair the damage. Keeping a spring in your step is not always easy, but there's one consolation. A drawing pin in a shoe is always better than one in a bare foot.

Mightier than the Sword

Somewhat out of breath, you change back into your dishevelled office shoes and enter the main building, waving the security badge at the door to open it. You leave the deflated trainers on the security guard's desk as a present. The lift door opens as soon as the button is pressed. Darting inside, you choose the sixth floor, to go straight to the meeting room. You're nearly an hour late, but the meeting should last at least 90 minutes. The doors slide open, but as you begin to walk briskly along the corridor, one of your colleagues appears ahead with a sheet of paper – can you sign the requisition form? Sidestepping him doesn't work. He's cornered you. Sighing, you feel in your shirt pocket for your favourite pen. The pocket is still wet from the rain earlier. Ever the professional, you bring out the pen ready to approve the form – and discover your hand has turned blue. The whole of the bottom of the pen is a gunky, fluffy mess of ink. The shirt pocket now has a large blue stain spreading over most of its surface. Ballpoint pens aren't supposed to leak! Why has it picked this morning to empty itself all over your clothes?

Even if your handwriting is impossible to read, it's unlikely you'll go more than a day or two without using a pen. Computers may rule the world, but pens don't need batteries, they fit in the smallest pocket, and they don't have new software to learn every 18 months. The humble ballpoint pen gives us the freedom to write almost anywhere, at any time.

It was not always this way. Thousands of years ago writing was a big deal. It was a way to leave a message for posterity, a magical way to speak to others when you were gone. Cavemen and -women learned the arts of grinding certain kinds of stones to make long-lasting pigments, which were sprayed from the mouth or painted with the fingers. In later centuries many cultures developed the art of stone carving, engraving their messages in rock for what must have seemed like eternity. These forms of writing were performed by the special few skilled enough to leave coherent marks and understood only by those trained in the magical art of reading.

It's one thing to leave your mark on a cave wall or a big rock, but murals are not helpful if you want to keep a record of everyday events, perhaps of who traded with you this morning. Something a little smaller and easier to use was needed. Book-sized clay tablets were one convenient solution, allowing symbols to be pressed into the wet clay and then dried into a more permanent form. Over 7,000 years ago the tablets were used to record pictograms (pictures that resembled the concepts they were supposed to represent). As the images were duplicated over and over again, they slowly turned from pictures into simplified symbols, which, by about 4,000 years ago, gradually became standardised into alphabets. Some 2,500 years ago alphabets that resembled the ones in use today had emerged. The Ancient Greeks even developed their version of a laptop: two tablets hinged in the middle, coated with wax to allow symbols to be pressed into their surfaces with an ivory or metal stylus.

While clay and wax were the methods of choice for relatively quick writing, the fine art of recording those special words for posterity had also been developed. Parchment (stretched and dried animal skin) and papyrus (made from strips of the stems of the papyrus plant, hammered, pressed and dried) provided excellent lightweight and clean surfaces for the words. Charcoal (burned sticks) would leave marks on these new surfaces, but in reality they did nothing more than leave a thick layer of black dust. With nothing but friction to adhere the black sooty particles to the tiny imperfections in the surfaces, the results were very temporary. Smudged text was unreadable, so an alternative was needed. The solution was ink – a dark, slightly viscous liquid that would stick to the primitive papers and dry, allowing permanent marks to be made.

Many varieties of inks were tried over thousands of years. It's likely that only those documents that remained readable were kept, so the examples of unsuccessful inks are lost forever. Perfecting ink was a real challenge. Make the colour from plant or animal extracts alone and the colour fades after a few years as the organic substances decay (or the molecules are excited by the energy in the light and undergo a chemical reaction with the oxygen in the air, making their colour fade away). Make the ink too watery and it will soak into the page and form wet puddles. Make the ink too oily and it will just wipe off the page. Make it too sticky and all you'll have is a coloured glue.

One of the earliest known inks was made in China, over 4,500 years ago. The dark pigment was made from the soot of pine smoke. Lamp oil and gelatin from boiled donkey skins gave it the right oily, sticky texture. (We call such burned carbon-based inks 'Indian inks' today, despite their Chinese origins.) The first use of the ink was to darken the surface of existing stone inscriptions, but before long it became popular for its ability to stick to parchment and papyrus, and dry (just as animal glue dries) as a perfect dark stain exactly where it was deposited.

Other recipes continued to emerge over time. Iron salts mixed with tannin produce a dark bluish-black colour and so were common ingredients (and still form the basis of many inks today). One method was to mix ground nutgalls with iron salts. Nutgalls are the bulbous outgrowths on trees such as oaks, often caused by burrowing insects, such as the larvae of certain wasps. The tree's growth mechanisms are hijacked by the substances produced by the wasps, and nutrient-rich cells grow, forming a gall on which the wasp larvae feed. As a side effect of the strange parasitic process, and possibly as a defence against being eaten, the nutgall becomes rich in tannin (a compound that can give animals and some insects indigestion). It's the same stuff used to help preserve skins when tanning them. Tannin from nutgalls mixed with iron salts produces a great black colour in ink.

While inks became better and better, writers still needed effective tools to place the ink on the parchment or papyrus. The ideal tool would have some kind of internal tube to carry enough ink within it so that several characters could be written before it needed to be refilled. The ink could trickle down under gravity to a pointy end, and by scratching the pointy end on the paper, a trail of ink would be left behind. There are many substances in nature that resemble this, and many of them were used as writing instruments. Hollow reeds, bamboo or, most commonly, feathers were used, their ends carefully cut at an angle to enable a fine line to be drawn. They were dipped in ink, the capillary action of the liquid making it climb a little way inside the internal tube, and then dragged across the paper. Although enormously successful and used for centuries, quills and other simple pens had short lives (perhaps only a week of use) and each needed careful crafting with a penknife before being ready for use. The other problem with quills was that they didn't hold much ink. The writer had to keep dipping the quill into the ink every few seconds to replenish the internal tube.

As writing became more common, the need for better writing instruments became greater. One sensible solution was to have an instrument that could hold much more ink. The first fountain pen was created in 1702, and it (and its later cousins) seemed to have the solution. They all had internal reservoirs that could hold enough ink for many lines of text. Some were refilled by carefully using eyedroppers to fill them from the top. Most had little rubber bulbs that would be squeezed to remove most of the air, then the nib would be dipped into the ink and the bulb released. As the bulb expanded it reduced the pressure of the remaining internal air, allowing the higher pressure air outside to push the liquid ink inside the bulb. Although we may call it suction, a lower pressure (fewer molecules) cannot 'suck'; instead a higher pressure (more molecules) must always push.

Later fountain pens used little levers to squeeze the internal rubber reservoir, or were designed to enable a coin or matchstick to do the same job. Nibs (the pointy bits at the end) were also refined, with air holes and grooves enabling an improved flow of ink to the paper with fewer messy mistakes. Eventually, self-filling fountain pens were replaced with cartridge pens, where disposable plastic ink cartridges could be easily swapped for new ones without needing messy inkwells at all.

Despite all the clever advances, the fountain pen still used the same principles as the quill. The writing instrument was a tube filled with ink that was designed to stain, with a pointy end, the nib, that guided the ink where you wanted it. Leave the pen for too long and the ink dries up inside. Flick the pen and out comes a spray of ink. Take the pen in an aircraft where the air pressure is lower and the ink will leak out everywhere (there is less pressure pushing against the liquid, so it expands). Increase the temperature and again the liquid expands (the molecules are moving about more quickly) and the ink leaks out.

What was needed was a magical kind of pen that contained its own ink, deposited the ink onto paper in a controlled and easy way and didn't leak! The very first attempt at a radical solution was in 1888, when an American leather tanner created a new device for marking leathers. It was a pen with a little ball in the tip. The idea was that the ball prevented the air from getting to the ink so it didn't dry out, and its seal prevented ink from leaking out. But as the tip was rolled over a surface, the ball rolled the ink from the internal reservoir to the outside and onto the paper. If the ink had the right consistency, then it would even act like a lubricant and make the ball turn smoothly, making writing a smooth and easy experience. That was the theory, but unfortunately the early designs had ink of entirely the wrong consistency, and so initial ballpoint pens would write at only one temperature and would leak or clog at any other. Either the ink was too runny and would leak around the ball, or it was too gloopy and would form lumpy, inky messes.

Some fifty years later a pair of brothers, one a chemist and the other a newspaper editor, decided to improve upon the design. Their names were Ladislas and Georg Biro, and their Biro pen eventually became the most successful ballpoint to date. In addition to improving the ink, perhaps the most important advance they made was to make the internal reservoirs into much thinner tubes. Instead of relying on gravity to push the ink to the ball (which meant you had to write with the pen held vertically), the thin tubes used capillary action to draw the ink to the tip. As the ink was deposited on the paper, the ink's clingy molecules pulled the remaining molecules towards the ball, meaning it could work at almost any angle. But even their invention was prone to regular leaks and failures. It took a Frenchman named Marcel Bich to develop the ideas further and produce a reliable and ultra low-cost pen with a six-sided, clear plastic body. He called it the Ballpoint Bic, and it became one of the most successful mass-produced products of all time. It also uses the capillary action of the ink to pull it towards the tip. You can see the process for yourself in every Bic pen through its clear plastic body – the little tube that holds the ink is clearly visible, and its end is simply open to the air. The capillary action of the gloopy ink molecules in the tube as they cling to each other and the walls of the tube is strong enough to keep them inside, even when held upside down.

Today's pens are amazingly well-designed implements that use inks specially formulated to write well and not leak. Pen manufacturers still continue to try and improve the design – for example, the pressurised ink cartridge of the 'space pens'. (There's a common story that claims that in the space race between the USA and the Soviet Union, the Americans spent millions on the amazing pressurised pen that writes upside down and the Russians simply used a pencil. In fact it's a complete myth. NASA did not pay for the development of the space pen, they simply bought the product from Fisher, which developed it to withstand the high temperature and pressure differences in space. Both the Soviet Union and the USA initially used pencils, and even an ordinary cheap ballpoint can work in zero gravity since it relies on capillary action and not gravity.)

Sadly, even the most expensive ballpoint pen can suffer from leaks. The design is rather like a tiny version of a roll-on deodorant – when left for a while, the ink dries on the ball and seals the liquid within. Rotate the ball and the liquid is rotated outside. It's a great design and copes with differences in pressure and temperature very well. But make the ball wet and the seal of dried ink is broken. With no seal, ink is free to leak out, being sucked into clothes just as water from the rain soaks your garments. Alternatively, keep a pen in a pocket and the fluff and grit may find its way onto the ball of the pen. The next time you use it, you may roll the dirt inside as you roll the ink outside. Now you're putting dirty ink onto paper, and the result is usually messy. Even worse, it takes only the smallest speck of dirt to become wedged between the pen and the ball for the seal to be broken and for ink to leak out. Use a ballpoint in a dusty environment or on dirty surfaces too often, and you may even damage the surface of the ball or its tiny socket, making the pen prone to leaving frequent inky splotches.

When you understand how the ballpoint pen works, it's easy to prevent leaks. All you need to do is keep it clean and dry and to write only on clean and dry surfaces. Even if your pen leaks, don't worry – the ink is designed to wash out without problems. Modern pens are unbelievably reliable compared to the long leaky history of quills or even fountain pens. They just have to be treated carefully.

Seeing is not Believing

The meeting door closes loudly. Everyone looks towards you. There's somebody standing at the front with a projected slide showing some kind of financial chart. Muttering apologies and trying to avoid their gazes, you make your way to the large table and find an empty chair. There are about fifteen people in the darkened conference room – the usual gang seem to be present, although there are a few faces that seem unfamiliar. For some reason everyone continues to stare. Perhaps it's the blue stain in your shirt. Or simply your lateness. Turning to the financial manager Dawn, you whisper conspiratorially to her, asking what you've missed. Her response is loud and clear, for the whole room to hear, 'I'm sorry, who are you? And what are you doing here?'

It's the sound of her voice rather than the words that suddenly make you realise you've never seen this woman before in your life. In a panic you look around and realise that there are, in fact, no familiar faces here at all. You've just gatecrashed a meeting of a group of complete strangers. Have you turned blind? No, your eyes are fine. How could you possibly make such a mistake?

We might all have eyes and a good-sized brain behind them, but we're not born with the ability to understand what we see. Instead we are born with an amazing ability to *learn* how to see and understand many useful things – and to learn very quickly. Before babies even have the ability to focus their eyes, they begin learning to recognise their world. Faces are often some of the first things they perceive clearly, and so babies of all ages are attracted to these strange patterns of eyes, nose and mouth. By the time they are seven months old, infants are able to understand the overall patterns of faces in much the same way that adults can.

Perception in all mammals is a very complex process. When we're first born, the neurons in our brains are highly connected, much more so than in adult brains. The first few months and years of our lives are spent pruning away unnecessary connections between neurons and removing unnecessary neurons, until we are left with coherent neural circuits that connect our eyes to our brains in ways that enable us to perceive our surroundings. It's a little like creating a computer by taking as many transistors as you can get (100 billion or so) and wiring as many together as possible, then carefully cutting all the unhelpful wires and removing the transistors that do nothing until you've sculpted your powerful computer.

The neural 'sculpting' process relies on testing: we must constantly interact with our environments and make sure that our developing brain is doing something useful. This means that the stimuli that occur frequently in our environments help stimulate our brains, which helps us to develop our brains better to respond to those stimuli. The more faces we see, the better we become at seeing them. Humans spend so much time looking at faces that significant parts of our brains become dedicated to recognising them. By the time we are adults our face-recognition centres are so highly developed that they can pick up a face almost anywhere. We can spot a face pointing in our direction out of the corner of our eyes. We even mistakenly see faces in random patterns: peering from forest branches, clouds or even the craters of the Moon.

The reason we know so much about the development of perception is not because we understand how the brain works exactly. We're still like cavemen looking at a supercomputer in terms of our understanding of the details. We understand what we do because of the unfortunate results when brains do not develop normally. If you like kittens, look away now.

In the 1970s biologists studying perception reared kittens in very carefully controlled conditions. These poor little cats grew up in rooms where all they could see were horizontal black and white stripes, vertical black and white stripes or diagonal stripes. No balls of wool, birds or mice to chase, no grass or trees or sky. All they saw from the moment they opened their eyes was stripes. But when the grown cats were exposed to other environments (moved from the horizontal stripy room to the vertical stripy room), they behaved almost as though they were blind. The cats' brains had developed to perceive and understand their limited environments, and when they were presented with something new they simply could not understand what they were looking at. Their eyes and brains were working, but the computer had been programmed wrongly and could not work for the radically different environments.

Enough torturing poor kittens. These were extreme examples of effects that we have observed many, many times since. One fascinating example was recorded by an anthropologist working in the Congo in the 1950s, who took a BaMbuti pygmy called Kenge from his home in the dense forest out onto a large open plain for the first time:

> And then he saw the buffalo, still grazing lazily several miles away, far down below. He turned to me and said, 'What insects are those?'
>
> At first I hardly understood, then I realized that in the forest vision is so limited that there is no great need to make an automatic allowance for distance when judging size. Out here in the plains, Kenge was looking for the first time over apparently unending miles of unfamiliar grasslands, with not a tree worth the name to give him any basis for comparison ...
>
> When I told Kenge that the insects were buffalo, he roared with laughter and told me not to tell such stupid lies.

Even the notion of something being smaller because it is further away must be learned. If you never see anything far away, you will never learn this trick and so you will not perceive your environment correctly. Another way to see the effects of environments is through optical illusions. For example, take a blank sheet of paper and draw an upside-down capital T, making sure the vertical line is exactly the same length as the horizontal line. Now look at it. Research has shown that people who are used to wide open spaces will perceive the vertical line to be longer than the horizontal line. When looking out over a large open space, the horizontal heights of trees and buildings give us more clues about distance, so we magnify these in our perceptions. Another example is the 'arrows' optical illusion – two lines of the same length side by side, one with normal arrowheads pointing outwards, the other with backwards arrowheads perched like Vs on the ends of the line. The second line appears longer than the first because we are used to interpreting these angles as cues for depth and the corners of straight-edged buildings. When the same illusion was presented to a tribe of Zulus in South Africa, who all lived in circular huts with circular doors and who had never seen straight-edged buildings, the optical illusion had no effect on them.

Clearly our environments play a tremendously important role in our ability to see. But so do our brains. Patients with damage to the occipital lobe and temporal lobes of their brains (the regions right at the back of your head and at the side by the ear respectively) can develop agnosia. Despite having perfect eyes, because of the malfunction in these important areas of the brain, they are unable to process what they see. There are many types of visual agnosia. Some people can perceive the separate parts of an object but cannot put them together in order to make sense of the whole (form agnosia). Some people can even copy pictures of an object like a spoon, and know exactly what a spoon is for and yet still be unable to recognise it, confusing it with a fork (associative agnosia). Some people cannot distinguish between the fingers of their own hands (finger agnosia) or lose the ability to recognise written words (alexia or visual aphasia). And some people lose the ability to recognise faces (prosopagnosia).

Patients with prosopagnosia provide us with some tantalising clues about how our brains recognise faces. For many years scientists have debated whether faces are 'special enough' to need their own region of the brain, one dedicated to recognising them. Some argue that faces are just other objects that we happen to see in our environments and that they become significant because all our emotional and physical needs are initially met by 'things with faces' (our parents or carers). Other scientists argue that evolution has clearly designed faces to enable us to communicate our feelings and emotions through expressions, so we should have a matching region in the brain to recognise and interpret the complexities of faces. The truth may be somewhere between the two, but it is clear that faces are recognised in very distinct parts of the brain.

One man suffered a gunshot wound to his head and developed prosopagnosia. Suddenly he could see and recognise everything except faces. He found himself living in a world of strangers, for he was unable to recognise the face of any friends or family – or even his own face. However, patients with prosopagnosia sometimes show a second form of unconscious face recognition. Although they are not consciously aware that they know a face, their emotional state is affected. They feel more comfortable in the presence of friends and more stressed when among strangers. The reaction indicates that humans use more than one mechanism in the brain to recognise faces. Another condition, known as Capgras's syndrome, may be the reverse of prosopagnosia (when arising from brain injury). People suffering from this weird condition are able to see and recognise faces, but they no longer have the correct emotional response. They become convinced that everyone around them has been replaced by identical strangers – everyone looks and sounds the same, but the sufferer feels nothing when perceiving them and so 'knows' that they cannot be the same.

Thankfully these conditions are very rare. Although there are different degrees of most conditions and some may be caused by genetic disorders (meaning you might have inherited it from your parents), if you are poor at recognising faces, the reason is much more likely to be environmental rather than neurological. Recent research has shown that most perception (including face perception) is not learned on its own. We often use other cues, such as sound and smell, to help guide us in our recognition. Indeed, scientists have shown that babies become more proficient at distinguishing between faces when they do not have the extra cues available to them. Like the hearing of a blind person becoming more sensitive because of the lack of help from vision, if we learn to perceive faces without the assistance of the sound of the voice, then the ability improves.

So if you are great at recognising faces, it may be because you were exposed to exactly the right kind of environment when you were growing up and you might also have a good brain to help you. If you struggle – particularly when stressed – don't worry, this is exceedingly common. The chances are that you have developed other unconscious methods for recognising people that work just as well, perhaps using their voices, body language or even their smell. Our brains are also highly adaptive organs, so it is quite possible to train yourself to become a better face recogniser. One handy method is to use your mobile phone to take pictures of everyone you have in your address book, and then every time you look for a number you will see their face. Before you know it, you will have trained yourself to be a face recognising expert.

Ripping Yarns

Your face glows with embarrassment, but by the time you reach your own floor in the building your mood has changed into anger. The open-plan office makes it easy to spot a victim on which to vent the frustration of the day. Unfortunately, mirth is the only response. Apparently everyone else knew the meeting had been cancelled; an email had been sent late yesterday. The free meeting room had been borrowed by the company two floors below that was short on space, with instructions not to disturb them. Feeling no better, you stalk to the bathroom in order to wash the blue stain from your shirt and hand. You take the opportunity to pull off the piece of shoe stuck to your thumb. A rough push on the bathroom door makes you feel slightly better, although you'd prefer to kick it a few times. As if sensing your anger, the sleeve of your shirt catches on the closing door latch. You pull roughly at it, in no mood to be tangled up. It stubbornly stays hooked. You give it another tug. It makes a horrible ripping sound. With a sinking heart you carefully unhook the material. Your sleeve now has a big hole in its fabric.

We're all so used to clothing that we never stop to marvel at its remarkable properties. But just imagine trying to get through the day wearing nothing but cotton wool for trousers and tissue paper for a shirt – within 20 minutes our clothes would be nothing but tatters. Our clothing is not made from anything particularly different from these substances, yet somehow it is enormously strong, able to withstand normal wear and tear for years. But if the strength of cloth does not only come from its material, where does it come from?

The answer is the twist. It's a trick that's very easy to see today: take a piece of tissue paper and tear off a long strip, about 3 cm wide. Try pulling it apart. It should be clear that tissue paper has very little strength. Now tear another long strip off, 3 cm wide, the same as the first. Turn one end one way and the other end the other way, twisting the tissue paper until it looks like a straight piece of string. Now fold it into two and twist it together again, making a fatter piece of string. Try pulling it apart now. You may well find it impossible to tear it into two.

The simple act of twisting creates enormous tensile strength (resistance to pulling) from potentially very weak substances. The cause of the strength is friction. Imagine two parallel conga lines of people, each holding onto their companion's waist in front of them. The strengths of the conga lines are only as strong as the two weakest links – whoever has the weakest grip on their companions will break their lines first. This is why tissue paper breaks so easily, for it is nothing more than a sheet of parallel conga lines of plant fibres. Now imagine the two conga lines are rather more complicated: the person in the left line is holding onto the waist of the person ahead on the right, the person on the right holds onto the waist of the person ahead on the left. All the way up the two lines, each holds onto the person on the other side, all their arms crossing over. Now if one person loses their grip it doesn't matter so much, for everyone is still locked together by their criss-crossing arms. This is what twisting does to a material. It winds the internal fibres around each other so much that even if a few individual fibres break, they are still locked by friction into the string and so they continue to provide strength. Twisting is so effective that it allows shorter fibres to become entwined together, locking them into strings of any length.

It should not be that surprising to discover that the friction of individual fibres can result in such strength. Every knot ever tied relies on exactly the same principle: the locking together of individual strands in clever loops designed to trap and squeeze them together. (You may have noticed that it's much harder to tie knots in really shiny, slippery cords because there is not enough friction to keep the knot tight.) In most materials all the tiny fibres have surfaces rougher than sandpaper when magnified, so when they are squeezed together they become locked together by all their bumps, like pieces of a jigsaw. Friction caused by twisting can give immense strength, regardless of the individual strengths of the constituent fibres.

Every rope and string, and every thread made from many shorter fibres, such as wool or cotton, is made in the same way. The process of creating threads from the shaven fluffy hair of sheep has been traditionally called 'spinning' because that's exactly what it is. The separate strands of wool are twisted with more and more strands slowly introduced in order to lock them into the existing twisted structure. Today there is a real science behind the twisting. Careful calculations are made to work out the amount of friction generated when certain fibres are locked together at different angles. From this we can figure out how many twists are needed to produce the strongest threads.

Twisting is not the only trick we use. Another is called weaving, and humans were certainly not the first animal to discover it. Birds commonly weave twigs and stems together to make intricately shaped nests, and beavers build huge dams by interlocking branches. The earliest example of woven cloth was discovered imprinted into clay by archaeologists. The simple fabrics were made from the stems or internal veins of plants, resembling the texture of a potato sack. They were over 25,000 years old, much earlier than the discovery of metals. Some archaeologists believe that Stone Age man may have learned to weave 40,000 years ago, and the technology might have been more useful than flint and rocks. It is possible that our view of the past has been distorted by the fact that stone survives so well over so many millennia, but cloth usually decays and vanishes in just a few months. Perhaps we should really call them Cloth Age man instead of Stone Age man.

Those early cloths were woven using a method known as twining. The horizontal 'weft' thread is passed over and under, over and under the parallel 'warp' threads, then the next weft thread is entwined with the previous one, passed under and over, under and over both the warp threads and the weft thread below, and so on. The result is a weave a little like a net – it's very tough and holds itself together quite well even if damaged. The problem with twining is that it's very hard to automate with a machine because each new thread is entwined or sewn into the previous ones. Because of this, modern weaves are actually a little simpler.

The plain or true, weave, which is most commonly used in our fabrics, follows a similar principle to twining. The first horizontal weft thread is also woven over and under, over and under the parallel warp threads. But the next weft thread is just placed on top of the first, woven under and over, under and over the same warp threads; it's not entwined with the previous weft. To automate the process you just need to lift all the odd-numbered warps with a stick and push the weft through, then for the next thread, lift all the even-numbered warps with another stick (called a heddle) and thread the weft back through again, pushing down (battening) the weft each time to make a dense weave. The other major kinds of weave are simply variations of the plain weave. Twill is made by weaving the weft over and under two or more warp threads at a time. Satin weave is made by weaving the weft under one and then over four or more warp threads at a time, making the weft 'float' and giving it softness. By changing the types of threads used and sometimes looping in other short threads (as in a pile weave) or weaving together different types at the same time, all cloths are made.

Whether the woven material is cotton, silk, wool or grasses, all are held together by friction. All those interlocking threads are enormously flexible, giving us soft and flowing cloths, but the only thing that stops them from unravelling into individual threads is the clever use of friction to lock the separate threads in place.

The whole idea of weaving fibres together to form a flexible and strong, sheet-like material is so successful that amazingly it is used within our own skins. Collagen fibres (the same stuff that is removed and transformed by boiling to obtain gelatin and make jelly or gluey substances) are actually woven together within skin to provide its strength. Like the cloth we make, leather has a natural grain that follows the direction of the fibres. In leather the grain is much more complex, often following the direction of the hair growth from the skin, but containing many fibres lying in other directions to give strength.

The grain of a woven cloth shows its biggest weakness. The weft and warp threads lie at right angles to each other providing the direction of its grains. Try to rip a cloth diagonally, not with the grain, and the separate threads all work together, locking up with friction. If a thread such as cotton or wool is used, the twists of the individual threads also add a huge amount to the strength of the cloth. But try to rip cloth with the grain and suddenly it's much easier. Because all the threads run parallel to each other, if you break the first weft thread between two warp threads, you have another weft thread directly in line below, between the same two warp threads to break. Now the separate threads are not all pulling together – instead, the entire strength of the cloth relies only on the strength of the individual weft threads one under the other. Even worse, because the cloth is no longer flat, all the threads in the two pieces of the tearing cloth are now supporting each other with all their strength while giving no strength at all to the weak point that is ripping. So tearing cloth along its grain is easy. All you have to do is break one weft thread or one warp thread and keep pulling. With little assistance from friction, the other threads all break one after the other and you've torn the cloth into two.

The solution to the tearing problem is to use more complex cloths that have weaves with grains in many directions at once. Now any direction you try to tear will always have a few threads running in a similar direction, so any tears will be very short and won't run through the cloth like a ladder in a pair of tights. This is what nature tries to do in our skins, which is why skin is very hard to tear. It's also the solution used in materials such as carbon fibre (used, for example, to make lightweight but super-strong bodies for sports cars). The fibres are all randomly woven together to eliminate grain, and then coated with resin to hold them in place. Carbon fibre will rip if enough force is generated, but tears are minimised by the random arrangement of fibres. But making cloths with such complex weaves is very expensive, so most hardwearing fabrics, such as denim or suit material, use twill weaves, the diagonal pattern of weft threads providing more resistance to tears along the grain.

Even the best cloth will always be susceptible to sharp objects that can snag and break the individual threads of the weave. Once the break has occurred, there is no more friction to support the threads in that area. Add a little pressure and the cloth will probably tear. Your only solution is to restore the friction by sewing up the damage, clamping the damaged weave together with a new weave called stitches.

Infectious Messages

You're surprised to see the guy from technical support sitting at your computer when you return to your desk a few minutes later. He scowls at you as you approach. You're still preoccupied with your ruined shirt and barely hear him telling you that you've caused a serious infection of the computers in the company. He's obviously mistaken. If anything, you probably saved the company from infection, for you remember receiving an email yesterday from an old friend who had warned you about a computer worm called 'I love you'. Apparently the program emailed people with fake messages and when they opened the mail it deleted a bunch of files and emailed itself out to new people. Your friend had mailed you instructions on how to remove the malicious program, although you couldn't seem to open the file he sent. What did you do that was so bad?

The IT person looks at you with disgust. The email wasn't sent from your friend, he explains. It was a fake message sent by a new version of the worm itself. By clicking on the file you had let the evil program install itself onto your computer, and from there it had gone on to infect everyone on the network and everyone else in your address book. They'd had to shut down the whole system to remove the virus. Meetings had been cancelled, hours of work lost. You are in trouble.

In 1970 the British comedy television show *Monty Python's Flying Circus* finished its final show of the season with a sketch featuring a couple in a restaurant asking what was on the menu. The chaotic answer (interrupted by a group of Vikings frequently bursting into song) was that the menu consisted of:

Egg and bacon
Egg, sausage and bacon
Egg and spam
Egg, bacon and spam
Egg, bacon, sausage and spam
Spam, bacon, sausage and spam
Spam, egg, spam, spam, bacon and spam
Spam, spam, spam, egg and spam
Spam, spam, spam, spam, spam, spam, baked beans, spam, spam, spam and spam
Lobster thermidor aux crevettes with a mornay sauce garnished with truffle pâté, brandy and a fried egg on top and spam

When the end credits rolled, most of the names had 'spam' inserted. It was only a short skit, so the comedy team were no doubt surprised to discover some twenty years later that their show had inspired the use of the word spam to mean unsolicited or junk emails.

Email is a wonderful invention – or at least, it used to be. When the World Wide Web was young (in the late 1980s and early 1990s) email was a fast, reliable and seemingly secure way to communicate using computers. In those days the main users were university staff and students. There were no online stores or Internet banks, no down-loadable music sites or social networking web pages. The word 'blog' was unheard of. But innovations move quickly in the world of technology. As the Internet was taken up for almost every conceivable type of information, emails became hijacked. Advertisements, then malicious programs and scams became hugely prolific. Just as the spam increased until it became overwhelming in the original Monty Python sketch, so email spam is now one of the biggest problems for networked computers today. In 2006 59 per cent of all monitored email traffic was spam.

Over half of all spam in that year was related to the financial services. One common trick used by 'cyber criminals' was to buy stock in a company, then send 'dump and pump' emails to thousands of people with fake predictions that the stock will perform well. Enough people believe the emails for the price of the stock to be pushed higher, allowing the criminals to sell their stocks at a profit. Another trick is known as 'phishing' – criminals send out emails that appear identical to legitimate emails sent from banks or online companies, asking you to confirm your security details or log-in information or even just pretending to charge you for a fictional product and asking you to log in to reply. Clicking on the link takes you to a webpage that also looks exactly the same as the one used by the bank or company, but in reality it's fake. When you type in your details, you are not able to proceed. Instead, your information is sent to the fraudster who uses it to access your bank account or steal your identity and perform criminal activities in your name. Other common examples of spam include messages that claim you have won the lottery, or that you can assist in the transfer of a huge inheritance and earn a percentage in the process. In the latter cases, those foolish enough to respond quickly find they have to pay 'administration charges' of thousands of pounds before they can obtain their 'huge payouts', which, of course, never arrive. Some people are even asked to fly to other countries to complete the transactions, where they have been kidnapped and ransomed back to their families. There are real criminals behind spam!

Other forms of spam are even more clever and just as malicious. One nasty kind is the email virus. Computer viruses have existed since the times of floppy disks. They are evil little programs that hide themselves inside ordinary programs (just as biological viruses hide inside cells) and are run invisibly whenever the legitimate programs are run. Instead of doing anything useful, viruses secretly copy themselves into other programs or onto disks so that they can infect other computers when the disk is read. Computer worms are similar except that they don't need to hide in other programs, they're full programs in their own right and they'll just worm their way into the heart of the computer and make sure they are run whenever the computer starts up. Viruses and worms used to be limited by having to be physically moved on floppy disks, but as email became popular it became a million times easier for viruses and worms to spread between computers. The problem was that files could be attached to emails, and those files could be viruses or worms. The trick was to fool the recipient of the email with the attached virus or worm into accidentally running the program. A double-click with a mouse serves the dual purpose of opening a text or image attachment and executing a program, so all that was needed was to disguise the program as a text or image document and then write something in the email to make the recipient want to try and look at the attachment.

In 2000 one of the most destructive email worms used a little basic social engineering to achieve exactly this. The worm hijacked the address books of infected computers and sent a sweet little message to everyone. The subject line was 'I love you', and the content of the message was simply, 'Kindly check the attached love letter coming from me.' The attachment looked like a text file, with the name 'LOVE-LETTER-FOR-YOU.TXT.vbs', but in reality it was a program. Double-clicking on it ran the program and infected your computer. Because the message came from someone you knew (your email was in their address book) and because the content of the message was just too tempting to resist, millions of people fell for the trick. Once running on your computer it copied itself to all the other computers it could find on the same local network, it overwrote image and audio files with copies of itself, it emailed the passwords from your computer to an address in the Philippines, and it mailed itself to everyone in your address book.

The 'I love you' worm spread across the whole Internet in one day. It followed the rising sun, flowing around the planet and infecting each new country as people woke up and checked their emails, ran the program and allowed it to copy itself further. It has been estimated that 10 per cent of all computers became infected with this worm, and the cost of cleaning out all the infected systems may have been billions in lost time for hundreds of different companies and governments.

Because viruses and worms are so prevalent today, every computer ships with anti-virus software as standard. The software runs in the background, often monitoring all programs you download or run, checking their code against lists of known signatures. Each virus or worm has some kind of unique fingerprint (a pattern of binary 1s and 0s) that can be used to identify them, so the anti-virus software must check that all potentially dangerous programs do not contain the fingerprints of any of the thousands of known viruses and worms. Researchers in computer science are attempting to develop artificial immune systems that would allow computers to detect harmful new programs that have never been seen before. But for now, current anti-virus software must be updated with the fingerprints of new viruses. When the software is up to date it is immune to the current viruses, just as you become immune to the latest version of the common cold once you've had it. But just as biological viruses mutate and change themselves so that they can infect you again, so computer viruses and worms are altered and mutated to avoid detection by the anti-virus software. (Some are even clever enough to mutate themselves.) For every new malicious program, many variants exist, each with a distinctive fingerprint.

The 'I love you' worm was no exception. Some of its variants claimed to be invoices for hugely expensive Mother's Day gifts or flights. Some pretended to be jokes or anxious messages from friends. But the nastiest variants contained warnings about the 'I love you' worm, with details about how harmful it was, and pretended to include a file with more details or even include a program that would remove the worm. Because so many people had become infected with the original worm, many millions more fell for the trick of 'curing' that worm, which allowed these variants to spread around the world all over again.

Until the computer scientists perfect their artificial immune systems, the only thing we can do is be vigilant and keep our anti-virus software up to date. If you receive an email from someone – even if it's someone you know – and the message seems a little strange, perhaps with a few weird spelling mistakes or capitalisations, then do not look at the attachment. No matter how curious you might be, just delete the email. (Better still, don't even read the email, for just the act of looking at it may be enough to cause some viruses to run.) If you receive an email from your bank or from an online company, and it asks you to click on a link in the email in order to go straight to their webpage – don't click on it! Just go to your web browser and find your own way to their webpage. If you're curious you can use the right mouse button (ctrl-click for Macs) and copy the link in the email, then paste it into notepad or TextEdit. There you will see what the link really points to. If the address looks even the tiniest bit different from the genuine web address, the email is fake and a criminal is phishing for your account details. Delete it! When browsing the Internet and a pop-up window suggests you should download a free program to speed up your computer, remove a virus, detect spyware or almost anything else – don't do it! It will only infect your computer, probably grab your passwords and mail them to a criminal somewhere.

The Internet used to be like a little country village where you could leave your doors unlocked and trust everyone around you. Today it is like a big city – full of people who will deceive you or steal from you if you are not streetwise enough. You wouldn't leave your door unlocked in a city or accept suspicious gifts from strangers, so don't do the same on your computer.

Tight Squeeze

The technical support guy takes hours. While he fixes the computer, you try to work at another desk. The tattered shoe and shirt are a constant distraction, but you are able to make some calls and make sure your car is OK. By lunchtime you're still feeling rather self-conscious, so you decide just to grab a sandwich and a bottle of juice from the cafeteria. Taking the bottle back to your desk, you realise there's really nothing to do while the computer is being repaired. You idly sit next to the technical support guy, pretending to go through some papers, drinking and nervously fidgeting with the glass bottle. Finally the technical support guy speaks to you. He's run a program to clean and optimise the remaining system. Apparently the computer should be fine in 10 minutes. You start to thank him and hold out your hand to shake his. At the last moment you realise your finger is trapped inside the neck of the bottle. He walks away shaking his head, as you frantically try to wrench the bottle from your finger. It's stuck at the joint. No matter what you do, it doesn't move.

People are naturally curious creatures, and one of the most natural things we do is use the sensitive tips of our fingers to touch the world around us. The tongue is another sensitive area and is often used by babies to explore new objects by placing them in their mouths as they do not have the ability to move their fingers well enough. Most people absently play with objects around them even while in conversation, just as their eyes flick around to obtain more cues about the world. You might trace the pattern in a table, fidget with a pen or unbend a paperclip. These are all subconscious activities that help your brain understand the feel of your environment.

Unfortunately, sometimes our curious fingers go places that they shouldn't. Accidentally getting a finger stuck in a bottle or a chain fence or a drawer handle is one of the most common mishaps to occur each day. Every day thousands of people manage to squeeze a ring onto their fingers only to find that it does not come off again. But sometimes the mishaps are a little more humiliating. In 2007 a shopworker managed to make the news by getting his finger stuck in the surface of a cast iron picnic table in front of his shop. The fire department had to spend over an hour cutting the table to pieces to free the embarrassed man in front of an amused crowd. On another occasion a professional bowler chose a bowling ball with holes a little too small for his fingers and sent himself flying after his ball when his fingers became stuck. The game was being shown live on television at the time.

It seems somehow unfair that our fingers are able to become stuck so easily. Surely if they can be pushed into something, they must come out again? If only it was so simple. Our fingers are not perfect tubes. They're lumpy, fleshy things with innards that can be pushed around. Even worse, they can swell up and become bigger.

Our anatomy causes some of the problems. Each finger has three visible joints (the thumb having two) with another within the wrist. The muscles that move the fingers are mostly wrapped around the forearm and attach to the joints of the fingers by tendons, like a string puppet moved by pulling its strings. We have some tendons running under the fingers so that we can clench them and grip things, and others running over the fingers, allowing us to unclench them. All are cleverly placed to give us amazing control, enabling us to spread the fingers wide, move each finger individually up and down and move most of the joints independently from each other. The bones in fingers may be thinner than pencils, so to stop them from slipping or bending too freely like little snakes, the joints between the individual bones are enlarged. Each joint is carefully shaped to keep the bones locked together, with cartilage inserts to provide a smooth, lubricated movement and ligaments to support the joints and stop them from moving too far. If you are double-jointed, this does not mean your joints are any different – it's simply that the ligaments that are supposed to limit the joint movements are a bit more elastic than they're supposed to be, allowing your joints to bend in directions that are not terribly useful.

Even the skin on fingers is special. On the fleshy underside of all the fingers and the palms we have friction-ridge skin. This special skin is covered with unique patterns of raised ridges that allow us to grip almost any surface, just as the pattern of grip on shoes allows our feet to grip the ground better. The patterns are so unique (even between identical twins) that forensic scientists use the fingerprint marks to identify criminals. This skin also has far more eccrine (sweat) glands than in other parts of the body, but not for keeping the hands cool. Water helps increase the friction by being attracted to hydrophilic surfaces (materials that like water and pull it towards themselves). So where dry skin might just slip over a surface, slightly damp skin can achieve a good grip. The skin also contains far more sensory nerves, allowing us to feel the detailed texture of surfaces in enormous detail. In contrast, the skin on the other side of the hand is completely different. It does not have friction ridges, it does not sweat much, and it does not have the same number of nerve cells. Instead it is designed to cope with all the bending at the joints, so has tough wrinkled surfaces to protect the knobbly parts from all the knocks they receive.

It's all a wonderful design, like everything else in our bodies. However, the anatomy of fingers does mean that they can become stuck in small places. Push a finger through the small neck of a bottle and although it may be a squeeze, it may well fit. But now the circular ring of glass settles behind the second joint. At the sides, the wider bones cause a problem. At the top, the wrinkled skin bunches up behind the ring of glass. At the bottom, the friction-ridge skin and sweat grips the glass. The combined friction may well be enough to stop the finger from coming out.

But friction caused by your anatomy is only half of the problem. The other half is caused by your circulation. Like every part of your body, the cells in your fingers are living entities that require a supply of oxygen and nutrients to give them energy, and they require waste products, including carbon dioxide, to be taken away. Our circulatory system takes care of this vital function. The heart pumps oxygenated blood from the lungs around the body. The oxygen seeps from the red blood cells in the arteries into the plasma, which seeps through the walls of the vessels to make up our interstitial fluid (the watery fluid that bathes all cells). From this our cells take up oxygen and nutrients and release waste. The interstitial fluid then seeps back into veins and is pumped back with the blood to the lungs, where we breathe out the waste gases and breathe in more oxygen to enrich the blood cells again. There's another system of vessels known as the lymphatic system, which also helps to suck up any leftover fluid and return it to the blood. It's also used by our immune cells to take a good look at anything nasty that might be trying to infect us.

We're watery creatures, and all the tubes and vessels within us need to be carefully controlled. There are valves in many of our major veins to prevent blood from falling back down in the wrong direction. If you have varicose veins, some of the valves have begun to leak and the blood is pooling within the veins, swelling them and making them discoloured and painful. Remarkably, many of the blood vessels also have muscles woven into them, allowing our brain to dilate or contract them. If we're running fast, we need to dilate as many vessels as possible to allow a fast supply of oxygen-rich blood to circulate. If we're very cold, the vessels to non-essential extremities, such as fingers and toes, will contract. In extreme circumstances, your body may sacrifice parts of itself using this method. Mountaineers trying to survive in subzero conditions may lose their fingers, toes and parts of their noses – their blood vessels constrict so much that the blood supply completely ceases in these areas. Any cells that do not receive a constant blood supply will quickly die. We call it frostbite, but the tissue may not be frozen – the mountaineers' bodies are simply making the judgement that it's better to keep organs such as the liver and kidneys alive, even if it means losing a few fingers.

So our blood supply changes depending on how much exercise we are having and how warm we are. The amount of leaky interstitial fluid also varies, especially if we're not moving around enough to help pump it back into the blood. Even gravity affects the amount of fluid present in different parts of the body. When you are in a very relaxed state, raise one hand above your head and let the other dangle down for 10 minutes and you might even be able to see the difference in size between the two.

If your finger is stuck inside a bottle, becoming hot and bothered is a natural reaction, but unfortunately it's the worst thing you can do. The increased blood supply will swell up your finger even more, locking it in place. You may also put the bottle between your knees in order to try and pull out the finger. But the lower your hand is, the more gravity will make the interstitial fluid pool in the fingers, and the more swollen they will be. If you become angry and still try and force it, you may bruise yourself or even strain ligaments or crack a bone. You're really in trouble if that happens, for your finger will swell up to try and fix the damage and may stay swollen for a long time.

The solution is to eliminate each of these problems. First, obtain something that will act as a lubricant – soap, oil, shampoo – and carefully work it under the rim of the bottle and ideally around that knobbly finger joint. Second, be calm, obtain some ice and place it on the finger to fool your body into contracting the blood vessels. The colder you are the better (within reason). Raising the hand high will also drain it of any extra interstitial fluid. Finally, don't just pull the bottle off – it may still be stuck on the bones or wrinkled skin and you do not want to hurt yourself. Slowly rotate the bottle left and right, and ease it off gently. Your fingers can change shape, and you can make them reduce in size if you need to. The fact that you got one stuck in a bottle means that it really will come out again, no matter how impossible it might feel.

① Fading Memories

Your finger is throbbing, but it's no longer in the bottle. Soap from the bathroom and a painful struggle for half an hour did the trick. Sitting down again, you look at the computer. You can see only a blank screen. Presumably it's finished doing whatever it was supposed to. Pressing buttons on the keyboard has no effect. You reach down and turn off the computer, wait 10 seconds and turn it back on again. There's a strange whirring noise, and then a message appears in white letters against a black background: *Fixed disk failure*. Nothing else happens. You try turning the computer on and off again a few more times. All it does is make the same whirring noise and show the same message. Your computer is dead.

Computers are everywhere, but how many people really understand how they work – or how they don't work? When a computer dies, what goes wrong? Surely if they're made up of electronic chips they can't wear out, so what would make a computer fail?

Modern computers are mostly solid-state. This means that most of the clever work that gets done is within the hugely complex processor chips, which contain millions of microscopic transistors all directing electricity in intricate paths within them. There are often several computer processors within each computer – one or two that run your software, a few to manipulate graphics and produce the output on the screen, and yet more to handle inputs such as USB devices, keyboards, mouse and disk drives. There are more chips used to hold all the data (called memory chips) and yet more to transfer data between all of the processors and the memory, on the 'bus' (there are no wheels or fares on this bus, though).

The combination of electricity flowing through chips and the heat produced by that flow can and does slowly wear out the chip. There are three mechanisms that cause this. One is electromigration, where atoms of the metal that conducts the electricity are swept along like pebbles in the bed of a stream. If too many are swept away from one area and build up in another, the chip may not conduct electricity in the way it was designed to and may fail. A second process is oxide breakdown, where one of the special oxide layers that make up the chip develops weak spots and melts away, causing tiny short circuits that destroy the chip. A third mechanism is hot-carrier interaction, where over-enthusiastic electrons pushed by an electromagnetic field may punch through the oxide layer and help form cracks and imperfections. Older chips did not have such tiny internal components and so had lifetimes of many decades. Modern super-miniaturised chips are now pushing the boundaries of physics, so they may only last about five years of continuous use. Not quite as reliable as you thought, perhaps!

But computers don't just have solid-state components within them. They also have a few moving parts as well. For example, when electricity flows through all the chips, some of it is turned into heat. Modern computers can become very hot indeed, so most computers also contain a fan to cool them down. Some may have several fans: one for the internal power transformer, which converts the mains alternating current into direct current, others sitting directly on the hot chips to cool them just as we put our faces in front of a fan to cool them. It's not uncommon to have a fan break down in a computer, and then for the chips to become so hot that they fail.

But that's not all. With current technology we can make memory chips with huge capacities, more than enough to store several encyclopaedias within them. (To give you an idea of the scale of information, this entire book is about 600,000 bytes of information, where a byte can store one character such as 'a' or '!'.) But the desire to store and manipulate more and more information means that even these chips are not enough. We now demand gigabytes of storage space, where each gigabyte is 1,000,000,000 bytes. For storing music and video we need many terabytes of data (1,000,000,000,000 bytes). At the time of writing, we cannot make memory chips with these kinds of capacities, although this may well change within a few years. The solution is to use some form of physical storage device instead of an electronic one.

We've been using physical storage for as long as computers have been invented. Before we even had memory chips, computer programs were stored on punched cards – pieces of card with holes punched into them. By the 1950s computers began to make use of the new technology of magnetic tape, which allowed different parts of its surface to be magnetised in order to store information, and that magnetic polarity could be detected in order to read the information. In the old movies you still see the tall cabinets with reels of magnetic tape spooling back and forth – these were just used for storage, the computer was elsewhere. As you might imagine, they tended to break down frequently, making the computers very unreliable.

Some home computers continued to use tape for storage, but by the late 1970s and early 1980s spinning magnetic disks had become recognised as a much better solution. Instead of needing to spool a tape back and forth to find the right information, to find something on a spinning disk you just need to move a reading head from the edge to the middle. Data are recorded in a series of circles on the disk, by magnetising little chunks of each circle. Just as you could skip to your favourite song by lifting the needle of a record player over the record, so a disk drive could skip to any chunk of data stored on the disk by moving its reading head. With some clever controllers, it could also keep track of any free space on the disk, wherever that might be, and fill it with new information to ensure the whole surface of the disk is used efficiently.

The designs of disk drives slowly improved. Initially the 'floppy' magnetic disks were 8 inches across; after many years of development they were able to store about 1 megabyte (1,000,000 bytes). They were bulky and unreliable, and so a smaller 5¼ inch 'mini' floppy disk was seen as a big improvement. The reduction in size meant that the smaller disks held only a few hundred kilobytes of data, but capacities slowly increased. The next step was the 3½ inch 'micro' floppy diskette, which introduced the sensible addition of a rigid plastic sleeve around the internal floppy disk to protect it.

While floppy disks and their disk drives were hugely successful for the 1980s and 1990s, by the turn of the century, memory chips were able to offer more reliable solutions. The problem was that floppy disks tended to become dirty quite quickly. The disk drives would frequently pick up a lot of dust and dirt on their reading and writing heads, and so it was very common for disks to stop working and all data on them to be lost.

The problems had always been known, so in parallel to the development of floppy disks, hard disks had been created. As you may guess from the name, hard disks are not floppy. They are rigid, non-removable magnetic disks, mounted within a hard disk drive and sealed inside forever. Because there was no need to make them easy to handle, hard disk drives contain more than one disk inside them, one above the other. The original hard disk built in 1956 had fifty disks (platters), each 24 inches across (not a small device) and could store an amazing 5 megabytes. As the years went by, the technology improved and the disks became smaller and more precise. Soon 3½ inch drives became standard for desktop computers, and 2½ inch drives for laptops. Amazingly, drives only 1.8 inches across were developed for tiny portable MP3 players. Within them is the same technology: several tiny magnetic disks one above each other, all spinning at high speed, with microscopic reading and writing heads flicking back and forth, magnetising the surfaces and reading the states. The technology is remarkable, because the tiny reading heads must float over the surface of the disks without touching them. To achieve this they maintain their own internal air pressure, they have their own air filtration systems to prevent dirt from getting inside, and they have sensors to detect if they're being bumped. If too big a jolt comes along, they'll park their heads out of the way. Modern hard disks can withstand unbelievable shocks – when switched off you could play football with one and it would probably still work just fine. The precision and accuracy of manufacture of a 1.8 inch hard disk would put the finest Swiss watch to shame.

However, hard disks are not everlasting. Many years of dramatic failures have resulted in extraordinary designs today, but any mechanical device will wear out eventually, and hard disks are no exception. One of the 'classic' types of failure is known as a head crash.

A sudden jolt while the drive is switched on, or a speck of dust in the wrong place, causes the read-write heads to hit the spinning surface of the disks and scratch them or even become stuck. At best, the disk has lost the information around the scratched area; more commonly, the whole disk will no longer work and may just lose the ability to read data, producing a repetitive clicking noise as the heads seek the right information and fail, again and again. Sometimes the bearings fail in a hard disk, stopping it from spinning smoothly and producing dust, which then causes a head crash. Or the internal platters become misaligned and can no longer be reliably read. Sometimes excessive humidity can cause corrosion with similar results.

To the trained ear, it is possible to hear the death rattle of a hard disk as it prepares to give up. You may start to hear a rougher whine above the noise of the fans. You may even hear a noticeable scraping noise. Sometimes a period of heavy use over several hours can exacerbate the problem. If the computer can still read it, try a disk repair program, which should be able to tell you if any parts are now unusable. If it has gone wrong and your computer is now complaining that it cannot see a hard disk any more, then there are various things to try. Check the power and data cables to the drive – sometimes they come loose and the drive is fine. Try holding the computer at different angles – sounds crazy, but if the read heads are scraping a misaligned platter, it can enable you to access the disk just long enough to retrieve your data. And for the really desperate, some people have found that removing the drive, placing it in a freezer bag and leaving it in the freezer for 30 minutes can bring the drive back to life for a few minutes. The internal components shrink in the cold, freeing bearings and stuck heads. Some have even found that a little tap with a hammer is enough to free the internal stuck heads and allow you to access the drive briefly. But these are all last resorts, likely to do more damage than good in the long term. If your hard disk has died and you have hugely important data on it, then the best solution is to send it to a specialist data retrieval company. They will open the hard disk in a clean-room to avoid the tiniest speck of dust contaminating the platters and can access the remaining data from each platter in turn. It's not cheap, and it's not something that can be done at home or even in a local repair shop.

Computers are just clever machines. We have to take our cars in for regular services or they break down. Computer components, such as processors and hard disks, can't be maintained like car engines, but they can be replaced. The important thing to remember is that they will not last forever. If you want to keep your data, it's best to assume that it will all go wrong tomorrow and make sure it's backed up today!

Shattered Hopes

Perhaps more out of a sense of guilt than anything, when the techies return from their lunchbreak you insist on helping to carry the dead computer downstairs to the IT department. It's heavy, but you are determined to show that you can do something useful today. The room is in the basement, a windowless techno-laboratory filled with parts of computers, shelves stacked high with cables and monitors. As you set the machine down on the floor, the heavy fire door begins to swing shut behind you. The technical support guy is following with the monitor, so you reach out to catch the door to open it for him. It's a much heavier door than you expected and you don't catch it in time. There's a distinct crunch as your little finger is caught between the heavy door and the edge of the doorway.

Bones are not essential for strength, flexibility and movement – the elephant has 40,000 muscles in its trunk and not a single bone – but they do have considerable advantages. A cage of bones provides useful support for all the fleshy internal organs. A shell made of bone can support and protect the delicate brain from being squished. Stiff, internal, stick-like bones can be used like poles within our limbs to push against the ground, allowing us to move at speed.

But how could tough stick-like structures grow inside a living creature? Animal cells are naturally quite squashy things, so they are not much good at forming hard substances on their own. The solution used by plants is to have rigid cell walls so that every cell provides its own support. But even rigid walls can be broken quite easily (we can cut plants with ease), and those that are really solid, like trees, are less good at repairing themselves as most of their solidity is created by the woody dead cells. We wouldn't want a series of new 'shoots' springing from a broken bone in the way that new branches grow from a broken tree.

Animal cells don't have cell walls as plants have, so they can't grow themselves into tree-like bones. Instead they can extrude various types of proteins, so our cells can knit together meshes of collagen and form cartilage (the stiffer stuff that makes up your ears and nose). If the bodies of animals are supported by water, 'bones' made only from cartilage can work quite well. Many ancient forms of fish (including sharks and rays) use cartilage for their bones with great success. But out of the water, cartilage is not quite strong enough. Cartilage leg bones are simply not tough enough to carry heavy organisms around. Some new invention was needed.

The solution came from the answer to a completely different problem. Living organisms require a wide range of inorganic nutrients to enable their cells to grow and survive. Plants need calcium to build those strong cell walls. Animals need iron to enable their red blood cells to grab oxygen from the air; plants use iron to help make photo-synthesis work and draw energy from sunlight. Both animals and plants need potassium, magnesium, sodium, sulphur and countless other substances in order to stay alive. Our planet is abundant in all of these substances (which is no doubt why we all evolved to make use of them), so most are absorbed by plants from the soil, which are then eaten by animals, which are eaten by other animals, and so on. The problem was that sometimes there was actually too much of a particular substance in an animal. Excessive sodium can cause hypertension or affect your nervous system, making you twitch. Excessive iron can cause fatigue, weight loss, arthritis and abdominal pain. If there is too much calcium in your blood your kidneys may start to fail, and muscles such as your heart will not pump properly. The solution used for excessive iron is for certain cells (often around the heart and liver) to exploit a protein known as ferritin, which grabs hold of the iron and stores it out of the way. The solution used for calcium is to store excess amounts in little hard deposits, often around areas where there is cartilage.

Suddenly, we had a way to make really hard structures in exactly the shapes we wanted them to be. We could grow scaffolding made of cartilage, eat lots of calcium and then our cells could deposit hard calcium structures to replace the cartilage. The result would be super-hard, inorganic structures that supported, strengthened and protected us. So this is exactly what our bodies do.

The process is known as ossification. It's a little like fossilisation, where organic structures are slowly replaced by stone. Inside us, cells carefully deposit substances, such as calcium, and remove the cartilage scaffolding as they go. As you might imagine, it's a long, long process that takes many years to complete. A newborn baby still has much of its bones made from cartilage – something quite obvious to see directly after birth as the process of being born often squashes the whole head into a slightly strange shape for a few hours. It's much better to have a bendy baby than a brittle one. They don't call them bouncing babies for nothing.

A gradual process of ossification is also important for another reason. Our bones have to grow in size as we grow up. It would be a real challenge to have completely finished bones when we were five years old, for many of them need to be more than twice that size in just a few more years. Growth is as fast as 20 cm (8 inches) a year during early childhood. But at the same time, the bones need to have tough surfaces at the joints or all the running about and playing would just wear down the cartilage. So our bones have different regions of ossification: some at the ends to make our joints strong, some in the middle to provide strength. The partial ossification makes it easier to expand and grow bones, cells dismantling and rebuilding the cartilage and the bone as the number of cells around them grow in the developing child. Small children start developing bones in their kneecaps only when they begin learning to walk. As we become older, the use of our bodies affects the growth of bones. Children who spend excessive amounts of time training as gymnasts can place so much stress on their developing skeleton that their growth is measurably slowed, only to spurt quickly when training ceases. At puberty the new hormones in our bodies cause the different areas of ossification to join up and our growth finally ceases. Our bones will have finished ossifying by the time we reach our mid-twenties.

Ossified bones are not just thick lumps of calcium phosphate. If our bones were solid all the way through, they would be much too heavy to move. Solid bones would mean that we'd either need very, very thin bones, which would not give us much protection, or we'd all need the muscles of a weight-lifter just to be able to stand up. So our bones have a dense layer of solid bone on the outside, but are just a fine network of sponge-like scaffolding inside. Like a modern skyscraper (which uses a metal skeleton with the rigid floors and walls put around the outside for strength), bones have a fine inner structure and a tough outer layer, making them both strong and lightweight.

Despite all the inorganic calcium, our bones are alive, packed full of cells. They have their own blood supplies, to keep all the cartilage and bone-building cells alive. They also have extensive links to our blood supply for another reason – bones are organs that make all the cells in our blood. Within our long bones is a yellow jelly called marrow. Inside other bones, such as the skull, hips, breast, ribs and shoulder blades, is a red marrow. The yellow marrow (or myeloid tissue) is made of millions of quickly reproducing generalist cells that are able to turn themselves into the different kinds of white blood cells of our immune system, ready to help remove nasty viruses and bacteria. The red marrow concentrates on making the red blood cells in our blood. When people suffer from leukaemia they have malfunctions or cancers in those generalist blood-making cells within their bone marrows. Because they cannot produce enough red blood cells (or because the red blood cells are not made properly and so are abnormal) they may become anaemic, their blood may not clot properly, and they may become very weak. With insufficient white blood cells, their immune systems become depressed, making them more likely to become very ill from relatively harmless viruses or bacteria. The treatment often involves exposing patients to radiation and chemotherapy to kill the abnormal cells in the marrow. The rapidly dividing cells in the marrow are particularly susceptible to the effects of radiation; most of the nasty effects of radiation poisoning arise because the cells in our bone marrow are the first to die. Chemotherapy – toxic chemicals designed to attack and kill certain types of cell – is another way to kill cancerous cells. Once the malfunctioning cells are gone, donor cells from the marrow of a healthy person can be injected to enable new healthy marrow to grow again.

At the same time as producing our blood, all the bone and cartilage-making cells within the bones never cease their building work. As quickly as some cells (osteoblasts) make new internal scaffolding, other cells (osteoclasts) absorb it again, so the insides and outsides of our bones are constantly being rebuilt throughout our lives. It's a clever strategy, for over a period of months it allows our bones to become stronger if we need to do more heavy lifting. The extra forces pushing on the bones encourages the internal cells to build stronger internal support systems and thicker outer shells. However, if you are an astronaut, this mechanism is a real problem. Those living in weightless conditions for several months have no forces pushing on their bones any more, so the rebuilding cells have no encouragement to keep the bones strong. The cells that absorb existing internal supports continue to do their work, but with little being rebuilt, the bones of these astronauts become lighter and more brittle. An astronaut in space for six months can lose as much as 10 to 15 per cent of their bone mass, much of it around the joints, which are the areas that normally are under the most pressure. It's a real problem with no cure at present, although scientists are working on machines that might induce forces on joints by vibrating the bones while in space. Astronauts must go through weeks of recuperation after their missions in space, to enable their bones to rebuild themselves.

As we become older, important hormones that regulate the balance between bone building and absorption may be low, so bones become thinner and weaker. There are also several diseases that affect the bone-building cells in similar ways. The resulting condition is called osteoporosis, and, just like astronauts, sufferers lose bone mass, with the result that their bones become weak and brittle, and fracture easily.

Thankfully, most of the time throughout our lives, the remarkable bone absorbing and rebuilding cells are in perfect balance and so our bones are exactly as strong and light as we need them to be. Should we ever fracture a bone, the same cells play the very important role of knitting the broken pieces back together and depositing nice fresh bone to remove all signs of the damage. The only minor problem with the cells is that they don't actually know what shape the bones are supposed to be – they always followed the original cartilage scaffolding. If you broke a bone but the fragments were left crooked, the osteoblasts would happily knit together the pieces into a solid, but rather crooked new bone. This is why we put broken bones into solid plaster casts or use splints to hold the fragments in the correct alignment while new bone is built to lock them together perfectly. Children before puberty often have 'greenstick fractures' where the bones partially bend and don't break all the way through (like a green stick of a tree). These heal especially quickly and well, for the bones of children are growing and being rebuilt at a fast rate anyway.

Bones are tough, but once ossification is complete it's not uncommon to crack them, especially by slamming fingers in doors. Sometimes cracked bones don't show up well on x-rays and so are hard to diagnose. One approach used by some doctors is to touch a vibrating tuning fork to the bone. If you feel a sharp pain, it may well be because the cracked piece of bone is vibrating. Always go see a doctor if you think you have a broken bone – it is important that a medical professional checks it out. Thankfully, a little crack may not even need a splint or cast, and as long as you don't put it under too much strain while it heals, new bone will grow to fix the problem in just a few weeks.

That Sinking Feeling

You're standing in front of your house again, exhausted. The taxi you'd taken home drives off. The medical officer at work had assessed you and decided a trip to the hospital was not necessary. She splinted the finger to the one next to it, gave you a mild painkiller, made you rest for a while and then sent you home. You're left with a right hand that is clumsy and painful. It's making the search for your front door keys with your left hand in your right pocket more difficult, but after much scrabbling you finally find them. Transferring them to the right hand, an involuntary clenching of the fingers sends a sharp pain shooting through the broken finger and you drop your keys. They tinkle when they hit the ground and then make a strange *ploink* noise. Looking down, you see why. They've dropped through a grating and fallen down the drain.

Why do things have to fall at all? Wouldn't it be great if, when you dropped things, they just hung in mid-air where you'd let go of them? Falling is a real pain in the backside, especially if we land on it. But if nothing ever fell, if there was no up and no down, we would not exist. Nor would any of the planets and stars in the heavens above us.

Even the ideas of up and down are confusing if you travel. The direction of 'up' in Europe is pretty much the same as the direction of 'down' in Australia. On that side of the planet, objects fall up from the perspective of Europeans. Yet, if you go there, objects clearly fall down. This strange paradox points to the truth behind up and down. The word 'up' really means 'away from the centre of the Earth', and the word 'down' means 'towards the centre of the Earth'. The force of gravity means everything nearby is pulled towards the Earth's core. The reason is simply that the Earth is a sphere (more or less) and so its centre of mass is in its middle. If the Earth was skittle- or bottle-shaped, then its centre of mass would be towards the more massive base. Standing on the surface near the thinner neck would feel like standing on a slope; we would stand at a strange slant as we would be pulled at an angle to the ground and not directly down into it.

The Earth does a lot more than pull us to its surface. It pulls all the separate rocks, metals, water and everything else together. Gravitation caused the Earth to form in the first place, out of clouds of dusty debris left over from the explosions of previous stars. The Earth's combined gravitation also reaches far beyond our atmosphere (a layer of gases also held in place by gravity). It catches stray meteors and asteroids and pulls them towards the Earth's surface. Gravitation even holds the entire Moon in its circular orbit, like a whirling toy aeroplane on a string, preventing it from flying away into space.

But the Earth is not so special. While its mass holds the Moon prisoner, the Moon has its own gravitational force. As it whirls around us, its gravity tries to pull objects on Earth towards it. The force is not strong enough to lift a feather, but it is strong enough to cause the water in our seas to bulge several feet towards it. (The molecules in water can move around more than those in a feather; when a vast enough number of water molecules have even a gentle pull on them, enough will move to cause a real overall effect.) As the Earth rotates, day to night to day, and the Moon orbits around us, the bulges move across the oceans, making the water levels rise and fall against the shores, creating our tides.

The Earth and Moon's gravitation is minuscule compared to that of the sun. Our nearest star is so massive that it holds many planets and whole ribbons of rocks in its grasp. All they can do is fly round and round the fiery object, their own gravity totally overwhelmed by its powerful force.

The same effect can be seen on a much smaller scale whenever we drop objects on Earth. Take a marble and a cannon ball and drop them from a tower. They will fall at the same speed and hit the ground together. Although the marble has its own microscopic gravitation, which could pull the Earth towards it, and the cannonball has a slightly larger microscopic gravitational pull, the gravity of the Earth is vastly more than both, so their own tiny gravitational forces have no measurable effect. What counts is that the two objects are pulled by the same Earth-gravity and so fall at the same rates.

Mass causes gravitation. The more mass an object has, the larger its gravitational field will be. Mass is simply how much there is of an object. It has nothing to do with size or weight. A large piece of balsa wood may have less mass than a much smaller piece of metal (like a key). There are simply more atoms in the metal compared to the wood (which has a lot of air in it). The balsa wood will also weigh less than the metal – there are fewer atoms being pulled by the Earth's gravity in the wood compared to the metal, so the combined force on the wood is less than on the metal.

It took a genius called Albert Einstein to figure out why mass creates gravitation. He realised that the whole of space and time is bendy. Imagine the universe is like the surface of a trampoline. Put a massive object – say a bowling ball – onto a trampoline and its surface is bent by the mass. Now roll a smaller mass – say a marble – towards the bowling ball, and you see its path is bent by the trampoline surface until it runs round and round the bowling ball. This is how the Earth forces the Moon to travel in circles around it. The mass of the Earth bends the space around it, forcing the Moon to 'roll' round and round. Just as the trampoline surface is distorted less and less the further you are from the mass, so the gravitational field generated by any mass has less effect the further you are from that mass. Climb a high mountain and your weight will be slightly less, for you are further from the Earth's centre of mass (although this effect depends on the shape and composition of the mountain).

Bendy space creates most of the effects we see in the night sky. It causes clouds of gases to spiral together and form spheres (stars and planets). It causes the stars to spiral together and form galaxies. Bizarrely, it's also the reason why all the galaxies seem to be flying away from each other at great speed.

At the beginning of the universe, every bit of mass, space and time in the universe was contained in a tiny, tiny point of energy. The 'big bang' created our universe, exploding space and time outwards from this tiny point, taking the mass with it. Draw dots on a balloon and blow air into it, and the dots seem to move apart from each other. Stretch space and everything in it appears to fly apart. So that initial explosion is still expanding space itself, taking all the galaxies, stars, planets, you and me with it. Outside our universe there is no space, no distance or position, so asking, 'What is our universe expanding into?' does not have any meaning. If you had a computer program that modelled a galaxy being stretched, the question, 'What is it expanding into?' also makes no sense in exactly the same way. There are no more things than there were before, so you don't need any more memory or a bigger computer. Neither the model nor the real universe is expanding into anything. It's just stretching.

Even light is affected by bendy space. If you were to take an astronomically long tape measure and extend it between our galaxy and another, it would always read the same distance, for it would be stretched as the space it is in becomes stretched. The light travelling from a distant galaxy is stretched in exactly the same way. Its wavelength is stretched, shifting its colour more towards a red colour. The 'redshift' effect allows us to calculate how far away the galaxies are.

But light can be affected in even more extreme ways. Hugely massive objects may have so much gravity that they collapse and compress themselves into tiny spaces. The resulting 'black holes' have such strong gravitational fields that they pull all matter into themselves, even light. If any light goes too close it will be sucked down to its surface (which is why they are black). Light that is a little further away will be bent as its path intersects the distortion in space, as if passing through a lens. So it is possible to detect a black hole by looking to see if the light from other stars in the sky becomes strangely distorted by the gravitational lens of a black hole passing between the stars and us.

As bizarre as it sounds, time is as bendy as space (they don't call time the fourth dimension for nothing). For example, a massive object slows time down. The closer you are to the large mass, the more time is slowed. Go too near to a black hole and time will become very slow for you. The same effect happens when you travel extremely fast – the closer you get to the speed of light, the more difficult it becomes to push yourself any faster, almost as though your mass increases. And just as if your mass was increasing, the closer you get to the speed of light, the slower time flows for you. It's why the speed of light is a fundamental limit in our universe, for in order to reach that speed you would have to push the equivalent of an infinite mass, which we can't do. If the whole thing sounds like science fiction, honestly, it's not. In 1971 two scientists called Hafele and Keating synchronised several caesium atomic beam clocks (the most accurate clocks available at the time) and placed some on board normal commercial passenger jet planes, flying round the world twice. When they came back they compared the clocks that had been speeding inside the planes with those on the ground and found that, as predicted, a time dilation effect (increased by the speed and lessened by the greater distance from the Earth) had indeed made the clocks tell different times. Today, the GPS (global positioning system), which consists of many satellites travelling at high speed some distance above us, only works because their clocks are constantly adjusted for the relativistic time dilation effects.

Thankfully, because we never really travel that fast and we never go near horribly massive objects, our lives are affected only by the masses of the Sun, the Moon and, most of all, the Earth. All the different gravitational fields are overwhelmed by the gravitational field of the nearest massive object, our home planet. Time and space appear constant because the mass of the Earth is constant throughout our short lives. So when we drop something like a bunch of keys, they are pulled 'down' towards the Earth's centre of mass, wherever we happen to be on the planet. There's nothing we can do about it, except hold on tighter or try not to drop small objects over drains. If the worst does happen and gravity does grab your precious keys from your fingers and pull them through a grating, you can always try using a different type of attractive field that happens to be stronger than gravity over short distances. A magnet on the end of a string can work wonders.

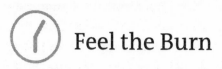 Feel the Burn

The drain is not deep so you decide to pull off the grating and reach down to retrieve the keys. It's tougher than you were expecting, especially using only your left hand. One almighty heave and the grating comes away. You lie down, reaching as far as you can and manage to hook the key ring with your fingertips, lifting it up. But when you try to move the grating back, a sharp pain shoots through your arm, and you cannot find the strength to move the grating again. What have you done to yourself?

About a third of an average woman and up to half of an average man is made from muscle. Without all that muscle we would not be able to move ourselves about, but even more importantly, we would not be able to digest food, process nutrients and waste, and we would not be able to circulate blood around our bodies. Plants rely on osmosis to pump their water and nutrients from the soil (and can even move their leaves and stems around by pumping water in and out of different cells). Animals do not have that luxury; they must push, pull and squeeze different organs and structures inside themselves day and night in order to stay alive.

We have three different types of muscle inside us to do all that work. One type is known as cardiac muscle. The cardiac muscle cells never stop pulsating; although they are regulated by signals from the brain, a single cardiac muscle cell will happily pulsate on its own. This is important, for these muscle cells make up your heart, and it's quite important that it never stops beating. Cardiac muscle cells are designed to be powered by oxygen and to be immune to tiredness. It's just as well, for your heart may well have to pulsate over 2.7 billion times in your lifetime without a pause. Try clenching and unclenching your hand once a second for more than 5 minutes non-stop and you'll quickly realise how impressive your heart muscle is.

A second type of muscle within us is known as smooth muscle. Like cardiac muscle cells, smooth muscle cells are involuntary – we cannot consciously control them. But smooth muscle is not designed to operate like the steady pump of our heart. Instead it often forms sheets that are within our skin, the walls of our blood vessels, reproductive, digestive, respiratory and urinary tracts, and even in the iris of our eyes. Smooth muscle cells sometimes emit collagen to keep themselves together in a nice stretchy, woven matrix, and they help support and adjust the operation of our organs and vessels. Smooth muscles dilate the blood vessels around our bodies when we're working hard or we're warm, and restrict them when we're cold. They squeeze our food and waste along the extensive tubes of our digestive systems, and allow us to breathe by adjusting the passages into our lungs. Like the heart muscle, smooth muscle is designed to be used for long periods without becoming fatigued and to recover very quickly if it is. Your brain does control many of the contractions of smooth muscles, but the control is totally unconscious. You will never be able to alter the way your stomach squelches your chewed-up food or the way your iris changes size in the same way that you can wiggle your fingers and toes.

The third kind of muscle is the type we're most familiar with, because we can consciously control it. Skeletal muscle is the biggest and strongest of our various types of muscles. Lying in bundles woven around our bones, one end of each muscle is fixed to a solid bone and the other end is fixed over a joint to the next bone, using tendons. We have around 639 skeletal muscles (it's hard to count them exactly for some seem to be in groups with others). There are thirty muscles in your face alone, and huge numbers bundled in your forearms to operate the fingers and wrist. There are powerful muscles in the legs and arms to help us run, and delicate muscles in the tongue and eyelids to help us taste and see. Each and every skeletal muscle is wired to our brains in much the same way that a computer is wired to the motors of a robot. And just as the computer doesn't power the robot's motors, it sends a 'move' signal to them, so our brain does not power our muscles, it merely sends a 'contract' signal to them. (Muscles also have spindle cells that sense movement of the muscles and send signals back to the brain like the sensors of a robot, providing proprioceptive information.)

Muscles may be told to move in a similar way to the electric motors of a robot, but they are not powered by electricity. Motion is generated through chemistry. Inside each muscle cell (no matter what kind it is) there are strings (filaments) of proteins running from one end to the other. In skeletal muscle these filaments are all lined up, giving them a striped appearance. The filaments are made from actin and myosin, but they are normally kept from touching each other when in a relaxed state. If a signal is received from the brain, the tiny electrical pulse from the neuron causes a chain reaction, releasing calcium and causing the signal to pulse through all the muscle cells nearby. The calcium forces other insulating proteins to move out of the way, exposing the actin to the myosin. The myosin then binds to the actin filaments, grabbing on like people in a tug-of-war planting their feet in the ground and heaving on the rope. The actin filaments are fixed at each end, so when the myosin pulls the actin towards the middle, the overall bundle of filaments contracts. Inside each skeletal muscle cell many sections of actin and myosin filaments are chained together, so when they pull at once, the typical result is that the filaments contract by a significant amount, shortening the overall length of the cell. When many cells contract at the same time the result is a contracting muscle. To relax the muscle, the calcium is pumped away, the binding between the actin and myosin filaments is broken, and the filaments separate and move apart again.

There are many different types of skeletal muscle cell; different because their chemical reactions are powered by different energy sources. Type I muscles, known as 'slow muscle', are powered by oxygen and so have rich blood supplies and special internal mechanisms inside each cell to convert the oxygen into energy (organelles known as mitochondria and proteins called myoglobin to hold onto the oxygen – these are what makes these muscles red in colour). Type I muscles are used during aerobic exercise; being powered by the air you breathe, they are able to work for long periods without fatigue.

Type II muscles are known as 'fast twitch' muscles, and in addition to using some oxygen, they also have a sugar-based power source called glycogen (and another called phosphocreatine), stored within the cells.

There are several kinds of type II muscles. Type IIa is still mostly powered by oxygen and used in vigorous aerobic exercise for several minutes. Type IIx is more powerful muscle, but relies on the glycogen and phosphocreatine much more than the oxygen, so can be used for only 5 minutes or less, for example when running an 800 metre race. Type IIb cells mainly use phosphocreatine and are used for anaerobic exercise as they need almost no oxygen. A 100 metre sprinter uses these ultra powerful muscles for their short bursts of speed.

Unfortunately, although the anaerobic type II muscles are very powerful, the chemical reaction that is used to generate energy also creates lactic acid as a side product in the absence of oxygen. Use of these muscles for more than two or three minutes will cause the lactic acid to build up dramatically. Without rest to let the cells dispose of the acid, the pH of the muscle cells can become so low that their metabolism fails, causing us pain.

The muscle cells, or fibres, are so powerful that we almost never use them all at once. For most everyday uses only a tiny percentage ever need to contract. When we heave with our muscles as hard as we possibly can, we're using about a third of the fibres. If we used 100 per cent of them we would tear our own bodies apart, ripping the muscles from the bone or breaking our own joints. Nevertheless, it is common for muscles to become painful, and not just because of a build-up of lactic acid.

One symptom all but the laziest of us have experienced is the stiffness and soreness of our muscles between one and three days after taking some vigorous exercise. The cause is nothing to do with lactic acid build-up or glycogen depletion. Instead, the pain is caused by actin and myosin filaments that have become ripped free from their normal positions within the cells by the intensive contraction of other filaments and other cells around them. If enough are ripped free, the muscle cells die and the body must rebuild fresh muscle cells, usually with stronger internal filaments. The process is normal and takes a week or so to complete, although the stiffness may disappear sooner. The solution to muscle stiffness (properly called 'Eccentric Exercise-Induced Muscle Damage') is simply to exercise regularly but not to overdo it each time. Studies have shown that just one period of exercise a week is sufficient to maintain the muscles and avoid stiffness. But it's better to exercise more regularly, to reduce the likelihood of straining the muscles.

For those who exercise rather more often, muscle cramps can be a problem. A cramp is a painful involuntary clenching of a muscle or group of muscles, sometimes occurring around the site of an injury in order to stabilise it, sometimes after strenuous activity or a period of being in one position for too long or sometimes seemingly at random. The exact cause of cramps is not always clear; it is possible that dehydration or a deficiency in one of the essential muscle-related chemicals (calcium, potassium, sodium, magnesium) may exacerbate the effect. A healthy, varied diet, plenty of water and regular but not excessive exercise should solve most problems.

Now and again, you may overdo it all at once. Instead of stiffness a day later, or the painful weariness of lactic acid, or even the sore spasming of a cramped muscle, you may instead feel a sudden sharp pain in a muscle. Perhaps you were trying to lift something a bit too heavy or you stretched a little too far when trying to reach something. Perhaps you were falling and wrenched your arm when trying to grab onto something. A 'pulled muscle' is immediately painful, and you may also feel an immediate weakening of the muscle. The cause is normally that you've torn a significant number of muscle fibres. The muscle cells have been ripped from each other, damaging a small area of the muscle. Rather sensibly, your body protests loudly, preventing you from using the same muscle for several days by making it hurt. While it rests, your body removes the torn and dead cells and replaces them with fresh, new and, hopefully, stronger muscle cells. Depending on how badly you've pulled the muscle, the repair may take two weeks or more to complete, the pain slowly becoming duller and more like the stiffness of exercise-induced damage. But you will recover just fine, and be strong again.

Muscles are amazing, chemical-powered contracting organs, but like everything in the body, they can be damaged if you don't respect them and take care of them. Use them often, but not excessively, and they will stay happy and healthy for your whole life.

Kitchen Fireworks

You finally manage to limp into the kitchen, muscles aching, feeling ravenous. You carelessly throw open the cupboard drawers and freezer, looking for something – anything – that you can eat quickly. Everything needs cooking, but you feel like something quick and easy. Your eyes fall on some microwavable pizzas. They will have to do. Most of your usual plates are dirty, so you grab one from the back of the cupboard. It's a nice-looking plate with swirling gold patterns around the edges. You drop the pizzas onto their little cardboard stands, put them on the plate and into the microwave, slam the microwave door and select 4 minutes.

Rather than tidy up, you decide that you need a drink to relax after this disastrous day, and get a bottle of red wine. Corkscrew in, you heave out the cork, fully expecting the liquid inside to spill everywhere. But no, just a satisfying pop and a healthy glug, glug, as you pour the wine into a glass. You suddenly notice that the microwave is making a strange crackling noise. As you turn back and look at it, your smoke detector starts shrieking. You realise there is smoke coming from the microwave, and sparks flashing from within, as though you have trapped your own evil thunderstorm inside it. You see another flash and realise the cardboard has caught fire inside the microwave.

Most people know that metal and microwaves aren't a good combination. Far fewer people know why. When you think about it, the whole notion may sound like a myth. After all, microwaves are actually made of metal. Some even have metal grills inside them to help toast the food you're microwaving. But it is no myth. If you're silly enough to place something into a microwave oven that contains even a tiny amount of metal, you may well see dangerous sparks flying from it. So why do these strange 'miniature waves' react so violently to metal placed into the oven, compared to the oven itself? Why does metal in a microwave oven spark?

Microwave ovens rely on electromagnetic radiation – the same stuff used by mobile phones to beam signals around, and the same stuff that is generated by lightning in the form of an electromagnetic pulse. The important thing about the waves of electromagnetic radiation used in ovens is their length. As you might guess from the name, microwave ovens use waves with a very small wavelength.

The origins of the microwave oven lie in the development of radar. It was 1904 when the first example of radar was demonstrated, showing that you could beam a radio wave at an object and listen to its reflection. The idea is not dissimilar to sonar, as used by bats and dolphins for millions of years. These creatures make very high-pitched noises and listen to the echoes. If there is no echo, there is no object there, but if there is an echo, then the closer that object is, the quicker the echo will come back. We can experience the same effect by shouting at a cliff face or large wall: the further away we are, the longer the delay between our shout and the echo.

Sound travels in waves, or repeated compressions of air caused, for example, by our larynxes (voice boxes) flapping about and making ripples in the air. Long wavelengths are low sounds, while short wavelengths correspond to higher sounds. Bats and dolphins use very high-pitched sounds, because the higher the sound, the shorter the wavelength is, and the shorter the wavelength, the smaller the objects that produce echoes. It's like needing a net with smaller holes to catch the smaller objects – if you want to 'see' tiny things in the dark, you need to make very, very high-pitched noises. Some bats (who like to eat little moths) make noises so high that the wavelengths don't affect our ears, so we can't hear them at all.

The same principles apply to radar, except that radar doesn't use sound waves, it uses electromagnetic waves. These are the same waves that we see as light with our eyes and feel as heat with our skin, except that our eyes can see only a small range of wavelengths (and our skin feels even less). Visible electromagnetic waves have a wavelength between 400 nm (violet) and 700 nm (red), or 0.0004 mm to 0.0007 mm. Waves with even smaller wavelengths are called ultraviolet light, even smaller still are called x-rays, and really small ones are called gamma rays. Waves with longer lengths than red are called infrared (as used in infrared remote controls). All waves with lengths more than about 15 cm are called radio waves, so for example, a radio station with frequency 100 MHz has a wavelength of about 3 metres.

Electromagnetic waves all behave in much the same way, except that their different wavelengths allow them to pass through certain objects, be absorbed by some and reflect off others. So when we're in a car listening to the radio and we go through a tunnel, we will lose reception because the radio waves cannot pass through the hill to reach us. If we're hot by the fire, a simple screen will absorb the heat and stop it radiating onto our faces. And as I once found out when playing as a little boy, if you have a bright enough torch, on a dark night you can light up the clouds above your head: the light travels all the way up and is reflected all the way back down to your eyes. The same principles also apply to sound waves – which is why moths are so hairy, because they're trying to use the fuzz to absorb the sound of the bat's calls rather than reflect the noise back and give away their positions. In general, if the object conducts the waves well, it will reflect them well. So a wooden floor conducts noise (put your ear to it and you will hear anything moving on it), and also reflects noise, producing good echoes. Similarly, a piece of metal conducts electricity and magnetism, and so also reflects electromagnetic waves extremely well.

Radar exploits these ideas. It's simply the use of radio waves beamed out, with a corresponding receiver to listen for the reflections. Because metal and other electrically conductive materials are so good at reflecting radio waves back, it's an ideal method for detecting aircraft, submarines or ships, which all tend to be made from a lot of metal. By 1940 the technology was being improved in a hurry by the British. In order to improve the ability of the radar to capture smaller objects, they needed to reduce the wavelength. Instead of using larger radio waves, slightly smaller waves with lengths between about 1 mm and 15 cm were used. These were called microwaves.

To produce them, a new gadget called a magnetron was invented. Although it sounds like a comic book superhero, this device is the key component in all radar systems and microwave ovens. It works by using a very high voltage (often more than 4000V), which causes electrons to be fired out from a heated internal cathode. Instead of zipping straight across to the anode in a big spark, cleverly placed magnets force the electrons into a spin. As they zoom round and round they pass by carefully placed metal vanes that begin to resonate at the right frequency. This electromagnetic resonation is channelled down a little antenna and out of the magnetron as high-power microwaves. It's connected to the radar transmitter (or it's connected to the interior space of your microwave oven).

Once designed, the British gave the Americans the plans for the magnetron and encouraged them to help develop and manufacture radar devices for the war effort. The Radiation Laboratory at the Massachusetts Institute of Technology began work on the development of more efficient radar, which became the second most important military project (the first was the Manhattan Project, which led to nuclear weapons). MIT asked the Raytheon company to develop a way of mass-producing the power tube of the magnetron. One of the chief engineers at Raytheon was a man called Percy Spencer.

Percy noticed one day while working near to a magnetron that the chocolate bar in his pocket had melted. He discovered that he could cook popcorn by placing it in front of the microwave beam, and by directing the beam into a container he found he could cook an egg. This discovery led to the development of the first microwave oven in 1947, which was called a Radarange. As well as having a silly name, it was a huge, water-cooled device costing thousands of dollars. Nevertheless, by 1967 the same company had developed the first low-cost, worktop microwave oven. It took only eight more years before the sales of microwaves were higher than sales of conventional gas cookers in the USA.

The design of microwave ovens has changed little since their invention. They all use magnetrons to produce the microwave energy (although modern designs are more efficient and more powerful). They all use a metal cage to trap the microwaves within the oven and force them to bounce around within the space without escaping. You will notice that your oven has metal walls and a metal grid in the door. Because the wavelength of microwaves used in ovens is 12.24 cm and the holes in the mesh are much smaller, the microwaves are simply reflected back inside. If your microwave has an internal electric grill attached to a wall, they'll bounce off that, too. The grill heats the food in the more traditional way.

Those objects that do not reflect microwaves will absorb them. Anything with water in it tends to be pretty good at absorbing microwave energy. The electromagnetic waves grab hold of the water molecules and twist them back and forth at enormous speed. It can do this because one end of every water molecule is positively charged and the other end is negatively charged, and the microwaves are producing an electric field that is oscillating at 2.45 billion times each second. The field permeates through the whole object, so all of the water molecules are grabbed and flipped at the same rate, vibrating each other and heating the object up. This is why food cooks so much faster in a microwave oven – every part of the food is being cooked at once. In a conventional oven or grill, the heat has to soak through from the outside.

There are some drawbacks, however. Because the microwave energy is introduced to the oven in one place, and it bounces around the inside, the waves can affect each other. Just like ripples in a bath, some waves may cancel each other out as they reflect from the edges, and others may reinforce each other. So there may be some parts of the food that receive stronger microwaves than others. To overcome this effect, most modern microwave ovens rotate the food, ensuring that, on average, each part receives the same waves. You may also notice that trying to defrost frozen food in a microwave can produce uneven effects. This is because ice does not have free water molecules, and the frozen ones will not be twisted and heated by the microwaves. So ice is not heated in a microwave, but water is. As soon as a few free water molecules are heated, they will melt their neighbours, causing them to respond to the microwaves and heat up. So you may end up with some parts of the food that are cooked, and other parts still frozen. The solution is to heat the food in short bursts, allowing it to rest for a few seconds and let melting occur before any hotspots are created.

Hotspots in food are one thing, but hotspots caused by unwanted fires are quite another, and if you want to avoid them you need to make sure you don't put any metal in your microwave. Metal reflects the microwaves, so tin foil would completely block the microwaves from heating your food. But even worse, metal conducts electricity very well. Inside the oven, where the electric field is oscillating at 2.45 billion times a second, anything that conducts electricity will have an electric charge pushed back and forth within it. In something like a spoon, this may be no problem. But if the object has sharp edges, then sparks may fly between them as the charge jumps between surfaces. Even worse, if it is a thin piece of metal, the charge may heat the metal up like the filament of a light bulb, and you may see sparks and even a flame. So if you are planning to use your favourite dinner plate with a gold pattern on it, the microwave is a bad idea. The chances are very high that the pattern contains real metal, and that thin coating of metal is perfect for conducting electricity, heating up and sparking. At best you may ruin your plate. At worst, if you've put something flammable like cardboard next to it, you might start a fire. Should that happen, stop the microwave, turn off the power and, if necessary, use a fire extinguisher.

Finally Cracked

Thankfully, after you turned off the power to the microwave, the sparks and fire immediately went out, leaving nothing but the blackened remains of your dinner and a kitchen full of smoke. You give up and decide to call the local restaurant and have something delivered. A glass of wine in one hand, you go into the living room and pick up the phone. As you try not to move the broken finger on your right hand or use the pulled muscle in your left arm, you manage to drop the glass. In your panicking eyes it falls as though in slow motion, finally hitting the wooden floor just next to your rug and instantly shattering into a thousand pieces. Red wine splashes everywhere, but even worse, sparkling shards now cover the floor like glitter.

There's a popular myth about glass. Go on a guided tour around an old house in Europe, and you may be told that the centuries-old glass in the windows is noticeably thicker at the bottom compared to the top. This, you will be told, is because glass is a super-cooled liquid and so over the centuries it continues to flow, falling under gravity and thickening the bottom of the glass. Sadly, no matter what the tour guide believes, the story is nothing more than a myth. It's the result of a misinterpretation of the evidence and a misunderstanding of the science. It turns out that window glass was sometimes made by blowing molten glass into a glass ball and then spinning the ball so that it flattened out like a plate with a knob in the middle. The outer pieces were cut to use as panes of glass, and because of the spinning process they were naturally fatter at one end and thinner at the other. The glass fitter would mount the glass with the fatter end at the bottom to make it stronger and look nicer. (Sometimes the central knob of glass was also used – you can still see this in the windows of some older buildings in Britain.) We know that the glass did not flow, for now and again the glass fitters made a mistake and mounted the glass upside-down, with the thin end at the bottom and the thicker part at the top. We also have examples of Roman glass over 2,000 years old that shows no signs of flowing at all.

So if glass is not a strange, slow-flowing, super-cooled liquid after all, what is it? In reality, the material is a solid, but that solid is made by 'super-cooling' a liquid extremely quickly. Glass is mostly made from silica, which is a molecule made from one silicon atom with two oxygen atoms stuck to it. Silica melts at a frighteningly high 1,723°C (3,133°F). If it's allowed to cool down naturally, it will slowly crystallise, following the shape of its silicon-oxygen molecules. As it cools, silica naturally forms itself into hexagonal shapes. (Look at a lump of quartz or amethyst to see it in its favourite forms, or indeed look at the sand on most beaches, which is made from tiny crystals of quartz.) But if molten silica is cooled down too rapidly (for example, when molten silica lava from a volcano meets the cold water of the ocean), its molecules do not have time to line up and form crystals. Instead they are locked together in their chaotic, random patterns, to form obsidian or 'volcanic glass'.

When we mimic the temperatures of a volcano by using a furnace, we can also melt silica and cool it in the same way. The result is glass: a transparent, brittle rock made from chaotic and randomly positioned silica molecules frozen in situ. Not a super-cooled liquid, glass is actually an 'amorphous solid' (its molecules are not arranged in any regular order). Most modern glass also contains other substances mixed in to make it melt at lower temperatures (sodium carbonate and calcium oxide, also known as soda and lime, and often magnesium oxide). Some glass has additives to make the mixture more transparent (for example, lead in lead crystal or flint glass). Other glass has additives to give it colour or to make it block certain types of light (such as UV light in sunglasses).

The molecular structure of glass makes it very special. In most solids the atoms are nicely arranged in regular patterns like bricks in a house. There's no way the light can make its way through, so it is reflected or absorbed or converted into heat. In glass all those randomly organised molecules are like the messy molecules of a liquid frozen in situ, leaving more spaces for light to make its way through. Even better, the electrons belonging to the silica molecules are particularly bad at interfering with visible wavelengths of light. The electrons can convert some wavelengths into heat, and others they reflect. But the wavelengths that our eyes can detect are unaffected and so are transmitted through the material. That's why glass is transparent to our eyes, even though it may absorb or reflect UV radiation.

The amorphous glass is also special for another reason. Unlike more structured materials, amorphous materials such as glass do not have a simple transition from solid to liquid when heated up. Heat a metal and when you reach its melting point, the temperature of the solid will remain at the melting point while its molecules detach and form a hotter liquid. But heat glass and it continues to become hotter and hotter, until it first reaches its glass transition temperature then reaches its melting point, and finally becomes a liquid.

Glass is not the only material to have this property; many polymers (such as plastics and rubbers) also have the same characteristics. Unvulcanised rubber also has a glass transition temperature, below which it becomes a brittle solid not unlike brittle glass. The glass transition temperature of rubber is much lower than everyday glass, so our normal experience of it is in this bendy, gloopy stage. Although its molecules are not really able to move past each other, they are able to move around, twist and stretch next to each other. As rubber becomes warmer and warmer, its molecules just move more and more, going from a bouncy rubbery texture to a gloopy texture, before finally melting and turning to a liquid.

Glass does exactly the same thing, only at much higher temperatures. Above the transition temperature it moves from being a brittle solid to a gloopy half-solid, half-liquid, before finally melting and becoming a proper liquid. The glass transition is enormously useful when shaping the substance. Instead of needing to heat the glass to over 1,500°C (2,732°F) and pour it into very heat-resistant moulds, we just need to heat it to a few hundred degrees until it goes past its glass transition and then it can be blown like a balloon, rolled or pulled into different shapes as though made of dough. However, since even the glass transition temperature of all common forms of glass is beyond anything experienced outside a furnace, the glass around us is fixed and unflowing in its solid, brittle state.

We can change the toughness of the glass by how quickly we cool it. One famous trick was to drip a blob of molten glass into a bucket of water. The sudden temperature change immediately solidifies the glass into a solid 'drip' shape, with a bulbous blob tapering to a thin tail. The bulbous end is enormously strong and can withstand hits from a hammer. But use your fingers to break the smallest piece from the end of the thin tail and suddenly the entire glass structure – including that tough bulbous end – explodes into fine dust. The mysterious exploding glass drops fascinated King Charles II in 1661 when he was presented with them by Prince Rupert of Bavaria. Now known as Prince Rupert's Drops, scientists have used slow-motion photography to film exactly what happens when the tail of a 5 cm (2 inch) drop made from ordinary soda-lime window glass is broken. A crack races at 7,000 kilometres an hour (4,350 mph) to the bulb and then spreads like the roots of a tree to encompass its whole surface, before the whole glass structure explodes outwards. The cause of this extraordinary behaviour is that initial rapid cooling. When the molten drop hits the water, its outer surface is instantly cooled and shrinks tightly around the still-molten inner core. Even when the entire structure is solidified, the tension remains like a balloon tightly filled with air. Breaking the tail breaks the tension just like popping a balloon, and the glass immediately tears itself apart. But unlike a rubber balloon, which might just tear itself into two pieces, the structure of glass is much more brittle. The molecular structure is haphazard, and there are many imperfections introduced by the other compounds. When under tension, just one crack is enough to trigger a catastrophic failure at countless numbers of the internal imperfections, resulting in the whole structure turning to dust.

Toughened glass (or 'safety glass') is made using the same process of rapid cooling to put the outer surface under tension. It makes the substance much harder than ordinary glass, but prone to the same kind of catastrophic failure. Shower screens, windows and car windscreens may be made of toughened glass. When damaged (perhaps by fatigue caused by heating and cooling in the shower or by a stone or piece of gravel) the glass shatters completely into tiny pieces. Sometimes the larger pieces will continue to pop and break into smaller fragments for some minutes. It's almost like popcorn popping as the stored tension releases itself, creating new cracks and little explosions of glass. Most modern toughened glass is now laminated with a layer of plastic to prevent all the pieces from flying everywhere and harming us.

It's easy to prevent the effect from happening. Once formed, glass can be allowed to cool more slowly in special ovens so that all the tension is released in a process called annealing. The resulting glass will just crack or break into larger pieces when broken, but may not be so strong.

Drinking glasses obviously need to be both strong and safe. More expensive glasses may be made with glass that has expensive additives to make it stronger and more shiny, and then annealed. Their rims may be cut with a hot blade or laser and then polished to remove all imperfections. It's an important step when the slightest imperfection will turn into a crack that will eventually cause the whole glass to fail. Cheaper glasses may be made of several types of glass. Toughened glass may be used for the base and stems, ordinary glass for the bowl. Rims may be 'rolled', giving a slightly fatter edge in order to resist chips and subsequent cracking.

Many glasses are designed to be tough enough to survive being dropped on a hard floor, but even the smallest chip will mean that they are weakened and ready to grow cracks. Few glasses survive being dropped regularly – unless you cover the floor of every room with soft bouncy carpet. If you manage to break a glass, there's really nothing you can do except pick up all the razor-sharp pieces with care and ideally take them to a recycling centre. From there they will be melted down and used to make new glasses, bottles or windows. Who knows, in a couple of years you might even break the same glass again in another form.

1   A Black Mark

After calling the local restaurant for a meal to be delivered, your attention returns to the fragments of glass everywhere. For some reason the base has shattered into tiny pieces, leaving the bowl as five or six jagged fragments. You find a paper bag and gloves and begin the work. Five minutes of careful clearing and a vacuum later, and the pieces of glass are gone. In their place is a horrible red wine stain, soaked into the rug and beginning to dry. You vaguely remember hearing something about pouring white wine on red to make stains disappear … but what if it just wastes more wine and makes it worse? Why is red wine so hard to remove from carpets?

A weed is nothing more than a plant in the wrong place. Similarly, a stain is nothing more than a dye in the wrong place. Bright colours obtained from the juices of certain fruits and berries were once common ingredients in dyes for clothing and carpets. Every time we spill some juice, sauce or wine, we reinvent another ancient dye.

On the surface, paints and dyes may seem to be very similar substances. They both change the colour of materials when applied. The differences are clear when you look a little closer. Paints are rather like inks: they're coloured glues designed to spread and then stick themselves to the surface. In contrast, dyes are designed to soak into a surface, fixing to each individual fibre of the material and changing their colour by absorbing some wavelengths of visible light more than others. Different types of dyes use different chemical processes to attach themselves to fibres. Over the years we've invented many types of fibres and equally many types of dye.

The oldest forms of dye were natural dyes, typically made from plant materials and occasionally some minerals and animals. Several thousand years ago most of our fabrics were made from animal hair, such as wool, angora, mohair and cashmere, or threads extruded from insects, such as silk. These fibres are all made from protein. (It's the main kind of chemical used in living cells, so it's easy for them to extrude.) Natural dyes are typically acid dyes. The vinegar-like acids (a natural result of using berries or plant materials) enable the molecules of the mixture to attach themselves to protein molecules. They stick to the protein because they happen to have regions on their complicated molecules that have an affinity to the shape of the protein, enabling their individual atoms to form bonds like magnets of different polarities sticking together. The molecules also are attracted to water molecules in a similar way, making them soluble. So if you wanted to dye an animal-based fabric or silk, you simply had to soak the material in the water that contained the dye and wait for the molecules to form their bonds.

There are many different types of acid dyes today, some with stronger acids that produce a lovely, even dye but that do not form very strong bonds with the fibres, meaning that they can be washed away (they're not wash-fast). These are often used for carpets and rugs, which don't usually go through the washing machine. Others may be more wash-fast, but because they bond so well to the fabric they may produce a less even colour, with too many molecules binding to one area and not enough to another.

Food dyes are also a type of acid dye. Because protein is so common within cells and because we tend to eat things made from cells (plants and animals), this kind of dye is ideal for changing the appearance of food. Today, most food dyes are artificial, made from ingredients as diverse as coal tar and mashed-up insects. Unfortunately, although they may provide vivid and appealing colours in foods (and cosmetics), many have been linked to cancers in more recent years and have been banned from use. There is no widespread international agreement about which food dyes are safe, with each country often regulating differently for their population. Colourings and dyes are still used in huge numbers of products, especially in products such as fizzy (soda) drinks, jams (jellies) and sweets (candies). It is known that some of the dyes in use today can cause allergies and behavioural problems in some children, so consumers are increasingly choosing 'natural' products without colourings and dyes.

There are many other types of dye. Some are 'fibre-reactive', which means that they chemically bond to protein or cellulose molecules of fibres, linking so closely that they become a single coloured molecule. Some require extra chemicals to be added to enable them to dissolve into the water ('vat dyes', such as the ones used to dye blue jeans). Some require chemicals to act as a 'mordant', fixing to the dye molecules and making them insoluble, preventing them from being washed away. Some rely on light to achieve this process, often showing a marked colour change as they become fixed into the fabric. Many modern dyes are combinations of many different types of dye, enabling them to stain more than one type of fibre at the same time.

Dyes are not just used to make clothing, carpets or foods look pretty. Much of modern biology and medicine relies on staining. If you've ever seen stained wood, you'll know that biological cells do not turn one even colour in the same way that fibres within fabrics do. Stained wood is attractive because the stain brings out the grain of the wood, darkening some regions much more than others. Biological cells are not like the fibres in cloth. Different cell types have different functions, and cells of each type may produce different proteins inside and outside their cell walls. Fibres within cloth are all made from the same stuff. Use a dye that is attracted to a particular kind of protein, and if the fibres of the cloth are made from that protein they will all take on the colour. But use the same dye on a group of cells, and only those cells that produce that protein will take on the colour, while all the others will be unstained (or stained less). In wood this produces a lovely highlighting of the grain. In biological laboratories it produces selective staining of certain cells, or even of certain structures inside the cells, depending on the stain. When you're using a microscope to identify how many cells of a particular type there are in a sample, the technique becomes absolutely indispensable. Often the difference may be completely impossible to detect with the naked eye, but by using 'markers' to stain specific regions, it becomes possible to identify cell types and structures with ease. Today much of the staining is done by robots, and computers are linked to the microscopes to count stained cells automatically, allowing us to analyse enormous quantities of microscopic biological features at high speed. The recent advances in DNA sequencing technology rely on staining the DNA molecules in order to analyse their structure and identify individual genes. During the development of new drugs, staining enables us to keep a close eye on different parts of cells to see exactly how the medicine affects them. Forensic scientists also use staining to identify blood or other bodily fluids at crime scenes.

Stains may be enormously valuable in many different areas of science, technology and industry, but what of your own home? If you do spill red wine onto a carpet or rug, what happens next depends on what the fibres of your carpet are made from. Grapes naturally contain tartaric acid, and some winemakers may even add more tartaric acid if the wine is too sweet. Red wine also contains pigments called anthocyanins, and as the wine ages it develops larger molecules that may react to form colours, such as browns, greens and purple. While the alcohol can inhibit the staining a little, all the other ingredients can combine to form a natural acid dye that has a strong affinity to protein fibres, such as wool, and also cellulose fibres, like cotton. So if your carpet is made from natural fibres, it will happily pick up the pigments and become stained by the wine. If your carpet is made from synthetic material, such as nylon or polyester, then it is much less likely to take up the stain, so water and soap should just wash it out.

For many years there has been a 'home remedy' to remove stubborn red wine stains. Even recommended by wine experts, the trick is to put white wine over the red wine stain and rub it in before the red wine dries. According to those who recommend this solution, the result is that the red wine loses its ability to fix to the fibres and washes out easily. Others recommend adding salt or milk or soda water or vinegar or detergent.

The difficulty with stain removal arises because the underlying chemistry is not identical. Each variety of wine tastes different because its chemical composition is slightly different – the grapes have grown in different soils, in different climates and have been treated differently with different additives. Likewise, the fibres in each new rug or item of clothing may have undergone different treatments, including dying and bleaching. The result is that each type of wine may have a slightly different affinity to the different fibres around you and may react differently when other ingredients are added to try and remove the stain. So, depending on the wine and the fibres, sometimes any of the above remedies may work, and at other times none of them may work.

As a last resort, bleach may remove the pigmentation. Bleach does not wash away a stain, instead it destroys the parts of the molecule that give the dye its colour. The colourful regions of dye molecules are called chromophores, and they work because the shape of the molecule causes some of the electrons whizzing around the atoms of the molecule to become very excited by certain wavelengths of light. So a red chromophore absorbs all the visible wavelengths except those between about 625 and 750 nm that we perceive as red, which bounce from the surface into our eyes. Bleach destroys some or all of those regions of the dye molecules, causing them to reflect more (or all) visible wavelengths and making bleached surfaces appear a different colour (or white).

Thankfully, today there are some excellent products available to avoid staining or remove stains. Some enable you to shampoo an invisible mixture into the fibres of the carpet, which coats the fibres, keeping those natural proteins locked away from dyes that are ready to latch onto them. Other specialist cleaning products are designed specifically to break the molecular bonds between the stain and the fibre, while (hopefully) leaving the dye of the carpet untouched. Most of the products are pretty good, but every time you spill a liquid onto a new surface and then try to remove it, you are performing a unique chemistry experiment, with no guarantees that it will be successful. The only real way to avoid stains is simply to avoid spilling liquids of any kind. That's why there are a lot of stains in the world.

Hot and Bothered

You give up on the stain when you hear the doorbell. Looking back at the soapy rug, the stain seems to have gone, but the area you've been scrubbing looks suspiciously paler than the rest of it. You bring the pizza back to the living room and go to find a fresh drink from the kitchen. Cold water will do fine. On the spur of the moment you decide to spice up the pizza by chopping a couple of chilli peppers and adding them to the top. Back in the living room you sprinkle them on, and then start eating the pizza with your fingers. Nice. You begin to relax, the exhaustion of the day hitting you. You tiredly rub your eyes, thinking that you should have an early night. Suddenly your eyes are burning, feeling hotter and hotter. You didn't wash your hands after handling the chillis. Your eyes are on fire! How can a tiny amount of vegetable juice possibly do this?

Chillis are the fruit of a family of plants known as capsicum. Not all capsicum fruit are hot. The (sweet) bell pepper (also known as paprika, capsicum or simply pepper) is a familiar red, green, yellow or orange fruit. The colour often depends on when it was harvested and how long it has matured. A common ingredient in recipes across the globe, bell peppers are no spicier than potatoes. The reason is a single gene, which prevents the production of a substance called capsaicin in these varieties. In contrast, the spicy member of the family is often called the hot pepper. As well as being smaller, these peppers produce capsaicin, the concentration of this irritant being highest in the pithy internal areas around the seeds.

Capsaicin (and five other very similar compounds with mostly unpronounceable names: dihydrocapsaicin, nordihydrocapsaicin, homodihydrocapsaicin, homocapsaicin and nonivamide) is the reason why chillis are 'hot'. In reality, chillis aren't at a higher temperature, nor do they increase the temperature of your mouth (eat something spicy and take your temperature if you don't believe it). Chillis have a 'hotness' or, more properly, a 'piquancy' because the compounds with those complicated names are especially designed to trigger the heat-sensitive cells in your mucous membranes.

In your mouth, eyes, nose, stomach and within most other mucus-producing membranes elsewhere, you have special sensory cells. These cells detect touch and temperature and send a pain signal to the brain if the heat is too intense. Capsaicin in chillis is designed to irritate those cells, fooling them into behaving as though they are being burned by something very hot. It's an evolutionary trick used by these fruits to prevent mammals from eating them and destroying their seeds. The digestive systems of birds do not affect the seeds, and by no coincidence, birds are immune to the compound and happily eat the fruit, spreading the seeds of chillis in their droppings.

Even cooking chilli peppers will release enough capsaicin vapours to irritate the nose and cause sneezing and coughing. But the piquancy or pungency of chillis is highly variable and depends on the type of chilli. Each variety produces slightly different amounts of the five compounds, so some produce an instant irritation, some take several minutes for the irritation to build up to full strength, some are very mild, and some are completely unbearable. The 'degree of hotness' used to be measured using the Scoville scale. Invented by an American chemist called Wilbur Scoville in 1912, the scale was based on the feeling experienced by tasters as they tried various dilutions of the chillis. The stronger the chilli was, the more it had to be diluted until it no longer felt hot, so the 'degree of hotness' was simply the level of dilution required. On this scale, the bell pepper had a score of zero, while pure capsaicin scored 15,000,000 to 17,000,000. Tabasco sauce (based on the tabasco pepper) scored around 2,500 to 5,000. Jalapeño peppers scored 2,500 to 8,000. Thai peppers scored between 50,000 and 100,000. But the Naga Jolokia wins the prize. Also known as Bhut Jolokia, Ghost Chili, Ghost Pepper or Naga Morich, it grows in northeast India and Bangladesh and is the hottest known pepper. It scores between 855,000 and 1,041,427. If chillis really did heat your mouth, these would make you breathe fire! Today the Scoville scale has been replaced with more objective chemical analysis techniques to measure the exact amounts of capsaicin, instead of relying on human tasters.

Eating substances designed to cause us pain may seem crazy. But while a European might be in agony after eating a curry containing the spicy Naga Jolokia, those people who are used to the spices develop tolerances. There is a real change to the sensitivity of the heat-sensitive cells in your mucous membranes if they come into contact with capsaicin regularly. So over the course of many years of eating hotter and hotter dishes every day, people in many countries lose the sensitivity to capsaicin in their mouths (and other regions) and can happily consume quantities that would make some of us cry in pain.

We've had a long time to become acclimatised to chilli. For 10,000 years people in South America have cultivated different varieties and used them to make their food spicy and hot. But surprisingly, even as recently as 500 years ago, most of the Asian countries that today are famous for their spicy food, such as Thailand, Korea and India, did not use chilli at all. Trading Europeans (who ironically use far less chilli in their foods), particularly the Portuguese and Spanish, introduced the fiery spices to Asia. There the climate was perfect for the farmers to grow their own chillis and produce their own fiery varieties, as you can taste for yourself in any Indian or Thai curry today. It has been suggested that chillis caught on in some hot countries because the spicy foods inhibit the growth of bacteria – or even disguise the taste of less-than-fresh meats. While these may have been reasons in the past, in modern times most chilli is eaten because it is a traditional and greatly enjoyed ingredient.

The painful, but temporary effects of chillis are so intense that capsaicin from chillis has become the active ingredient in 'pepper sprays'. Becoming more and more popular with police forces around the world, these sprays are used to incapacitate people by spraying them in the eyes. The score of a pepper spray on the Scoville scale is about 2,000,000 to 5,300,000. When just a tiny amount of capsaicin from relatively mild chillis is accidentally rubbed into an eye, an unpleasant sensation of heat and pain is felt. The liquid from a pepper spray may be a thousand times worse. Victims feel intense pain, and may even lose their sight for ten or fifteen minutes. It often takes the body at least forty-five minutes to flush the capsaicin (or artificial compound based on capsaicin) from the affected areas, with lots of tears. The symptoms are so intense that in rare cases when used on people with respiratory conditions, such as asthma, pepper sprays have caused death, the irritated mucous membranes of the respiratory passages swelling until the passage of air becomes cut off. The use of pepper sprays is strictly limited in most countries of the world, where they are often classed as restricted weapons. In 1972 the use of pepper sprays was banned for warfare by the Biological Weapons Convention, but it remains legal for use in internal security. As horrible as the symptoms are, the effects are normally temporary, and they are almost always less harmful than a bullet.

Thankfully, there may be rather more pleasant uses for capsaicin. Recent research has shown that the spicy compound may be the answer for a new kind of anaesthetic. Traditional anaesthetics block a huge range of neurons, causing loss of pain, but also numbness, a loss of touch, movement, coordination and mental alertness. The best kind of anaesthetic would block only the neurons that are receptive to pain signals and nothing else. In 2007 scientists at Harvard announced that the combination of a compound called QX-314, which blocks electrical activity in neurons, with capsaicin, which opens up channels in the cell membranes of pain receptors, produces a targeted anaesthetic that only switches off pain and nothing else. The new combination of compounds may be the beginning of a revolution in anaesthesia, allowing us to eradicate pain wherever it occurs, without the side effects of conventional painkillers.

Capsaicin and the related compounds produced by chillis are not soluble in water, but they do dissolve in oil. This is why you sometimes only feel your mouth heating up towards the end of a meal. While you were eating, the oils in the food were dissolving the capsaicin and carrying it to your stomach. Once you've finished, the oils are gone and water-based drinks will not have much effect on the remaining capsaicin sticking to the inside of your mouth. Research has been carried out to find the most effective way of removing the spicy heat from your mouth after a 'curry overdose'. One study found that while rinsing with water took 11 minutes to reduce the heat, and sugar-water or fruit juice was 2 or 3 minutes faster, the outright winner was milk. It's thought that the combination of the protein casein and the fat breaks down the bonds between the capsaicin and the cells of your mouth, and helps flush them away. Milk chocolate and some beans and nuts have a similar effect.

If you do accidentally chop some chillis and then rub your eyes, you have much the same options as if you've eaten something too spicy, for the same effect occurs in your eyes as it does in your mouth. The safest is unfortunately to let your eyes flush themselves clean with tears over the next few minutes. Although your eyes may go red and feel awful, they are not being damaged by the capsaicin, they are simply being fooled into behaving as though they are being burned. If the pain is unbearable, flushing the eyes with cold water (keep your eyes open) may help speed up the process of capsaicin removal. If you have enough spare milk, you could even try flushing the eyes with this, although you should flush them with water afterwards. As usual, the best remedy is not to do it in the first place. Whenever you have been handling chillis always wash your hands thoroughly with soap and water (not just water, for remember that capsaicin is not soluble in water). Treat chillis as though they contain a dangerous chemical weapon – because they really do.

Taking it All in

Your eyes feeling a little less inflamed after running the cold tap over them, you come back to the living room. The remains of your pizza are sitting on the wooden floor where you accidentally spilled them in your hurry to flush your eyes. At least you'd only just cleaned the floor. You pick up the pieces and seeing nothing wrong with them – by some miracle the pieces landed dry side down – you dust them off and continue eating. As you begin the final piece you feel something strange in your mouth. A gritty kind of crunchy texture. You pick the gritty pieces from your mouth and discover they are tiny pieces of glass you must have missed earlier. Taking the slice of pizza closer to the light you realise it is covered in tiny fragments of glass, dust and a few hairs. But if this piece is so dirty, how bad were the pieces you've just eaten? What happens if you accidentally eat dust, dirt and glass?

Animals, fish, reptiles, insects and, indeed, almost all multicellular animals are designed along very similar principles. We all have a mouth at one end, an anus at the other, and a windy internal tube linking the two. Our ancient descendents were simple worm-like organisms, and it shows. We're all still nothing more than over-complicated worms, our internal tubing ornamented with different limbs, organs and skeletons.

In humans, our internal digestive tubing is anywhere from 5 to 12 metres (16–40 feet) in length. (The length often depends on the weight of the person rather than the height, with larger people having more tubing inside them to cope with the extra food.) All stretched out, we would be very long worms indeed. To make it all fit, most of it is coiled up inside our lower abdomens.

When you consume food, the first thing you do is liquidise it in your mouth. Your teeth mash up as much of the solids as they can, and your saliva helps turn the result into a gloopy sludge. The beginnings of digestion occur at the same time, for the saliva contains many proteins designed to break down carbohydrates in food. You produce around 0.7 litre (1¼ pints) of saliva each day from three large glands (some the size of your nose) behind the throat and under the tongue, which squirt the fluid through little valves into the mouth. You also have minor glands in the inside of your mouth, at the back of the tongue and even inside your lower lip (that's what the funny little lumps are that you can feel with your tongue). As well as providing a good coating of mucus in your mouth and down your throat, saliva also contains many minerals and compounds designed to kill some types of bacteria and even reduce pain. (This is why we instinctively lick our wounds – our saliva may well be cleaning, protecting, reducing pain and helping the wound to heal.)

Once your mouthful of food has been turned into a nice slimy mush, your tongue gathers it together to form a little gooey ball called a bolus. It then pushes the bolus to the back of your throat, muscles close off the tubing to your nose (you don't want to push it up there if you can help it), and the tissues in your throat begin the process of squeezing the bolus down. In a process known as peristalsis, the smooth muscles in the lining of the tubular walls rhythmically contract, squeezing the food along just as we use our fingers to squeeze out the contents of a tube of toothpaste. Along the way, a flappy lid of cartilage tissue (the epiglottis) hinges down to cover the entrance to your airways (trachea) and guides the bolus down the tube (oesophagus) towards your stomach. The impulse to breathe is temporarily halted as the food passes by. Then the smooth muscles of the oesophagus squeeze the food all the way down. The squeezing process is so effective that it can even push pure liquids into your stomach when you are upside down, which is pretty important if you are bending down to drink from a stream. Normally it takes eight or nine seconds for the bolus to reach the stomach. (If you pour liquid down your throat, gravity may take it there even faster, but peristalsis usually still takes eight or nine seconds to catch up and let the liquid flow into the stomach.)

Next a little valve opens (the lower oesophageal sphincter, or cardiac sphincter, named because it is situated fairly near to the heart), and the food is pushed inside the stomach. When things become a little messy here and stomach acid accidentally spills up through this valve, we experience 'heart burn', the unpleasant feeling of stomach acid irritating the lower oesophagus.

Inside the stomach conditions are very different. Just the smell and anticipation of food on its way is enough to begin the secretion of gastric acid in the stomach. It's a highly acidic mix, mainly consisting of hydrochloric acid. Once food is within the stomach, acid production steps up further, and the muscles of the stomach wall pulsate, slowly churning the contents like a cement mixer. The acid breaks down proteins in the food, and many other compounds assist in tearing the molecules apart. The acid also helps inhibit the growth of any bacteria or viruses that you have swallowed with the food. After anything from 40 minutes to a few hours (depending on what you've eaten), the stomach slowly releases the resulting fluid, known as chyme, into the outgoing tube, called the duodenum. (We don't normally get to see chyme, except when something makes us vomit, in which case the stomach convulsively squirts its contents up and out in an attempt to expel anything nasty that we ate accidentally.)

The duodenum, a tube between 25 and 30 cm (10–12 inches) long, receives the acidic chyme and triggers the gall bladder to excrete an alkaline bile and the pancreas to produce sodium bicarbonate in order to neutralise the acid. The gloop is then pushed further along, mixing with yet more enzymes, which further break up the molecules into smaller pieces. Its next destination is the small intestine, a coiled and lengthy tube (several metres long) where nutrients are absorbed. The walls of the tube are wrinkled and covered in microscope finger-like protuberances, increasing the surface area of the inside dramatically. Water, vitamins, minerals, fats, sugars and all the other useful nutrients are absorbed through the walls and into the blood supply. What's left is then pushed through into the large intestine or colon. Here live over 700 species of bacteria, and they like to eat the gunge that comes through. The bacteria help break down the remaining undigested substances, such as fibre, and produce some vitamins for us in the process. They emit gas as they eat, which consists of nitrogen and carbon dioxide, with small amounts of methane, hydrogen sulphide and hydrogen. So the 'wind' you may produce is all made by bacteria in your colon feasting on the remains of your food, nothing else. The bacteria also play an important role in our immune systems. Because they are foreign organisms within us, our immune cells quickly learn to produce antibodies against them and prevent them from entering our bloodstream and harming us. There are so many types of bacteria down there under controlled conditions that our immune systems are given an excellent chance to learn what the latest designs of bacteria look like. So when a new and nastier variety tries to infect us, 'cross-reactive' antibodies that were originally designed to control the harmless bacteria in our colons can be modified quickly and used to wipe out the new danger. Recent research suggests that the appendix, which is attached to the colon and was once thought to be a useless and vestigial structure, plays an important role here, for it is rich in immune cells. Some scientists have discovered that the appendix can also store a small supply of useful bacteria and help repopulate the colon after illness has flushed away the normal population.

Finally, the remaining vitamins and water are absorbed, and the brown sludge that we call faecal matter (or poo), is compacted over the next few hours. Around twenty to thirty hours after eating, the solid waste is finally pushed from the opposite end of our bodies and the process is complete.

Our digestive systems are remarkably adept at handling a huge variety of substances, and, of course, they need to be. It's only in the last hundred years that we've understood that dirty food and contaminated water will make us ill. For most of the billions of years of our evolutionary history, we've eaten raw or badly cooked foods. We've eaten foods covered in dirt and gravel. We've eaten foods containing hair, feathers, bone, cartilage, seeds, bark and everything else you can think of. So our bodies are designed to break down and absorb anything that will help keep us alive and simply expel anything that is indigestible from the other end. Eat tiny fragments of grit or glass, and as long as there is nothing sharp enough to perforate our internal tubing, they will just go straight through us. (Normally if we are foolish enough to put something with sharp edges in our mouths we will feel it and spit it out long before swallowing.) Eat dust, which is likely to comprise fibres from clothing, dirt from outside and dead skin cells, and what your body cannot absorb it will expel. If we were very unlucky, or very stupid, we could eat something poisonous. But we have excellent senses of taste and smell and a vomit reflex for exactly this reason. Most common, naturally occurring poisons taste horrible and immediately make us want to spit them out or vomit them up again.

The most likely causes of problems after eating something dirty are bacteria and viruses. These little 'germs' are everywhere. They live on our skins, on our dishes, in our beds; they cover the home (and indeed the world). Most are completely harmless. Many are extremely useful to us, like the vast populations living in our colons. And therein lies the problem. Humans and bacteria have evolved to cooperate. We need to be able to introduce useful bacteria into our colons to help us digest foods, so it is not in our interests for our digestive systems to kill all bacteria. A newborn baby must be able to introduce bacteria into its intestine, and adults benefit from replenishing their bacteria now and again, perhaps even deliberately with probiotic yogurts. Unfortunately, once in a while a new breed of bacteria or virus breaks the truce and tries to use the half-open door to infect us. Our colons (and sometimes even our stomachs) are lovely places for them to live, with lots of nice food and warmth. The colon even provides a nice escape route through which some of the bacteria and viruses can escape, ready to infect another victim.

The result for us is typically a condition known as gastroenteritis. Our bodies react against the infection, increasing our temperature in order to kill off the invaders, but also flushing the intestines with water to wash out the harmful invaders. The result is fever, diarrhoea and sometimes vomiting. If it lasts, it's an extremely serious condition, for the intestine is extruding water instead of absorbing it. Sufferers become dehydrated enormously quickly and, depending on the severity of the condition, may not be able to absorb water properly by drinking, meaning that they require fluids from an intravenous drip in order to survive. Sufferers also lose essential salts and sugars. It is so easy for our internal tubes to become infected in this way that worldwide hundreds of millions of us suffer from the condition every year. Even today the

179

total number of people who die from the condition may be as many as 3 million each year.

Luckily, gastroenteritis is not a new condition either, and our bodies are designed to recover fast. As long as sufferers are kept hydrated and the missing salts and sugars are replenished, then in just two to six days their bodies will have removed the unwelcome visitors to their colons, and their amazing digestive systems will be back to normal. If you have eaten anything bad and you are experiencing symptoms that alarm you, then always see a doctor. But remember, we are designed to eat a huge variety of things, including bacteria. The proper development of our immune systems relies on us being exposed to new bacteria every day. It is important that our foods and water supplies are kept entirely separate and uncontaminated by waste that may have come from the colons of others (so wash your hands after going to the toilet). However, we'll usually be just fine after eating a bit of dusty or gritty food.

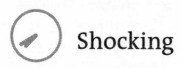

Shocking

The rain from earlier in the day has returned with a vengeance. You can hear torrential rain falling outside, and perhaps a distant rumble of thunder. Feeling better, even with dusty food in your stomach, you turn on the television to see if there's anything worth watching. Flicking through the channels, you're distracted by a bright flash outside. A loud rumble of thunder follows after less than a second. That sounded close. You look out of the window and another bright flash dazzles you, the thunder making the windows shake. At the same time all the lights go out and the TV becomes black and silent. Heart pounding, you feel your way to a cupboard and find a torch, then locate your fuse box. A circuit-breaker has tripped. You flick it back on, and the lights come back. Back in the living room, the television remains dark and silent. No matter what you try – even changing the fuse in its plug – the TV set does not work. It's been killed by lightning. But how?

In the heart of a giant thunderstorm, the dazzling flashes of lightning and their accompanying crashes of thunder can be awe-inspiring and frightening natural phenomena. A bolt of lightning is pure electricity sparking across the sky. The power of that electricity may be as much as 120,000 amps at 3,000,000,000 volts, flowing for a few millionths of a second. It's enough power to run a 100W light bulb day and night for several months. Because all that power is concentrated into a huge spark, its heat is hotter than the surface of the sun and is more than enough to turn sand into glass. As air is superheated and blown apart by the lightning, a shockwave expands from the electrical explosion. This wave of compressed air expands out like ripple, moving at the speed of sound.

If the lightning is many miles away, when the shockwave finally reaches our ears it has had a chance to bounce and echo off many other surfaces and so sounds like a long rumble of thunder. If the lightning is overhead, you hear the ear-splitting *crack* of that initial fearsome electrical explosion followed by the rumble of its echoes coming back. (Another cause of the longer rumble is the fact that some bolts of lightning are several thousand metres long, so the noise from superheating more distant air takes longer to reach your ears than the noise from heating the closer air.) Either way, in air the light always travels much faster than the sound, so there's always a gap between seeing the flash and hearing it. The further away the lightning, the bigger the delay between flash and rumble.

At all times, day and night, somewhere on the Earth there is lightning ripping its way across the sky. The remarkable amounts of energy are all generated inside clouds. There are no batteries or generators involved. All that energy originates from the sun and the rotation of the Earth. Evaporation of water from the oceans causes the formation of clouds, huge, expanding bodies of floating water droplets swirling and rising through the atmosphere. As the droplets in the clouds move, some turning to ice, others combining to form larger droplets or breaking up into smaller droplets, something mysterious happens. Some of the particles become positively charged and others negatively charged. The positively charged particles mostly cluster towards the top of the cloud, and the negatively charged ones gather at the bottom. The more of this charge separation that occurs, the more the cloud becomes charged like a giant battery, with the positive terminal at the top and the negative terminal at the bottom. At the same time, a large positive charge also develops on the ground, the force of the negative charge in the bottom of the cloud pushing away the extra electrons like magnets of the same pole repelling each other.

There are currently at least twelve different theories about why charge separation takes place within large clouds. The most commonly cited reason – that ice crystals rub against each other to create static electricity – may well be true (particles of dust in the cloud from an erupting volcano do exactly this), but it doesn't really explain why the whole cloud separates the charges, positive at the top and negative at the bottom. When static electricity builds up in a woollen jersey, the negative charge is fairly evenly distributed throughout the material. If you touch a door handle you may well see a spark, like a little bolt of lightning. But if the woollen jersey was like a cloud it would be positively charged around your shoulders and negatively charged around your stomach. Every so often sparks would fly from shoulders to stomach. Clearly that doesn't happen. (When you remove the top you may well see lots of little sparks and crackles, but this is caused by slight random variations in charge throughout the material and by charges combining in newly touching folds jumping to other regions with less charge. There is no clear separation of charge as in a cloud.) At present we're still trying to figure out why charge separation occurs. It seems likely that the cause is partly because smaller ice crystals are blown higher than larger ones, and the smaller ones may somehow have a positive charge. Unfortunately, scientists find it very hard to do experiments on anything as big as a thundercloud, so the phenomenon remains an unsolved mystery at present.

Charge separation creates an imbalance. When it occurs there are water molecules at the top of the cloud with too few electrons and molecules at the bottom with too many electrons. If you fill a container with high-pressure gas (or low-pressure gas), beyond a certain pressure the container will fail and the pressure will equalise itself, the force of the higher pressure molecules overcoming the resistance of the container. Similarly, when the negative charge builds up enough in a cloud, eventually the pressure of the voltage becomes high enough to overcome the resistance of the air. When that happens, electrons start to force their way through the air, often proceeding downwards in 50 metre (165 foot) steps towards the positively charged ground as they cut negatively charged channels through the air. These 'leaders' are pushing electrons as they go, so are significant electrical currents themselves. At the same time, electrons belonging to the atoms of the highest points of the ground (closest to the cloud) are pushed away, and positively charged 'streamers' start to reach up through the air. These are fingers to the sky made from electrical current of many tens or hundreds of amps. When the negatively charged leader from the cloud makes contact with a positively charged streamer from the ground, the circuit is made, and all that pent-up electrical charge can flow in a bolt of lightning. The energy of this 'return stroke' is so great that the air is superheated and produces a huge amount of heat and light. (Lightning also flies inside the cloud between the positive and negative regions following the same process.) Because the leader and streamers have carved their ionised channels through the air, it is common for four or five lightning strikes to occur in quick, flickering succession down the same paths. Lightning frequently strikes in the same place twice!

The formation of streamers from the ground is more likely to occur from higher objects (which are closer to the encroaching negative charge) and also from good conductors, such as metal objects (which have plenty of free electrons able to move easily). This is why golfers are frequently hit by lightning – their metal golf clubs or umbrellas may be the highest point on a large, open golf course. It's also why you should not shelter near a tall tree in an electrical storm. The height of a tree may well make it more likely to create streamers and attract the lightning, and when it is struck its sap may explode because of the furious heat and injure you. It's also why, if you find yourself in exposed conditions under an electrical storm, the recommended position to take is the 'lightning crouch'. You should crouch on the balls of your feet with your heels pressed together, preferably wearing rubber-soled shoes, and hug your knees. This way you are low down, but not touching too much of the ground which might be about to conduct a great deal of electricity. If you feel a tingling sensation and your hairs are standing up, then take the position immediately for you are in a large electric field and are in immediate danger. Otherwise, the best solution is to jump in the car. If struck, the metal body of the car conducts the electricity straight past you to the ground, and you will be fine. (Of course if you have an open-top car or a carbon-fibre sports car, it won't work quite so well.)

The powerful blast of electromagnetic radiation from lightning does more than create a flash and a crack of thunder. It radiates a quick but very intense electromagnetic field. Just as a radio antenna in an electromagnetic field (radio wave) has an electric current induced in it (which is how radios turn the invisible signal into audible sound), so the electromagnetic burst from lightning can induce significant electric currents in metal objects or wires that are nearby. So while a direct strike from lightning on a power line may produce a significant surge of power, even a lightning strike nearby is enough to induce a power surge because of the electromagnetic field.

Most of our technology is designed to cope with the effects of lightning, with many protective circuit-breakers designed to 'trip' if they detect excessive surges of power. But sometimes lightning is a little unusual. In 5 per cent of lightning strikes, the positively charged top of the cloud is blown forwards and overhangs the ground. Now negative streamers rise from the ground, and positive leaders creep down, until a positive lightning strike occurs. Having much further to travel to reach the ground, the charge has to build up much more, so positive lightning is five or six times more powerful than ordinary negative lightning. It can also sometimes seem like a 'bolt from the blue' as the main bulk of the storm cloud may be some distance away and the skies might appear fairly clear. All that extra power produces a huge electromagnetic pulse (EMP), which can be strong enough to induce excessive electrical currents to flow in electronic equipment nearby, melting their components and destroying them.

EMPs are more commonly associated with nuclear weapons. The blast from a nuclear detonation produces a huge emission of electro-magnetic radiation called gamma rays. These are strong enough to knock electrons from air molecules and cause a large pulse of electricity to travel through any nearby electronic equipment. The cause is slightly different compared to lightning, but the effect is the same – your electronics are fried. The military have developed nuclear weapons for exactly this purpose, and they would be deliberately set off in the atmos-phere to cause the effect. Special 'EMP hardened' electronics are now standard for all military applications, using shielding to redirect the induced current away from the delicate components.

At home we don't have expensive EMP-shielded electronics. At most, our gadgets have shielding to prevent them from emitting too much radiation and so interfering with other gadgets. While they may have fuses and circuit-breakers to stop the power entering their components through the plug in the wall, they have little or no protection from the EMP of a nearby positive lightning strike. Thankfully these occurrences are very rare. Modern buildings have lightning conductors to keep the surge away from the interiors, so at home the most common causes of lightning damage are spikes or surges of power caused by a distant strike on a power line. The momentary increase of power is sometimes so quick and so great that before the circuit-breakers have a chance to cut the power, it's already made it to any electric device that is switched on and fried its circuits. If you have a strike on your unprotected home or a tree right to next to your home, it's also more likely that the current from the strike itself will find the power cable and run straight through the wiring of the home. Sometimes a strike this close will spark straight over the circuit-breakers, blow all the bulbs from the ceiling, melt all the electrical sockets and may well start an electrical fire. However, if you live next door to someone who has just suffered a lightning strike like this, the gadgets in your own home may have been invisibly fried by the EMP from the same strike.

Lightning is still full of mysteries and surprises, but while we don't know exactly how clouds can make it, we certainly know it's dangerous. Many people die every year from lightning strikes. Always try to avoid being in an exposed location during an electrical storm. When at home, if you are concerned by a fierce electrical storm nearby, switch off and unplug important electronic items, such as computers, to protect them from power surges. If you're unlucky enough to have your equipment fried by an EMP, your only choice is to replace it.

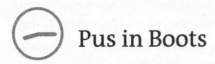 # Pus in Boots

Your feet are tired, so you remove your shoes and socks and massage your toes. You decide to make a hot drink to help you relax. In the kitchen the kettle seems fine – no leaks, no dangers – so you boil some water and add a sachet of instant hot chocolate, stirring it well. You try to ignore the mess still in the sink; you can clean it up in the morning. While the hot chocolate cools down enough to drink, you return to the living room. Perhaps some music would be nice. You have a favourite CD somewhere. As you search for the disc, cup in the other hand, you inadvertently spill some of the hot liquid. It lands on your bare foot, scaldingly hot. Crying out with the pain, you put down the cup and hop to the bathroom, putting your foot in the bath and pouring cold water over it. The pain dies down to a dull throbbing but in minutes you can see the damage. A blister is rising on the skin where the liquid fell.

We have been drinking hot liquids for thousands of years. Tea was drunk in China over 4,000 years ago, hot chocolate by Mayans over 2,500 years ago, and coffee was discovered in Ethiopia a thousand years ago. Apart from the stimulation provided by the ingredients, warm drinks have served several useful purposes. The process of boiling the water kills off any harmful bacteria and parasites that might infect our digestive systems. The warm liquid literally heats us up from the inside, stimulating the dilation of blood vessels in the walls of the oesophagus and stomach to carry the heat around our bodies, and making us feel more relaxed as a result. But there is also another less pleasant side effect of our habit of preparing and drinking hot liquids. Boiling water can burn us quite seriously if it touches our skin.

What happens when we're burned? When anything too hot touches our skin for too long, the membranes of the skin cells burst and the cells die. The more heat that is applied and the longer the heat is there, the more it is conducted into our skin and the flesh below, so the more cells that die. Burns are measured using a scale. A first-degree burn is the mildest. Just the top layer of the outer skin (the epidermis) has been damaged. As those cells die, they release chemical messages, which trigger the dilation of nearby blood vessels and attract immune cells. The pain receptors in the skin also send their signals to the brain. So the area becomes red, swollen and painful. Your body begins the process of cleaning up the dead cells to allow new ones to grow in their place, and also tries to teach your brain a lesson – don't do that again!

A second-degree burn is more serious. Now more cells of the epidermis are destroyed, and some cells in the top of the dermis are also killed. After a few minutes, or a few hours depending on the severity of the burn, a void forms within the epidermis, and lymphatic fluid (not pus) leaks into it. The result is a swelling like a balloon in the skin, which we call a blister, and it usually causes enough pain to make us want to avoid letting anything touch the blistered skin.

Blisters are a design feature of our clever skin. They're an emergency response designed to provide a protective environment rich in immune cells for new skin cells to grow. Generally initiated when the upper layers of the epidermis are failing, they protect against any infection that might try to take advantage of the dead outer layer and gain entry into us. Blisters do not separate the epidermis from the dermis, they actually occur within the epidermis itself. They form when a deep layer of the epidermis, known as the stratum spinosum, loses its ability to stick to the layer below, known as the stratum germinativum or basal cell layer. This may happen because the cells have become damaged or destroyed through excessive temperature.

A blister may also form when repetitive friction loads are placed on the skin – not just rubbing, but rubbing with pressure. The constant pressure causes tears to form in the stratum spinosum, which will open up to become a void in which lymphatic fluid pools, forming a blister. Just like the friction of your feet causing an old linoleum covering to separate from the floor in wrinkles or puckers, so the friction of ill-fitting shoes on your skin can cause the upper layer of skin to tear from the lower layer.

It's important that blisters occur above the basal cell layer, for this deepest layer of the epidermis is the one that contains all the fast-growing cells that make the layers above. So while the blister forms and provides a protective cushion, the basal cell layer underneath is stimulated into action. When blisters are the result of friction damage, instead of simply growing new layers of skin exactly as they were before, the basal cell layer is also stimulated to do a more thorough job. It grows a much thicker layer of skin, which we call a callus. The result, after about twenty-eight days when the whole area has been regenerated, is a tougher, thicker area at exactly the place where the damage had occurred. This is your body's way of protecting you from future damage in the same area. The next time the same friction load is experienced on that spot, your skin won't be damaged.

Blisters forming because of second-degree burns are performing an important job, and should be left alone. Many studies have investigated what happens to patients who have blisters that are left intact compared to those that have blisters 'deroofed' or drained with a needle. Generally, as soon as the seal of the blister is broken, infection is much more likely, pain is worse and often healing is slower. Of course, blisters frequently form in exactly the places most likely to receive friction loads or further accidental damage. It is quite common for them to pop, exposing the delicate inner layers of the skin and producing an open wound. Should this happen, it's very important to keep the area clean and preferably cover it with sterile bandaging. A popped blister takes longer to heal, and an infected one takes a lot longer.

Third-degree burns are even more serious. Now the heat has been so intense for so long that the epidermis has become charred and destroyed. A blister cannot help here, for the basal cell layer has been killed and damage extends deep into the dermis. Pain may be much less compared to a second-degree burn, but this is only because the nerve cells that would send the signals to the brain have also been destroyed by the heat. Often second-degree burns occur around the edges of the third-degree wound, so the injury is far from painless. Blood naturally flows to the site of the wound, and all the body can do is form a scab over the area and try to rebuild the many layers of skin from scratch. Scarring is common after these types of burns, for the body simply creates a kind of generic skin covering to patch the hole. For more severe burns it cannot match the pigmentation or hairs that should be there, for all those cells were destroyed. Sadly, the process of embryogenic development that made the skin, its follicles, pigments and pores when we were in the womb is not switched back on again when we're adults, so many original characteristics are lost. This can be made worse if large areas of the skin are burned, resulting in large, thick scabbed areas called eschars, for blood may find it hard to reach the areas and feed the new skin cells as they try to grow. Sometimes surgery is needed, or skin grafts from other parts of the body (slices of skin epidermis taken from a healthy area and moved to cover the area with no skin).

Third-degree burns are often measured in terms of the percentage of the body surface area affected. For example, each leg including the foot counts as 18 per cent, an arm counts as 9 per cent, the front of the torso is 18 per cent as is the back, and the head and neck is 9 per cent. Anyone with burns covering more than 10 per cent (or less on sensitive areas such as face, hands or genitals) is considered critical. A large percentage means that the burn becomes more likely to be life-threatening as the body's fluids simply leak from the open wounds. Infection is also exceedingly common. And some third-degree burns are worse still. Instead of just charred skin, the flesh below can be cooked or burned away. In devastating cases, even the bone may be charred.

There are many causes of burns. Scalding from hot water is very common, whether from kettles, radiators or even bathwater. Fires cause many third-degree burns as the human body is made from plenty of flammable oils, fats and proteins, despite the high water content. Breathing hot smoke can produce serious internal burns to the lungs. Acids can eat into our skins and cause chemical burns. Electricity can also cause severe burns, as the high current heats our tissues up like the hot wire in a toaster. Those struck by lightning may have only minor burns visible on the surface of their skins, but internally may have horrible burns following the path of the lightning within them.

Children are particularly susceptible to burns, for their skin is more delicate. Just being exposed to water of 66°C (150°F) for two seconds is enough to cause a nasty burn. Burns may also be produced by longer exposures to cooler temperatures, for example 5 minutes at 49°C (120°F) will also cause a burn.

If you have been burned, the first step is to remove the source of the burning. Get away from the hot water, put out the fire and extinguish any smouldering clothes, but *never* remove clothing stuck to the burned skin or you'll simply peel off the skin as well. Wash off any chemicals causing a chemical burn and remove clothing that they may have soaked into. Put the burned flesh under cold water for long enough to cool down the area but no more. Take care: after a severe burn, even running water has enough force to wash away the skin. Never put butter or oils on a burn; the old 'remedy' can be harmful as it traps heat and prevents oxygen reaching the injury. Don't burst blisters, try to bandage the area (over clothes if necessary) with sterile gauze, but never use a sticky plaster or band-aid – again, it may just take off the skin when unpeeling it.

A minor first-degree burn will heal on its own. A minor (coin-sized) second-degree burn will also be fine if the blister is left alone. Larger second-degree burns or third-degree burns require immediate medical attention, especially if a child has been affected.

Burns will always be a serious danger. The Centre for Disease Control and Prevention in the USA reports that burns and fires are the fourth most common cause of accidental death in the USA, with over 4,500 of these tragedies occurring each year. Thankfully, the human body is an amazing piece of engineering, able to repair and regenerate itself, even after some unbelievably serious burns. Make sure all burns are looked after properly, and you'll heal and be as good as new again before you know it. Just leave those blisters alone.

Jumping Tunes

After carefully putting a little antiseptic cream on the burned area, you return to the living room and collapse onto the sofa. At least you found the CD you were looking for. It had been lying on a pile of others that you hadn't got around to putting away. You reach over and insert the CD into the machine, then lean back to listen. After five minutes of crystal-clear music, suddenly the sound deteriorates into a noise that sounds like hail falling on a tin roof. The music returns briefly, then skips thirty seconds ahead in the song. It then starts repeating the same split-second of music continuously, a guitar machine-gun with unlimited ammo. You eject the disc and take a look at it. As the light glints over its rainbow silver surface you see that it has some tiny scratches across its shiny surface. Surely CDs are supposed to be indestructible. A few scratches shouldn't matter, should they?

The first optical storage discs were created in the early 1970s. Known as laser discs, they were 30 cm (12 inches) in diameter (about the size of vinyl records) and stored video as well as audio. They went on sale in 1978 and were reasonably successful for the next twenty years, with millions of people worldwide using the read-only format. But their introduction was two years after VHS video cassettes, which were a cheaper and more flexible format, allowing consumers to record their own videos, so laser discs never reached the same popularity or gained a significant share of the market. Four years after the laser disc came another competitor, the cheaper and smaller cousin known as the compact disc. It began life as a read-only, audio-only disc. Its small size and unrivalled clarity of sound made it a hit. Before long, CDs had made laser discs, audio cassettes and vinyl records obsolete.

Both the CD and its parent the laser disc rely on many important inventions. Perhaps the most significant was the laser. Today a familiar part of our lives – laser printers, optical storage, fibre optic tele-communications, laser pointers – lasers are incredibly important demonstrations of physics in action. Essentially, a laser is simply a device that produces light. However, unlike an ordinary light bulb, which produces a wide range of different frequencies (which is why its light looks white to our eyes) and pushes light out in all directions (which is why we can light a whole room with one bulb), a laser is much more specific. Laser light is normally just a single frequency of light, and it is normally pushed out in one focused line. The clue to how a laser works is in its name: Light Amplification by Stimulated Emission of Radiation. It relies on the behaviour of atoms when stimulated.

Atoms are extremely tiny particles, and they make up all molecules. Proteins, as so commonly used in living organisms, are made from a super-complicated ball-of-string of atoms. Water is much simpler, being made from one hydrogen and two oxygen atoms stuck together. Substances known as 'elements' are made from a single type of atom, like hydrogen, oxygen or carbon. Each atom is made from a bunch of protons and neutrons with electrons whizzing around them like planets orbiting the sun. Different elements simply have different numbers of protons in the middle. Hydrogen has only one, lead has eighty-two. This is known as the atomic number of the element. All atoms of a certain element have the same number of protons, so carbon always has six. However, they may have different numbers of neutrons in the middle – these are known as 'isotopes' of the element.

When an atom is 'excited' it means that energy has been transferred to the electrons whizzing around those internal protons and neutrons. An electrical charge or light (electromagnetic radiation) is enough to kick those electrons and make them zip around with a bit more energy. If the electrons are kicked too hard, they'll simply fly away and join another atom, making the first atom more positively charged and the other atom more negatively charged. But kicked a little, the electron will be pulled away from its normal comfortable place around the atom. When it bounces back to its normal orbit again, it generates electromagnetic radiation, or light.

The laser exploits these subatomic behaviours in a very precise way. Atoms of a special substance (the lasing medium) are 'pumped' using flashes of bright light or electrical current. They then emit their own light at a frequency that depends on how excited they have become. This light is trapped between two little mirrors that bounce it back and forth, further triggering the atoms of the lasing medium to emit light at the same frequency and direction. The more radiation that is emitted in the right direction to bounce off the mirrors, the more the lasing medium produces more radiation in the right direction. Because one of the mirrors is only half-silvered, once enough light is bouncing back and forth, it is strong enough to escape through the half-silvered mirror as a straight beam of one frequency of light. Out shines the straight laser light.

Anyone who has seen a CD will know that the surface of these discs is a shiny silver colour. They need to be shiny because they are read by bouncing laser light from their surfaces. Information is stored on a compact disc in one very thin and surprisingly long spiral of bumps. If stretched out straight, the spiral on one little disc would be 5 kilometres (3½ miles) long. The tiny trail of bumps is much too small to see with the naked eye (although they do produce a nice rainbow effect on the silvered aluminium surface). Lasers are essential for CD players because they allow a tiny beam of light to be focused onto the microscopic silver bumps, so they can be read by a little sensor. If the light was not a focused spot it would hit a larger area of the disc and it would not be possible to detect if a bump was there or not, for light would reflect off many bumps at once. With a laser, and unbelievably precise tracking by a motor to push the laser into the right place, the CD player can shine a point of light at bump trails and see if individual bumps are there or not. When each bump is 0.0005 mm wide and the spirals are only 0.0016 mm apart, you can understand why precision is essential. Even the speed of the disc is changed, slowing down from about 500 to 350 rpm as the laser moves towards the edge to ensure that the same number of bumps pass under the laser each second at all times.

CDs store information in a similar way to vinyl records: by having a spiral of undulations on a disc, which is read and turned into audio. The difference is that vinyl records use a wiggling groove cut into their surfaces. As a needle scratches over the surface, the wiggles vibrate the needle, and the vibrations are turned into a tiny electrical signal, which is amplified into full-volume audio. So records store music very directly, as analogue wiggles in their spiral tracks.

CDs also store information as spirals of undulations in their surfaces, but the information is not analogue, it is digital. Instead of wiggles in the track corresponding to wiggles (compressions) in the air, the bumps and spaces on a CD spiral represent 1s and 0s in binary numbers. The audio on a CD is nothing more than millions of numbers all written in binary (for example, 4 is written 00100000 and 37 is written 10100100 in binary). The numbers describe the shape of the sound wave every 0.000023 seconds (that's 44,100 samples each second for left and right channels). Those numbers are just saying, 'up a bit, now down, now up a little more, now down a lot ...', which, when converted by a digital to analogue converter, produces a wobbly waveform. This is amplified and pushed to your speakers or headphones, which then vibrate the air exactly according to that waveform and produce sound in your ears.

Using numbers to define waveforms is not perfect; it will only ever be an approximation. If there are not enough numbers to define a tiny change in the waveform, or if the sampling rate is too slow (if the waveform changes significantly in less than 0.000023 seconds), or if the 'smoothing' process (to change the stepped wave defined by the numbers back into a smooth wave) introduces unwanted artefacts, the recorded sound will not be quite the same as the original. However, in order to tell the difference you'd need some exceedingly good speakers and some excellent ears to match.

The binary numbers on a CD don't only define numbers. Every number is stretched with extra binary 1s and 0s to ensure there are never long gaps with no bumps and help the computer to make sense of what it is seeing with its laser vision. The numbers are also interlaced out of order, so an entire revolution is read in order to figure out the next chunk of audio waveform. The interlacing makes sure that a scratch that is wide enough to distort the reading of many bumps in succession will not be disrupting several numbers in succession and causing an audible glitch. Instead, a series of numbers from completely different parts of the waveform will be disrupted, making the corruption inaudible to our ears. As if this wasn't enough, there are also error correction bits added to the numbers, which the computer uses to check that the numbers all make sense. One simple example of error correction would be to follow a number with a second number that says how many 1s there were supposed to be in the previous number. So 10100100 (37) would be followed by 110 (3). The error correction is sufficiently clever that the computer can figure out simple mistakes in reading and correct the numbers on the fly.

The result of the extraordinary precision of laser reading and error-correcting digital to analogue converters is pure crystal-clear sound at all frequencies audible to the human ear. But good as the technology is, it can only cope with CDs that are looked after reasonably well. Those little bumps are read by bouncing light from them. Although the aluminium surface is protected by a tough layer of clear plastic, its optical characteristics will be affected by dirt, oil, scratches or even dust. However, what most people don't realise is that the more delicate side of the CD is the side with the label. CDs are created from the back – the layer of bumpy aluminium is pressed onto the clear plastic, then a thin layer of acrylic is sprayed on, then the label is printed. While scratches on the clear plastic side may distort the light from the laser, scratches on the label side can go through the layer of acrylic and actually damage the aluminium layer, destroying the little bumps that define those essential binary numbers.

If your CD is not playing correctly it means that the laser vision of the reading computer can no longer make sense of what it sees. It may interpret some of the lumps and bumps of scratches as numbers and try to play them, resulting in nasty hissing or crackling noises. If it becomes sufficiently confused it may even be fooled into reading the same circle of data over and over again instead of following the outward spiral, causing that machine-gun-fire sound.

Scratches may be caused by not keeping the discs in their protective cases, handling them without enough care or even by the CD players of cars as the CDs rattle about in the mechanism. If minor scratches are visible on the clear plastic side, it is possible to polish them out using metal polish (always polish at right angles to the spiral, from the middle to the edge, to avoid creating your own confusing spiral pattern of polish). But if the scratch is on the label side, the CD is irretrievably ruined. You cannot put back the little bumps of aluminium once they've been scratched off.

Scratches can and do mess up CDs. Look at a CD 'jewel' case and you'll see how it carefully holds the surfaces of the CD in the air and away from anything that might scratch them. You should try to do the same. Always hold a CD by its edges and always keep it safe in its case. It will live as long as you, if you look after it.

Chewing it Over

At times like this, there's only one solution. You return to the kitchen and find a rich chocolate gateau. You cut a generous slice of the rich, gooey cake. It smells divine. So that you don't make a mess with the creamy, runny chocolate you find a fork to eat it with – no more spills today. You start eating it, letting the chocolate melt in your mouth. It's delicious. Each forkful is a delight. Before you know it, you're putting the last little piece in your mouth. Perhaps another slice ... But somehow you accidentally bite down on the fork. There's a horrible jarring feeling, a strange throbbing in your front tooth, and then your tongue feels something hard and sharp in your mouth. You run over and take a look in the mirror. A piece of your front tooth has just broken off.

Humans are designed to be omnivores. Our digestive systems are good at coping with plant material and meat. It's one reason why we are so successful and have spread across the face of the planet. We can eat a lot of the things that live around us. One important reason why we can eat and digest such a variety of foods is the range of teeth we have.

At the very front of our mouths we have flat cutting teeth called incisors, which move together a little like the flat blades of scissors to cut through larger foods and separate a bite-sized chunk. We can also use these teeth a little like rodents and gnaw through tougher foods. Perhaps the most extreme adaptation of incisors is found in elephants, whose tusks are hugely overgrown and pointy incisors; also in narwhals, which have a single incisor adapted into a unicorn-like horn.

On either side of our incisors we have canine teeth, named after dogs and their particularly good, long, pointy examples. In humans, these teeth have longer roots than the incisors, making them stronger, and they usually protrude slightly beyond the incisors. Canine teeth (also sometimes known as eye teeth and stomach teeth) are not for cutting; they are for tearing the flesh of animals. Carnivores, which eat nothing except meat, normally have much more impressive canine teeth (or fangs) compared to their other teeth. One of the best examples was the now-extinct sabre-tooth cat *Smilodon fatalis*, which had fangs the size of large kitchen knives. Research has shown that the cat probably killed its large prey with a quick tearing bite to the throat; surprisingly, its bite was much less powerful than that of the modern-day lion, which kills by grabbing the throat of its prey and holding on despite the struggling.

The next teeth along in our mouths are the premolars, followed by several sets of molars. These teeth are lumpy grinding teeth, the premolars resembling the canines a little more and so able to help with some tearing if necessary. The molars are designed to lock together with only small gaps between them when our jaws are closed. Their lumpy and sharp surfaces mash up all foods pushed between them by our tongues. (The English word molar derives from the Latin *mola* meaning 'millstone'.) The chewing action is assisted by our jaws making slight circular motions instead of simply moving up and down, resulting in the food being ground down into tiny pieces that are then mushed together by our saliva ready for swallowing. These teeth have to be firmly anchored into our jaws, for they must withstand the same kinds of forces that the jaws of pliers endure. To help them stay in place they have not one, but two or three long roots. (The roots of all teeth are long, typically twice as long as the length of the tooth visible in your mouth, but they are conical in shape, nothing like tree roots.) Molars are very common in animals that eat plant material, such as cows or horses. Elephants have extraordinary molars, many bigger than your fist, which give them the ability to chew up bark or wood.

When they are biting, tearing and chewing food, teeth must withstand tremendous pressures and must not be worn down from chewing tough plant or bony materials. As our species evolved, somehow we needed these amazingly well-shaped structures to be as hard as stone and yet to be able to act like living structures. We needed them to grow from nothing, to embed themselves securely in the bone of our jaws. We needed nerves within them so that we had some feeling of what we were chewing. Ideally, we would like them to repair themselves if damaged or even replace themselves. How could organisms create living stone inside themselves?

Astonishingly, evolution managed to work it all out. Our teeth are indeed as hard as (some kinds of) stone. To be more precise, they're much harder than gold, silver or copper, harder than most types of iron, and very nearly as hard as window glass or steel. Stones vary in hardness, depending on the minerals that they are composed of. Hydroxylapatite (made from calcium and a few other elements) is one such mineral, naturally occurring as partially translucent crystals in rock. Hydroxylapatite is also the main component of tooth enamel, giving our teeth their hardness and brittleness. You really do have stones in your mouth.

But teeth are much more than solid lumps of rock. If they were, they would be so brittle that they would crack into pieces every time we bit down on something hard. So each tooth has only a couple of millimetres of enamel to provide the outer coating on the surface above the gum. Underneath is a softer layer called dentine, which provides a more resilient and shock-absorbing substance for the tooth. Unlike the super-hard enamel, only 70 per cent of dentine is hydroxylapatite; the rest is water and proteins (mostly collagen). Dentine has an amazingly complex structure, with trillions of tiny tubes radiating from the inner core out to reach the enamel. These help to provide strength and conduct sensations inwards towards the nerve. Within the gum, surrounding the dentine surface of the root is a similar mixture known as cementum, which is a little higher in water and collagen. It provides an excellent surface from which collagen fibres tie the root of the tooth onto the nearby bone of the jaw. Although the fibres are very short, their natural elasticity provides a slight cushioning effect, allowing teeth to move slightly rather than break themselves or the jaw bone.

Within the core of the tooth is the pulp. It may just sound like a mess, but the tooth pulp is a complex organ in its own right, supplied by blood from a hole at the bottom of the root and also filled with nerves and specialist cells for producing dentine. There are also immune cells lying in wait, just in case the enamel and dentine above should fail and expose the pulp to bacterial infection.

Twenty of these amazing structures grow in our jaws, and then after a few years they are reabsorbed, discarding the outer enamel shells to leave room for up to thirty-two more to replace them. It's a sensible strategy from an evolutionary perspective. We spent most of our history without toothpaste, so it's a good idea to replace teeth after a while. But the second set of teeth only needed to last until we reached our thirties; life expectancy was less than forty years for most of us, a few thousand years ago. One or two rotten teeth falling out didn't matter so much, and our diets contained few sugar-rich foods (unlike today), so our teeth lasted as long as we needed them to. There's no particular reason why we couldn't have more sets of teeth in our lives – other animals do. The incisors of rodents never stop growing, to compensate for the huge amount of wear caused by their constant gnawing. Sharks just keep growing row after row of new jagged teeth because their violent feeding often results in teeth being lost. Humans grow only two sets because that's all we ever used to need.

The ability to grow stone in our mouths is a remarkable feat, when you think about it. Cells in our jaws form tiny buds, which slowly grow bigger, building the different layers of the tooth and extruding the calcium-based minerals in exactly the right places. As they form, bone in the jaw forms around them and cartilage 'ropes' linking bone to root slowly push the tooth upwards. Even once a tooth is fully developed and surrounded by bone, it continues to develop and adjust itself. Place constant pressure on the tooth and the bone socket reshapes itself, absorbing anything in the way and developing new bone to fill any gaps. When braces are placed around teeth, this is exactly what happens. Your teeth are pushed into a different alignment and your jaw rebuilds the bone around them to lock them into place.

Even the stone-like substance of our teeth is under constant repair. New dentine is constantly produced from within, but even that outer super-hard enamel layer is replaced. Within your saliva is exactly the right mix of calcium compounds to enable remineralisation. So while acids may soften or even erode away the enamel, your saliva helps to harden the surface and make new deposits. Your teeth can repair themselves!

This is just as well, because in modern times our diets have become enormously high in sugars. There are always plenty of bacteria in our

Chewing it Over

mouths ready to feast on the sugary residues left behind in the crevices of teeth and gums. Unfortunately, these bacteria (which form that white gooey coating that we call plaque) produce acidic waste products that eat away our precious enamel, and, indeed, the dentine underneath. This can be a real problem, for once a cavity has formed in a tooth, it can become a lovely comfortable hole in which the bacteria can live. The longer they live there, the more their acid may tunnel deeper into the tooth, causing more and more damage. Once a patch of enamel is removed to expose the dentine, we have 'sensitive teeth'. Those little tubes within the dentine are now exposed to the inside of your mouth, and they conduct temperature rather too efficiently into the nerves within the pulp. If too much dentine is eaten away, the nerves begin to feel pain. In the worst case, even the pulp may become infected and the entire tooth may need to be removed before it simply dies and disintegrates. It's not a pleasant feeling to have infected teeth. If you've ever had toothache you'll know exactly what it feels like when the nerves of a tooth become agitated.

Luckily, we have toothpastes to redress the balance. These pastes are composed of several useful ingredients: an abrasive powder to help scour away the bacteria, sometimes an antibacterial agent to kill some of the bacteria, perhaps a whitening agent to make the teeth appear whiter, and even some compounds designed to fill the little tubes in exposed dentine and prevent the conduction of hot and cold to the nerves from being so intense. But the most important ingredient is fluoride, a compound that reacts with the calcium in your saliva and helps remineralisation of enamel. It forms a slightly different compound called fluorapatite, instead of the natural hydroxylapatite, but this is a good thing. New enamel made from fluorapatite is just as tough, but it is slightly more resistant to erosion from acids. This is why all good toothpastes should contain fluoride – they are helping your teeth to rebuild themselves and make them harder again.

Because teeth are good at keeping themselves healthy, often the best thing to do is to keep them clean, give them a regular dose of fluoride and let them get on with it. Dentistry work is often damaging to teeth, involving significant drilling and loss of enamel and dentine. Researchers recommend that restorative work (fillings) should be performed only on larger cavities. You may not always see the effects of remineralisation on the surface of your teeth, for it is slow and subtle, but if you have tartar or calculus deposits on your teeth you are seeing one side effect of the process. Tartar is mineralised plaque. Fossilised bacteria, if you like.

Our teeth become softer after eating sugary food or drinking acidic juices. It is at these times that cleaning using an abrasive toothpaste may actually scrub away enamel rather than help rebuild it. Research has shown that after exposure to very acidic conditions it takes at least an hour for your saliva to partially harden the surface again and six hours for it to be back to full strength. But even when at maximum hardness, enamel is a naturally brittle substance, so it is possible to chip off a piece or even break a tooth in half if you are careless and bite too hard on something tougher than your tooth. A minor chip in the enamel will probably not hurt beyond a feeling of sensitivity as the dentine is exposed. It's not serious and a new layer of enamel will be deposited as long as you keep it clean. A more serious crack or split will need a trip to the dentist and may well result in the whole tooth needing to be capped or extracted. Dentistry is very advanced these days, and even a chip can be covered with special veneers to make it look perfect again. But rather than having to rely on artificial fillings or substances glued onto your teeth, the best solution is to help them look after themselves. Flossing removes the bacteria between the teeth. Toothpaste with fluoride will keep them clean and allow them to remineralise. And watch what you bite!

Patience and Pain

It's been a long day and you still feel on edge. Perhaps a relaxing hot bath will help prepare you for sleep. You go to the bathroom, turn on the water and leave it to fill the bath while you put your clothes in the laundry pile for washing. After the day's events they're all in need of cleaning, as are you. You sit on your bed for a few moments, recalling the litany of today's mishaps. The sound of splashing snaps you out of your reverie – the water must have filled the bath by now. You make a quick dash to the bathroom. But in your haste you don't watch where your feet are. Your toe thuds against the side of the bath. For a split-second you think it's fine, but then a sharp pain shoots up your leg. The sharp pain quickly fades, to be replaced by a throbbing ache, which slowly increases as though its volume is being turned up. It hurts enough to make you sit down. You're sure it's not broken, but why does it have to hurt like this?

It's hard not to grow up without accidentally hitting an elbow, head or toe against something now and again. The painful result is a reminder that we need to take more care to avoid damaging our bodies. Interestingly, there are some people who are born with a malfunction in a critical gene that prevents pain signals from ever reaching their brains. They grow up without any idea of what pain is, often resulting in them causing serious harm to themselves or even killing themselves accidentally.

The perception of pain is so fundamental to our survival that it affects our brains in profound ways. There is not one single pain centre; instead, the whole brain lights up like a Christmas tree when pain is perceived. In the short term we are immediately prompted to protect the painful area, to remove it from the source of the pain and often to cease all use of the affected area while we examine it. In the longer term, our subconscious behaviour is altered. If we hit our head on a specific low beam or handle, next time we'll duck. An experience of pain that lasts for long, continuous periods may affect our emotions and attitudes. We may develop depression and become less active. Alternatively, a severe experience of pain and a conscious awareness of exactly what led to that pain may result in the development of an aversion to anything resembling the cause. We call that aversion fear. It may become a long-term sub-conscious memory that lasts far longer than your memory of the event that caused the aversion. You may no longer remember the time you fell off the high wall and painfully twisted your ankle as a child, but your fear of heights may still be with you.

We don't always perceive pain. Even when the nerve cells are sending us pain signals, there are times when it is more important for us simply to run away, rather than roll about on the ground in agony. So there are regions of the brain that actively inhibit our perception of pain, sometimes for just a few minutes, sometimes for several days. But there are also areas of the brain that do the reverse, and make us hypersensitive to pain. When we're safe and recovering, such heightened sensations might, for example, encourage us to avoid using the painful part while it heals.

Astonishingly, there used to be considerable confusion about when we first start experiencing pain. A hundred years ago it was widely accepted that newborn babies simply did not perceive pain at all, because their brains had not developed sufficiently. Perhaps rather cruelly by today's standards, for decades many 'pin-prick' experiments were conducted on sleeping infants in attempts to understand the onset of pain perception. Much confusion was caused in those early experiments by the seeming lack of sensitivity of babies straight after birth, which turned out to be because the mothers had received anaesthetics while giving birth, and the babies received a small dose via their umbilical cords. Today (as anyone with children can affirm), it is well understood that a baby in pain will show clear discomfort. Crying, wriggling, fisting, large muscle movements, accompanied by clear respiratory and hormonal changes and erratic sleep, are all clear signs of pain. But those early scientifically flawed experiments sadly resulted in a culture that disregarded the pain of babies for much too long, despite the true scientific findings. Until recently even major operations on premature babies were performed without any anaesthetic at all. In 1985 a mother made the headlines by explaining the routine operation that was performed on her premature baby. He had holes cut in both sides of his neck, another in his right chest, an incision from his breastbone around to his backbone, his ribs prised apart, and an extra artery near his heart tied off. Another hole was cut in his left side for a chest tube. The baby was awake and conscious; the only drugs provided were to paralyse him. While the little boy may not remember such experiences, what kinds of emotional traumas induced in his young brain were simply unknown. Thankfully, most modern medicine does now consider the perception of pain by babies, and this kind of treatment is a lesson from the history books.

Our brains experience pain throughout our lives, but despite its huge significance to us, its source is simply a few little signals from some tiny nerve cells. These cells are no more special than those that signal temperature or touch, but our brains are designed to treat them differently. Pain receptors, or nociceptors, may use fairly ordinary sensors, but they're wired up to the alarm bells in our heads.

The 'wiring' in the human body is called the nervous system. Your brain and spinal column are known as the central nervous system. All the other nerves are known collectively as the peripheral nervous system. Like all cells, nerve cells (whether the neurons in your brain or sensory nerves in your skin) are little living chemical factories that are provided with energy by the blood supply and perform their specific jobs by producing the right kinds of proteins at the right times. Nerve cells happen to have the trick of using some clever chemistry to alter the electrostatic charge within them enough to produce little pulses of electricity. They have sometimes enormously long 'wires' connected into them like the roots of a tree (dendrites) and a wire leading out (the axon). In the brain a mixture of chemical and electrical signals produces all the thoughts and memories you will ever have. The output of little electrical pulses, through the spinal column and into your muscles, enables you to move. The input of little electrical pulses from the sensory nerves, through the spinal column and into your brain, enables you to sense everything.

To sense pain we have nociceptors throughout our skin and on the surfaces of ligaments, tendons, bones, blood vessels and even other nerves. We also have some (but far fewer) pain receptors within the body cavities and internal organs. The different numbers and locations of the receptors produce different feelings of pain. In the skin, where we have the highest density, we feel cutaneous pain – a sharp, immediate and easy-to-locate sensation. In areas such as the blood vessels, tendons and bones we feel somatic pain – a longer lasting, dull pain that does not have such an obvious location. In the internal organs we feel a visceral pain – an ache that is extremely hard to locate and sometimes seems to come from a completely different area.

There are no nociceptors at all in the brain, despite it being full of neurons. When you feel a headache, you're actually feeling the nociceptors in the membrane and blood vessels surrounding the brain, not within it. There is perhaps little reason to have pain receptors inside the brain – it's not something you can rest by using less, it doesn't really repair itself very well if damaged (in fact you'll probably die without medical attention), and the chances are that if your skull has been damaged enough to damage your brain, you're going to feel more than enough pain already.

The nerve cells that respond to pain do not send signals if they are damaged themselves. They can't – they've been damaged. Instead, they have little sensors that respond to chemical signals produced by damaged tissue nearby. When other cells die unnaturally, they emit protein signals such as histamines and bradykini, which trigger a chemical change in the pain receptor cells. Additionally, extreme temperatures or excessive forces (caused perhaps by tearing) trigger the cells. Like the neurons in your brain, the nerve cells then send a little electric signal up their long 'wires'.

Just like the wires in your home, the wiring of nerves is made from bundles of cables (axons) surrounded by a sleeve or sheath to insulate them. In your body that sheath is made from different substances depending on the nerves. The very fastest nerves are quick because they have a sheath made from myelin, which helps the little electrical pulse to be conducted along at a much faster rate. Our best nerves can move the signal at 120 metres (394 feet) a second, so your brain receives the first signal from a stubbed toe just over one-hundredth of a second after the event. But some nerves are much slower for they do not have the special myelin sheath. Called C-fibres, these may propagate the signal at only 50 cm (25 inches) a second (the electrical charge is moving because of the movement of ions and not electrons). So a signal from your toe might take over a second and a half to reach your brain from these nerves!

This is the reason why stubbing your toe causes such a strange and noticeable delay between the damage and the sensations. In just over one-hundredth of a second you will feel the pressure of the impact and perhaps an initial sharp pain if you managed to damage the skin (perhaps by hitting the toenail). But then you may have a second and a half to wait before the aching pain from the internal blood vessels and bone reaches your brain. The damage was all done at the same time, it just takes different times for the different nerves to tell your brain about it.

It all makes sense when you understand how you are wired up inside. Many of the fastest nerves are on the skin, to enable you to react very quickly before serious damage is done. Some are even wired via your spinal column direct to certain muscles, bypassing your brain altogether. These give you super-fast reflexes, making you snatch your hand away from fire before your brain realises what's going on. The slower, unmyelinated nerves are mostly reserved for those long-lasting, dull, aching pains. These don't need to be fast, for the damage is clearly already done if you've hurt something inside yourself. They provide a long reminder that you're damaged, telling you to take it easy while your body repairs the mess.

It's not much comfort if you are suffering, but pain caused by tissue damage is there for a reason. Pain is a perception that is designed to be unpleasant. Without pain we'd never learn how to look after ourselves properly and would damage or kill ourselves far too easily. So we suffer now and again and, hopefully, learn because of it.

Eureka!

Still sitting on the edge of the bath, you realise the water level is now very high. You reach over and turn the taps off. It's a tricky procedure with a broken finger, a sore toe and a pulled muscle in your arm. You feel as if you've fallen down the stairs. As you lean over you remember slipping on the tiled floor this morning. Perhaps it's precognition, for at that moment your hand slips and you fall back into the full bath. It's actually a nice feeling of warmth. You're floating in the deep water, feeling light and relaxed, a pleasant ending to an exhausting day. But when you look around, you see that water has overflowed all over the bathroom floor. Surely if you're floating, the level of the water in the bath shouldn't rise that dramatically – should it?

That famous moment, about 2,250 years ago, when Archimedes was taking a bath (and no doubt being anointed with oils by his servants) has become a legend. This eminent mathematician had been asked by Hiero II, the king of Syracuse, to figure out a way of telling if a gold crown was pure or not. Archimedes realised while he was in the bath that his body was displacing an amount of water that corresponded to his volume. The larger the object immersed in the bath, the more the water level rose. Since the impure metal of the dodgy crown probably weighed less than a crown of solid gold, he now had a way of working out the density of the metals. All he had to do was measure exactly how much water was displaced by the crown and how heavy the crown was, and divide weight by volume to discover how dense the metal was (how much mass per unit volume). Then he could do the same with a lump of gold, dividing its weight by its volume to discover the density of the valuable metal. If the density of the crown differed from the density of the pure gold, the crown could not be made from pure gold.

Archimedes was so excited by this revelation that he jumped from his bath and ran down the streets of Syracuse, shouting, 'I've found it! I've found it!' which in Ancient Greek sounded like, 'Eureka! Eureka!'

It's a good story, but it's highly unlikely to be true. Archimedes was an accomplished mathematician and inventor, who wrote many books (or parchments as they were in those days) detailing his discoveries. He never wrote about this incident, nor did any other Roman writers who lived at the time. Instead, the story was first written 200 years after the death of Archimedes by a Roman architect called Vitruvius. Perhaps Vitruvius read the accounts of another Roman writer called Plutarch (who was contemporary with Archimedes) about bathing:

> Oftimes Archimedes' servants got him against his will to the baths, to wash and anoint him, and yet being there, he would ever be drawing out of the geometrical figures, even in the very embers of the chimney. And while they were anointing of him with oils and sweet savours, with his fingers he drew lines upon his naked body, so far was he taken from himself, and brought into ecstasy or trance, with the delight he had in the study of geometry.

So it is clear that while Archimedes was a famous mathematician, he didn't actually like taking a bath very often and probably never jumped out and ran around the streets of his home, shouting. Vitruvius almost certainly made the whole thing up.

Archimedes was unlikely to be so pleased with the idea of water displacement and density, for he was a very practical early scientist. He probably knew that the displacement of water would indeed be the same volume as an object placed into the water, but if you tried to measure the displacement with enough precision to distinguish the densities of metals, the distortions caused by surface tension of water would make life very difficult. Light objects are partially supported by the surface tension, and with heavy objects the way the water sticks to the side of glass containers makes it hard to measure the tiny, tiny differences you'd need to find. Even measuring weights accurately enough would have been exceedingly difficult.

Archimedes probably knew these things because he'd written a two-volume book on buoyancy and was the first person ever to do so. Today Archimedes' Principle is named after him because of his important ancient work. Think of it like a law of nature that says: 'When a solid body is partially or completely immersed in water, the apparent loss in weight will be equal to the weight of the displaced liquid.' It's a hugely important principle, because it explains why things float (or sink) in liquids.

We know intuitively that some things like to float and others don't – push a light piece of polystyrene foam under water and you can feel the force it exerts on your hands as it tries to rise back up to the surface. Hold a brick under water and you will feel that it wants to sink. Its weight exerts a force downwards on your hands. But compare the weight of that brick when you are holding it in the air with its weight when you are holding it under water, and you will notice Archimedes' Principle: it does not feel quite so heavy when it's under water. Even though both the piece of foam and the brick are being pulled downwards by the same gravitational force of the Earth, somehow their interaction with the water makes the foam rise in the opposite direction to gravity and the brick to have less force pulling it downwards.

It all makes sense when you think about all the tiny atoms. For its size, foam has not got many atoms. Most of it is simply air trapped in bubbles. So foam is a little more dense than air, but much less dense than water. There are far more atoms in the same volume of water, compared to the foam. When you push a piece of foam under water, all the atoms of the water are still being pulled downwards by Earth's gravity, but there are more atoms in the water than there are in the foam, so the water experiences a stronger pull (it's heavier). As all those atoms are being pulled downwards, and the foam experiences less of a pull (it's lighter), there is only one direction it can go: in the opposite direction to the water. You'd see the same thing if you filled a cup with little poly-styrene pieces and glass marbles, then shook it. All the marbles sink to the bottom and the polystyrene pieces are pushed to the top. The force exerted by the heavier liquid on those lighter objects when submerged in that liquid is known as buoyancy.

Place a heavier object, like a brick, in water and the reverse happens. Now there are more atoms in the same space compared to water, so the brick experiences more downwards force than the water (it's heavier). As it sinks, the water is forced out of the way and has to go upwards. But forcing water upwards takes some effort, for the water has a significant weight itself. So the water atoms resist being pushed out of the way, in proportion to how many are being pushed. As they resist, they push in the opposite direction to the falling motion of the brick, so they make the brick fall more slowly. In effect, the weight of the brick is reduced in proportion to the number of water atoms being displaced.

The same effect occurs in air as well, but air happens to be much less dense than water. That's why water finds it hard to float about in the air, and can only manage it for short amounts of time as tiny droplets in clouds before turning into rain and sinking down below the air. It's also why the piece of foam may float to the surface of the water, but will not float beyond the water and up into the air – it's lighter than water but heavier than air.

We exploit buoyancy in every boat and ship ever made. Sometimes we use buoyancy to achieve the seemingly impossible. For example, some giant cruise ships in use today weigh over 50,000 tons, but that's nothing compared to the massive oil tankers that cross our seas every day. The largest of these was a terrifying 650,000 tons in weight when full of oil. Clearly, this much weight would sink like a stone if the density of the vessel was the same as a stone. So the trick is to make these ships *big*. The heaviest ship was also the largest ship, at 458 metres (1,504 feet) in length and 69 metres (226 feet) wide. Even though her hull was made of many layers of thick steel, the huge size meant that the average density was less than that of the seawater outside. That's all you need in order to create enough buoyancy to float, and so even these monsters of the oceans float just as happily as a toy boat in your bath.

Buoyancy relies on enough volume to ensure that the average density is less than water. But problems arise if that volume changes. For example, if the pressure exerted on a submerged object is enough to crush the object and reduce its volume, suddenly its average density increases, and its buoyancy is reduced. It's extremely important for submarines to minimise this kind of compression of their hulls, so their metal shapes are made circular in cross-section to allow them to shrink a little but not to bend and then suddenly crush inwards like a tin can. A submarine is perhaps the only form of boat that has complete control of its own buoyancy. Since they can't adjust their volumes, instead they adjust their average densities by storing compressed air. When they want more buoyancy, they release the pressurised air into special ballast tanks, forcing out the water in them. With more air in the same volume, the average density of the vessel is reduced, so the seawater pushes the submarine upwards.

When the force of gravity is exactly balanced by the buoyancy of a submerged object, the object is neutrally buoyant and floats exactly as if it is experiencing zero gravity. For this reason, special 'neutral buoyancy facilities' are used to train astronauts before they go into space. Identical-looking and -behaving versions of their spacesuits and all equipment are constructed and carefully made neutrally buoyant. The astronauts then spend many hours submerged in the giant pools, learning how to operate the equipment and complete their missions.

We all tend to be naturally quite buoyant, for the density of oils and fats is lower than water, and we all have fatty deposits under our skins. Those of us who are a little more cuddly will float better for this reason. Water with more salt in it has a greater density, so we all float better in salty seas. We can also adjust our buoyancy by holding more or less air in our lungs, just like a submarine. When we swim, proper breathing helps power our movements but also helps keep us buoyant. The whole idea of buoyancy and floating is so important that it's perhaps a little sad that Archimedes may be remembered more for something that never happened than for Archimedes' Principle, which is as fundamental to science and technology today as it was over 2,000 years ago when he discovered it. The next time you float in a bath after a long and tiring day, spare this ancient scientist a thought.

Bibliography

7.00 Oblivious Beginnings (sleeping through alarm)

Susan Blackmore, 'Lucid Dreaming: Awake in Your Sleep?', *Skeptical Inquirer* 15, 1991, pp. 362–70.

F. Crick and G. Mitchinson, 'The function of dream sleep', *Nature* 304, 1983, pp. 111–14.

W.C. Dement, *Some Must Watch While Some Must Sleep*, New York: W.W. Norton, 1978.

I. Feinberg, 'Changes in Sleep Cycle Patterns with Age', *J. Psychiatr. Res.*, 1974, 10:283–306.

MayoClinic, *Fatigue: When to Rest, When to Worry*, Mayo Foundation for Medical Education and Research (MFMER), 2007.

PhysOrg.com, 'Clever "Clocky" Combats Oversleeping', PhysOrg.com, 6 April 2005.

J.P.J. Pinel, *Biopsychology*, Needham Heights, MA: Allyn & Bacon, 1992.

Andrea Rock, *The Mind at Night: The New Science of How and Why We Dream*, Basic Books, 2004.

Robert L. Van de Castle, *Our Dreaming Mind*, New York: Ballantine Books, 1994.

Tsuneo Watanabe, 'Lucid Dreaming: Its Experimental Proof and Psychological Conditions', *Journal of International Society of Life Information Science*, 2003, 21(1): 159–62.

7.10 Bathroom Skating (slipping on soap)

Katrin Boschkova, *Adsorption and Frictional Properties of Surfactant Assemblies at Solid Surfaces*, YKI Institute for Surface Chemistry, 2002.

Hans-Jürgen Butt, Karlheinz Graf and Michael Kappl, *Physics and Chemistry of Interfaces*, Wiley Publishers, 2006.

John S. Evans, 'How Does Oil Work?', Technical Bulletin Issue 23, Wearcheck Division of Set Point Technology, 2002.

Patrizia Garzena and Marina Tadiello, *Soap Naturally – Ingredients, Methods and Recipes for Natural Handmade Soap*, Programmer Publishing, 2004.

Edwin Roy Hinden, Water-wet Bar Soap Preserver, United States Patent 20060266907, 2006.

Harold Hopkins, 'All that Lathers is not Soap', *FDA Consumer*, US Food and Drug Administration, 1979.

Journal of Synthetic Lubrication, John Wiley & Sons, Ltd.

NIIR Board, *Modern Technology of Cosmetics*, Asia Pacific Business Press Inc., 2004.

C.A. Patrides (ed.), *Sir Thomas Browne; The Major Works*, London: Penguin Books, 1977 edn.

Derrick Pounder, 'Postmortem Changes and Time of Death', *Forensic Medicine Course Lecture Notes*, Department of Forensic Medicine, University of Dundee, 2006.

Taylor and Francis, 'Tribology Transactions', *Journal for the Society of Tribologists and Lubrication Engineers*.

7.20 Sword Fighting (cutting yourself shaving)

Bruce Alberts (ed.), *Molecular Biology of the Cell*, Garland Publishing Inc., 2005.

Tim Dowling, *Inventor of the Disposable Culture King Camp Gillette 1855–1932*, Short Books, 2001.

R.K. Freinkel (auth. and ed.) and D.T. Woodley (ed.), *The Biology of the Skin*, Taylor & Francis Ltd, 2000.

P.L. Giangrande, 'Six Characters in Search of an Author: The History of the Nomenclature of Coagulation Factors', *British Journal of Haematology*, 2003, vol. 121: 703–12.

Philip L. Krumholz, *A History of Shaving and Razors*, Adlibs Pub. Co., 1987.

H. Peter Lorenz and Michael T. Longaker, *Wounds: Biology, Pathology, and Management*, Stanford University Medical Center, 2003.

T. Romo and L.A. McLaughlin, 'Wound Healing, Skin', Emedicine.com, 2003.

L. Rosenberg and J. de la Torre, 'Wound Healing, Growth Factors', Emedicine.com, 2003.

7.45 Dark Clouds (toast on fire)

William J. Beaty, articles about electricity, *Science Hobbyist*, amasci.com, 1995–2000.

I. Berman-Levine, 'Burnt Toast – Is it Dangerous?', Dr Irene's Nutrition Tidbits, newsletter published by HealthandAge.com, vol. V, issue no. 20, 2004.

William D. Callister, *Materials Science and Engineering*, Wiley Publishing, 1997 (4th edn.).

Dougal Drysdale, *An Introduction to Fire Dynamics*, John Wiley and Sons Ltd, 1998 (2nd revised edn.).

Alok Jha, 'Close Encounters', special report: Chemical World, *Guardian Unlimited*, 22 May 2004.

Steuart Kellington, *Reading about Science: Heat, Electricity and Electromagnetism*, London: Heinemann Educational Publishers, 1982.

US Department of Health and Human Services, Public Health Service, 11th Report on Carcinogens, National Toxicology Program, 2005.

D.E. Volk, V. Thiviyanathan, J.S. Rice, B.A. Luxon, J.H. Shah, H. Yagi, J.M. Sayer, J.H. Yeh, D.M. Jerina and D.G. Gorenstein, 'Solution Structure of a Cis-opened (10R)-N6-deoxyadenosine Adduct of (9S,10R)-9,10-epoxy-7,8,9,10-tetrahydro-benzo [a]pyrene in a DNA Duplex', *Biochemistry*, February 2003, 18;42(6): 1410–20.

8.00 Flash in the Pan (exploding pan of liquid)

Barron, James, 'Steam Blast Jolts Midtown, Killing One', *New York Times*, 19 July 2007.

D.A. Crowl and J.F. Louvar, *Chemical Process Safety. Fundamentals with Applications*, Englewood Cliffs: Prentice, 1990.

T.J.R. Francis and D.F. Gorman, 'Pathogenesis of the Decompression Disorders' in P.B. Bennett and D.H. Elliott (eds.), *The Physiology and Medicine of Diving*, London: W.B. Saunders, 1993 (4th edn.), pp. 454–80.

Nigel Hawkes *et al.*, *The Worst Accident in the World: Chernobyl: The End of the Nuclear Dream*, London: Macmillan, 1986.

Lou Ann Jopp, 'Superheated Water', University of Minnesota Regional Extension Educator, Food Science, Extension Regional Center, St Cloud, 2004.

John Knox, 'The Physics of Pressure Cookers', Physics 100, Physics Department, Idaho State University, 2003.

Ira N. Levine, *Physical Chemistry*, University of Brooklyn: McGraw-Hill Publishing, 1978.

Mark Peplow, 'Special Report: Counting the Dead', *Nature* 440, 2006, pp. 982–3.

Mark J. Uline and David S. Corti, 'Activated Instability of Homogeneous Bubble Nucleation and Growth', *Phys. Rev. Lett.*, 99, 2007, 76102–76400.

US Food and Drug Administration, *Microwave Oven Radiation*, Center for Devices and Radiological Health, Consumer Information, 2007.

8.10 Cheesy Grimace (milk gone bad)

O. Adolfsson *et al.*, 'Yogurt and Gut Function', *American Journal of Clinical Nutrition*, 2004, 80: 2: 245–56.

Ricki Carroll, *Making Cheese, Butter, and Yogurt*, Storey Publishing, 2003.

U. Desselberger and J. Gray (eds.), *Viral Gastroenteritis*, Perspectives in Medical Virology, Elsevier Science, 2003.

T.L. Dormandy, 'Biological Rancidification', *Lancet*, 27 September 1969, 2(7622): 684–8.

Marina Elli, Maria Luisa Callegari, Susanna Ferrari, Elena Bessi, Daniela Cattivelli, Sara Soldi, Lorenzo Morelli, Nathalie Goupil Feuillerat and Jean-Michel Antoine, 'Survival of Yogurt Bacteria in the Human Gut', *Appl. Environ. Microbiol.*, July 2006, 72(7): 5113–17.

Sven-Olof Enfors, *The Food Microbiology Compendium*, Industrial and Environmental Microbiology 3A1315, KTH–Biotechnology, Stockholm, 2007.

Janet Fletcher, 'The Myths about Raw-milk Cheese', *Speciality Food* magazine, 2005.

Donald B. Katz, Miguel A.L. Nicolelis and S.A. Simon, 'Nutrient Tasting and Signaling Mechanisms in the Gut IV. There is More to Taste than Meets the Tongue', *Am. J. Physiol. Gastrointest. Liver Physiol.*, 2000, 278: G6–G9.

Lucius L. Van Slyke, *The Science and Practice of Cheese-making*, Cornell University Library, 1909.

8.20 Drowning Out Noise (wet MP3 player)

Charles K. Adams, *Nature's Electricity*, Pennsylvania: Tab Books, 1987.

David Linden, *Handbook of Batteries and Fuel Cells*, McGraw Hill Higher Education, 1984 (2nd edn.).

Kazunori Ozawa, *Lithium Ion Rechargable Batteries: Materials, Technology, and Applications*, Wiley VCH, 2008.

RAE Systems Inc., 'Lithium-Ion Batteries', Technical Note TN-166, rev. 1 cw.01–02, 2005.

Wayne M. Saslow, *Electricity, Magnetism, and Light*, Toronto: Thomson Learning, 2002.

Jim Stingl, 'iPod vs. Water: All May not be Lost', *Milwaukee Journal Sentinel*, 29 August 2007.

Clive D.S. Tuck, 'Modern Battery Technology', Ellis Horwood Series in Applied Science and Industrial Technology, New York and London: Ellis Horwood, 1991.

8.30 Warm Snow (bird droppings)

Jules M. Blais, Lynda E. Kimpe, Dominique McMahon, Bronwyn E. Keatley, Mark L. Mallory, Marianne S.V. Douglas and John P. Smol, 'Arctic Seabirds Transport Marine-derived Contaminants', *Science*, 2005, 15, vol. 309, no. 5733, p. 445.

D.A. Campbell, 'Some Observations on Top Dressing in New Zealand', *New Zealand Journal of Science and Technology*, 1948, vol. X.

Mary H. Clench and John R. Mathias, 'Intestinal Transit: How Can it be Delayed Long Enough for Birds to Act as Long-distance Dispersal Agents?', *The Auk*, 1992, 109(4): 933–6.

D.A. Croll, J.L. Maron, J.A. Estes, E.M. Danner and G.V. Byrd, 'Introduced Predators

Transform Subarctic Islands from Grassland to Tundra', *Science* 25, 2005, vol. 307, no. 5717, pp. 1959–61.

Jorge Domínguez *et al.*, *Boundary Disputes in Latin America*, Washington, D.C.: Institute of Peace, 2003.

Steve Ford, 'Preserving Your Car's Paint Finish', *The Car Guy*, 1995–2007.

Anne Fowler, 'Looking at Bird Poo', fourthcrossingwildlife.com, 2006.

Edward F. Frank, 'History of the Guano Mining Industry, Isla de Mona, Puerto Rico', *Journal of Cave and Karst Studies*, 1998, 60(2): 121–5.

Stephen K. Lower, 'Introduction to Acid-Base Chemistry', A Chem1 Reference Text, Simon Fraser University, 1999.

'The Perfect Shine', LLC, Car Polish Clinic, Autopia Detailing Library, 1999–2007.

Casey Quan, 'Guano, History and Trade', *TED Case Studies*, January 1994, vol. 3, no. 1.

Cagan H. Sekercioglu, 'Increasing Awareness of Avian Ecological Function', *Trends in Ecology & Evolution*, August 2006, Vol. 21, issue 8, pp. 464–71.

E. Skadhauge, K.H. Erlwanger, S.D. Ruziwa, V. Dantzer, V.S. Elbrond and J.P. Chamunorwa, 'Does the Ostrich (*Struthio camelus*) Coprodeum have the Electrophysiological Properties and Microstructure of Other Birds?', *Comparative Biochemistry and Physiology – Part A: Molecular & Integrative Physiology*, Elsevier, April 2003, vol. 134: 4, pp. 749–55.

Jimmy M. Skaggs, *The Great Guano Rush*, New York: Saint Martin's Press, 1994.

Steven S. Zumdahl, Susan A. Zumdahl and Paul B. Kelter, *Chemistry*, Houghton Mifflin Co., 2002 (6th edn.).

8.45 Losing Track (forgetting bag)

Alan D. Baddeley, *Essentials of Human Memory*, Psychology Press Ltd, Taylor & Francis Group, 1999.

P.J. Bayley, R.O. Hopkins and L.R. Squire, 'Successful Recollection of Remote Autobiographical Memories by Amnesic Patients with Medial Temporal Lobe Lesions', *Neuron*, 10 April 2003, 38: 135–44.

M. Boutla, T. Supalla, L. Newport and D. Bavelier, 'Short-term Memory Span: Insights from Sign Language, *Nature Neuroscience*, 2004, 7(9), pp. 1–6.

N. Cowan, 'The Magical Number 4 in Short-term Memory: A Reconsideration of Mental Storage Capacity', *Behavioral and Brain Sciences*, 2001, 24, 1–185.

K.A. Ericsson, W.G. Chase and S. Faloon, 'Acquisition of a Memory Skill', *Science*, 1980, 208, 1181–2.

S. Lehrl and B. Fischer, 'The Basic Parameters of Human Information Processing: Their Role in the Determination of Intelligence', *Personality and Individual Differences*, 1988, 9, pp. 883–96.

S. Maeshima, Y. Uematsu, F. Ozaki, K. Fujita, K. Nakai, T. Itakura and N. Komai, 'Impairment of Short-term Memory in Left Hemispheric Traumatic Brain Injuries, *Brain Injury*, 1997, 11:4, pp. 279–86.

Randi C. Martin, 'Components of Short-term Memory and Their Relation to Language Processing. Evidence from Neuropsychology and Neuroimaging', *Current Directions in Psychological Science*, 2005, vol. 14, no. 4.

Catherine E. Myers, 'Anterograde Amnesia. Memory Loss and the Brain', the Newsletter of the Memory Disorders Project at Rutgers University, 2006.

NICHCY, 'Traumatic Brain Injury', Fact Sheet 18 (FS18), Washington, D.C.: National Dissemination Center for Children with Disabilities, 2006.

M. Poirier and J. Saint-Aubin, 'Memory for Related and Unrelated Words: Further Evidence on the Influence of Semantic Factors in Immediate Serial Recall', *Quarterly Journal of Experimental Psychology*, 1995, 48A, pp. 384–404.

M. Poirier and J. Saint-Aubin, 'Immediate Serial Recall, Word Frequency, Item Identity and Item Position', *Canadian Journal of Experimental Psychology*, 1996, 50, pp. 408–12.

Eugen Tarnow, 'The Short Term Memory Structure in State-of-the-art Recall/Recognition Experiments of Rubin, Hinton and Wentzel', 2005.

K.M. Visscher, E. Kaplan, M.J. Kahana and R. Sekuler, 'Auditory Short-term Memory Behaves like Visual Short-term Memory', Public Library of Science – Biology, 2007, 5: 3.

8.55 Losing Grip (skidding on road)

J.B. Dunlop, *The History of the Pneumatic Tyre,* Alex Thorn and Co. Ltd, 1924.

Five Years of the Electronic Stability Program ESP, Web Publications Pty Ltd, 2000.

D. Hosler, S.L. Burkett and M.J. Tarkanian, 'Prehistoric Polymers: Rubber Processing in Ancient Mesoamerica', *Science*, 1999, 284 (5422), pp. 1988–91.

Don Iannone, 'Corporate History: Goodyear Tire & Rubber', *Economic Development Futures Journal*, 2006.

Ronald K. Jurgen, 'Electronic Braking, Traction and Stability Controls', Progress in Technology, Society of Automotive Engineers, 1999.

John Loadman, *Tears of the Tree: The Story of Rubber – A Modern Marvel*, Oxford University Press, 2005.

Mark Peralta, Limited slip differential, United States Patent 6402656, 2002.

Charles Slack, *Noble Obsession*, London: Hyperion, 2003.

Society of Automotive Engineers, *Advancements in ABS/TCS and Brake Technology*, Society of Automotive Engineers, 1995.

Various, 'Charles Goodyear – The Life and Discoveries of the Inventor of Vulcanized India Rubber', *Scientific American Supplement*, 31 January 1991, no. 787, pp. 19–24.

9.10 Mixing Your Drinks (diesel instead of petrol)

Paul K. Dempsey, *Troubleshooting and Repairing Diesel Engines*, Tab Electronics, 1995.

Rudolf Diesel, Patent no. 7241, 1892

Michael Kemp, 'A Costly Mistake', *Daily Telegraph*, 27 August 2005.

Herbert Kroemer and Charles Kittel, *Thermal Physics*, W.H. Freeman Co., 1980 (2nd edn.).

Crawford MacKeand, *Sparks and Flames: Ignition in Engines – An Historical Approach*, Tyndar Press, 1997.

R.H. Perry and D.W. Green, *Perry's Chemical Engineers' Handbook*, New York: McGraw Hill, Inc., 1984 (6th edn).

Royal Automobile Club of Queensland, *Mis-fuelling*, Maintenance and Repairs, Fact Sheets, 2007.

9.20 An Unpleasant Trip (tripping over)

Charles W. Anderson, 'Strategy Learning with Multilayer Connectionist Representations', *Proceedings of the Fourth International Workshop on Machine Learning*, Irvine, CA, 1987, pp. 103–14.

H.H. Ehrsson, T. Kito, N. Sadato, R.E. Passingham and E. Naito, 'Neural Substrate of Body Size: Illusory Feeling of Shrinking of the Waist', *PLoS Biology*, 2005, 3(12).

S.M. Highstein, R.R. Fay and A.N. Popper (eds.), *The Vestibular System*, Berlin: Springer, 2004.

J.R. Lackner, 'Some Proprioceptive Influences on the Perceptual Representation of Body Shape and Orientation', *Brain*, 1988, p. 111.

M.L. Lenhardt, R. Skellett, P. Wang and A.M. Clarke, 'Human Ultrasonic Speech Perception', *Science*, 1991, vol. 253, issue 5015, pp. 82–5.

Ely Rabin and Andrew M. Gordon, 'Influence of Fingertip Contact on Illusory Arm Movements', *J. Appl. Physiol.*, 2003, 96: 1555–60.

G. Robles-de-la-Torre and V. Hayward, 'Force can Overcome Object Geometry in the Perception of Shape through Active Touch', *Nature*, 2001, 412 (6845): 445–8.

David A. Winter, *A.B.C. (Anatomy, Biomechanics, Control) of Balance During Standing and Walking*, Waterloo Biomechanics, 1995.

9.30 Coming Unstuck (chewing gum in hair)

Ho Khai Leong, *Shared Responsibilities, Unshared Power: The Politics of Policy-Making in Singapore*, Eastern University, 2003 (rev. edn.).

Debora MacKenzie, 'Chewing Gum gave Stone Age Punk a Buzz', *New Scientist*, 18 September 1993, 1891, p. 7.

Cris Prystay, 'At Long Last, Gum is Legal in Singapore, but there are Strings', *Wall Street Journal*, 4 June 2004.

Michael Redclift, *Chewing Gum*, London: Routledge, 2004.

Clarence R. Robbins, *Chemical and Physical Behavior of Human Hair*,' New York: Springer-Verlag Inc., 2002 (4th rev. edn.).

Wrigleys, *All About Wrigleys*, Peoria, Il.: Wm Wrigley Jr Co., 2004.

9.40 Staying Afloat (rain-soaked clothes)

G.K. Batchelor, *An Introduction to Fluid Dynamics*, Cambridge University Press, 1967.

R. Gomes, H.F. Levison, K. Tsiganis and A. Morbidelli, 'Origin of the Cataclysmic Late Heavy Bombardment Period of the Terrestrial Planets', *Nature*, 2005, 435, 466–9.

Rebecca Harman, *The Water Cycle*, London: Heinemann Library, 2005.

James Kasting, 'How and When did Water Come into Existence on our Earth?', NASA Astrobiology Institute, 2002.

Jörn Müller and Harald Lesch, 'Woher kommt das Wasser der Erde? – Urgaswolke oder Meteoriten', *Chemie in unserer Zeit*, 2003, 37(4), pp. 242–6.

John R. Philip, 'Plant Water Relations: Some Physical Aspects', *Annu. Rev. Plant Physiol.*, 1996, 17, 245–68.

William G. Pollard, 'The Uniqueness of the Earth', *Air University Review*, July–August 1971.

Martin A. Silberberg, *Chemistry*, New York: McGraw-Hill, 2006 (4th edn.).

Various, 'Wrinkly Skin', *BMJ* fillers, 2003–4, 327: 1328-a.

Various, 'Moisture and Humidity: Measurement and Control in Science and Industry by Its Measurement and Control', *International Symposium Proceedings of Sci Symposium on Moisture and Humidity*, Instrument Society of America, 1985.

9.50 Knowing Your Place (being lost)

T. Alerstam, 'Detours in Bird Migration', *Journal of Theoretical Biology*, 2001, 209, 319–31.

Peter Berthold, *Bird Migration: A General Survey*, Oxford University Press, 2001 (2nd edn.).

S. Carrubba, C. Frilot 2nd, A.L. Chesson Jr and A.A. Marino, 'Evidence of a Nonlinear Human Magnetic Sense', *Neuroscience*, 2006, 144(1): 356–67.

Hugh Dingle, *Migration: The Biology of Life on the Move*, Oxford University Press, 1996.

David J. Griffiths, *Introduction to Electrodynamics*, Prentice Hall, 1999 (3rd edn.).

J. Marvin Herndon, 'Substructure of the Inner Core of the Earth', *PNAS*, 23 January 1996, Vol. 93, Issue 2, pp. 646–8.

Dominik Heyers, Martina Manns, Harald Luksch, Onur Güntürkün and Henrik

Mouritsen, 'A Visual Pathway Links Brain Structures Active during Magnetic Compass Orientation in Migratory Birds', *PLoS*, 2007, ONE 2(9): e937.

B. Hillier and J. Hanson, *The Social Logic of Space*, Cambridge University Press, 1984.

D.F. Hollenbach and J.M. Herndon, 'Deep-Earth Reactor: Nuclear Fission, Helium, and the Geomagnetic Field', *PNAS*, 25 September 2001, vol. 98, no. 20.

R.N. Johnson, B.P. Oldroyd, A.B. Barron and R.H. Crozier, 'Genetic Control of the Honey Bee (*Apis mellifera*) Dance Language: Segregating Dance Forms in a Backcrossed Colony', *Journal of Heredity*, The American Genetic Association, 2002, 93: 170–73.

F. Papi, P. Luschi, S. Akesson, S. Capogrossi and G.C. Hays, 'Open-sea Migration of Magnetically Disturbed Sea Turtles', *Journal of Experimental Biology*, 2002, 203: (22) 3435–43.

A.T. Scholz, R.M. Horrall, J.C. Cooper and A.D. Hasler, 'Imprinting to Chemical Cues – Basis for Home Stream Selection in Salmon', *Science*, 1976, 192: (4245), pp. 1247–9.

F. Urquhart, *The Monarch Butterfly: International Traveler*, Nelson Hall, 1987.

Rfidiger Wehner, '"Matched filters" – Neural Models of the External World', *Journal of Comparative Physiology A*, 1987, 161: 511–31.

W. Wiltschko, U. Munro, H. Ford and R. Wiltschko, 'Bird Navigation: What Type of Information does the Mahnetite-based Receiver Provide?', *Proc.R.Soc.*, 2006, B.272: 2815–20.

10.05 Pain in the Neck (bee sting)

Benjamin Lester, 'Honey Bee Defense Leaves Hornets Breathless', *ScienceNOW Daily News*, 17 September 2007.

J. Meier and J. White, *Clinical Toxicology of Animal Venoms and Poisons*, CRC Press, Inc., 1995.

E.C. Mussen, 'Wasp Stings', Bee and Pest Notes, No. 7449, IPM Education and Publications, UC Statewide IPM Project, University of California, 1998.

Alfred Neugut, Anita Ghatak and Rachel Miller, 'Anaphylaxis in the United States: An Investigation into its Epidemiology', *Arch. Intern. Med.*, 2001, 161.108, pp. 15–21.

Hye Ji Park, Seong Ho Lee, Dong Ju Son, Ki Wan Oh, Ki Hyun Kim, Ho Sueb Song, Goon Joung Kim, Goo Taeg Oh, Do Young Yoon and Jin Tae Hong, 'Antiarthritic Effect of Bee Venom: inhibition of inflammation mediator generation by suppression of NF-kappaB through interaction with the p50 subunit', NCBI, 2004, vol. 50, issue 11, 3504–15.

R. Resiman, 'Insect Stings', *New England Journal of Medicine*, 1994, 26: 523–7.

F.E. Russell, 'Venomous arthropods', *Vet. Hum. Toxicol.*, 1991, 33(5): 505–8.

J.O. Schmidt, 'Allergy to Venomous Insects', in J. Graham (ed.), *The Hive and the Honey Bee*, Hamilton, Il: Dadant & Sons, 1992.

P. Visscher, R. Vetter and S. Camazine, 'Removing Bee Stings', *Lancet*, 1996, 348 (9023): 301–2.

10.15 Lost Underfoot (sticking yourself with superglue)

Michael Ashby and David Jones, *Engineering Materials*, Oxford: Butterworth-Heinemann, 1996 (2nd edn.).

Kellar Autumn, Metin Sitti, Yiching A. Liang, Anne M. Peattie, Wendy R. Hansen, Simon Sponberg, Thomas W. Kenny, Ronald Fearing, Jacob N. Israelachvili and Robert J. Full, 'Evidence for Van der Waals Adhesion in Gecko Setae', ed. Thomas Eisner, *Proceedings of the National Academy of Sciences of the United States of America*, Ithaca, NY: Cornell University, 9 July 2002.

J. Brandrup, E.H. Immergut and E.A. Grulke (eds.), *Polymer Handbook*, New York: Wiley-Interscience, 1999 (4th edn.).

F. Jueneman, 'Stick it to 'um', Industrial Research & Development, August 1981, p. 19.

Sharon Caskey Hayes, 'Discovery of Super Glue Helped Land Coover in National Inventors Hall of Fame', *Kingsport Times-News*, 11 July 2004.

P. Montagne *et al.*, 'Gelatine', *Larousse Gastronomique*, New York: Clarkson Potter, 2001.

P.C. Painter and M.M. Coleman, *Fundamentals of Polymer Science,* CRC Press, 1997.

Robert O. Parmley, *Standard Handbook of Fastening and Joining*, McGraw-Hill Professional, 1989.

E.M. Petrie, *Handbook of Adhesives and Sealants*, McGraw-Hill Professional, 2000.

J. Quinn and J. Kissack, 'Tissue Adhesives for Laceration Repair During Sporting Events', *Clinical Journal of Sports Medicine*, 1994, Vol. 4, No. 4, p. 245.

Nathan D. Schwade, 'Wound Adhesives, 2-Octyl Cyanoacrylate', eMedicine article, 10 April 2002.

H.V. Vinters, K.A. Galil, M.J. Lundie and J.C. Kaufmann, 'The Histotoxicity of Cyanoacrylates. A Selective Review', *Neuroradiology*, 1985, 27(4): pp. 279–91.

A.G. Ward and A. Courts, *The Science and Technology of Gelatin*, New York: Academic Press, 1977.

10.35 Crossed Connections (electromagnetic interference from phone)

Jon Agar, *Constant Touch: A Global History of the Mobile Phone*, Totem Books, 2005.

Keith Armstrong and Tim Williams, 'Radiocommunications Agency EMC Awareness', Ofcom (the independent regulator and competition authority for the UK communications industries), 2007.

Association of Radio Industries and Businesses, *IMT-2000 DS-CDMA System*, 2002.

Australian Radiation Protection and Nuclear Safety Agency, Commonwealth of Australia, *Mobile Telephones Scientific Background*, 2006.

Zhi Ning Chen (ed.), *Antennas for Portable Devices*, John Wiley & Sons, 2007.

Zhi Ning Chen and M.Y.W. Chia, *Broadband Planar Antennas: Design and Applications*, John Wiley & Sons, 2006.

Peter Glotz and Stefan Bertsch (eds.), *Thumb Culture: The Meaning of Mobile Phones for Society*, Transcript Verlag, 2005.

David J. Griffiths, *Introduction to Quantum Mechanics*, Prentice Hall, 2004 (2nd edn.).

Simon Haykin, *Communication Systems*, John Wiley & Sons, 2001 (4th edn.).

Friedhelm Hillebrand (ed.), *GSM and UMTS, The Creation of Global Mobile Communications*, John Wiley & Sons, 2002.

Siegmund M. Redl, Matthias K. Weber and Malcolm W. Oliphant, *An Introduction to GSM*, Artech House, 1995.

Various, 'Inter BSC – Intra MSC Handover Call Flow', EventHelix.com Inc., 2000–2004.

Andrew J. Viterbi, *CDMA: Principles of Spread Spectrum Communication*, Prentice Hall, 1995.

10.45 Hissy Fits (puncture)

AVM Industries, 'What is a Gas Spring and How does it work?', Gas Spring Technical Guide. AVM Industries OEI Division, 1997–2006.

Donald Bastow, Geoffrey Howard and John P. Whitehead, *Car Suspension and Handling*, John Wiley & Sons, 2004 (4th edn.).

Tubal Cain, *Spring Design and Manufacture (Workshop Practice)*, Special Interest Model Books, 1998.

EUROPA, 'Climate Change: Commission Welcomes Political Agreement in the Council to Reduce Emissions of Fluorinated Greenhouse Gases', Press release IP/04/1231 from EUROPA, the portal site of the European Union, 2004.

Charles L. Perrin, 'Nike AIR Technology Explained', Charlie's Sneaker Pages, 2007.

Marion F. Rudy, Footwear (A shoe embodying a multiple chambered pneumatically inflated insert encapsulated in a yieldable foam), United States Patent 4219945, 1980.

Marion F. Rudy, Diffusion pumping apparatus self-inflating device, United States Patent 4340626, 1982.

Marion F. Rudy, Load carrying cushioning device with improved barrier material for control of diffusion pumping, United States Patent 4936029, 1990.

Marion F. Rudy, Load carrying cushioning device with improved barrier material for control of diffusion pumping, United States Patent 5042176, 1991.

J.B. Strassner and Laurie Becklund, *Swoosh: The Unauthorized Story of Nike and the Men Who Played There*, New York: HarperBusiness, 1993.

Ian Turner, *Engineering Applications of Pneumatics and Hydraulics*, London: Butterworth-Heinemann, 1995.

10.55 Mightier than the Sword (leaking pens)

Geoffrey Berliner, 'Leaking, Flooding and Other Such Inconveniences of the Fountain Pen', Berliner Pen, 2003.

Christoph Cuppers, 'On the Manufacture of Ink. Ancient Nepal', *Journal of the Department of Archaeology*, August–September 1989, No. 113, pp. 1–7.

Raymond P. Dougherty, 'Writing upon Parchment and Papyrus among the Babylonians and the Assyrians', *Journal of the American Oriental Society*, 1928, 48, pp. 109–35.

Editorial, 'Pencil Us in for the Next Y2K Disaster', *Moscow Times*, 14 January 2000.

Henry Gostony and Stuart Schneider, *The Incredible Ball Point Pen: A Comprehensive History and Price Guide*, Schiffer Publishing Ltd, 1998.

Megan Lane, 'Did Biros Really Revolutionise Writing?', BBC News Magazine, 2006.

R.A. Leng, 'Potential Rôles of Tree Fodders in Ruminant Nutrition' in *Tree Foliage in Ruminant Nutrition*, Rome: Food and Agriculture Organization of the United Nations, 1997.

C. Ainsworth Mitchell, *Inks and Their Composition and Manufacture*, Charles Griffin & Co. Ltd, 1904.

Joe Nickell, *Pen, Ink, and Evidence: A Study of Writing and Writing Materials*, University Press of Kentucky, 1990.

R. Reed, *Ancient Skins, Parchments and Leathers*, Seminar Press, 1972.

Peter Tyson, 'Fading Away', inquiry article for Saving the National Treasures, NOVA Science programming, 2005.

11.05 Seeing is not Believing (mistaken identity)

R.M. Bauer, 'Autonomic Recognition of Names and Faces in Prosopagnosia: A Neuropsychological Application of the Guilty Knowledge Test', *Neuropsychologia*, 1984, 22, pp. 457–69.

V. Bruce and A. Young, 'Understanding Face Recognition', *British Journal of Psychology*, 1986, 77 (3), pp. 305–27.

V. Bruce and A. Young, *In the Eye of the Beholder: The Science of Face Perception*, Oxford University Press, 2000.

Daniel Chandler, *Visual Perception 4*, UWA, 1997.

Leslie B. Cohen and Cara H. Cashon, 'Infant Perception and Cognition', *Comprehensive Handbook of Psychology*, vol. 6, Developmental Psychology, New York: Wiley, 2001.

M.J. Farah, *Visual Agnosia: Disorders of Object Recognition and What They Tell Us about Normal Vision*, MIT Press, 1990.

A. Glennerster *et al.*, 'Humans Ignore Motion and Stereo Cues in Favor of a Fictional Stable World', *Curr. Biol.*, 2006, 16(4): 428–32.

N.G. Kanwisher, J. McDermott and M.M. Chun, 'The Fusiform Face Area: A Module in Human Extrastriate Cortex Specialized for Face Perception', *Journal of Neuroscience*, 1997, 17 (11), pp. 4302–11.

I. Kennerknecht, T. Grueter, B. Welling, S. Wentzek, J. Horst, S. Edwards and M. Grueter, 'First Report of Prevalence of Non-syndromic Hereditary Prosopagnosia (HPA)', *Am. J. Med. Genet. A.*, 2006, 140(15): 1617–22.

R. Lickliter, M. Vaillant-Molina, L.E. Bahrick, L.C. Newell and I. Castellanos, 'Intersensory Redundancy Impairs Face Perception in Early Development', paper presented at the annual meeting of the XVth Biennial International Conference on Infant Studies, Westin Miyako, Kyoto, Japan, 2006.

C.A. Nelson, 'The Development and Neural Bases of Face Recognition', *Infant and Child Development*, 2001, 10 (1–2), pp. 3–18.

F. Newcombe, E.H.F. de Haan, M. Small and D.C. Hay, 'Dissociable Deficits after Brain Injury', Andrew W. Young (ed.), *Face and Mind*, Oxford University Press, 1998.

Y. Xu, 'Revisiting the Role of the Fusiform and Occipital Face Areas in Visual Expertise', *Cerebral Cortex*, 2005, 15, pp. 1234–42.

11.15 Ripping Yarns (torn clothing)

J.M. Adovasio, O. Soffer and B. Klíma, 'Upper Paleolithic Fibre Technology: Interlaced Woven Finds from Pavlov I, Czech Republic, *c.*26,000 Years Ago', *Antiquity*, 1996, 70(269): 526–34.

E.J.W. Barber, *Women's Work: The First 20,000 Years*, New Jersey: Princeton University Press, 1991.

Mary E. Black, *Key To Weaving*, New York: Macmillan Publishing Co. Inc., 1957.

Deborah Chandler, *Learning to Weave*, Loveland, Col.: Interweave Press, Inc., 1995.

Julie Chen, Joey Mead, Johannes Leisen, Ning Pan and Steve Warner, 'Substrate-Coating Interaction' in *Coated Fabrics*, NTC Project: F00-MD06 National Textile Center Research Briefs – Fabrication Competency, June 2003.

Wendy Chatley Green, 'Frequently Asked Questions about the Stringy Stuff Hanging from Needles and Hooks', Wool Works, 1995.

B.M. Haines and J.R. Barlow, 'The Anatomy of Leather', review, *Journal of Material Science*, 1975, 10: 525–38.

John W.S. Hearle, N. O'Hear and H.A. McKenna, *Handbook of Fibre Rope Technology*, CRC Press, 2004.

Pankaj K. Porwal, Irene J. Beyerlein and Stuart Leigh Phoenix, 'Statistical Strength of Twisted Fiber Bundles with Loadsharing Controlled by Frictional Length Scales', *Journal of Mechanics of Materials and Structures*, 2007, vol. 2, p. 4.

Sundara S. Rajan, *Modern Practical Botany*, Anmol Publications Ltd, 2002.

Anthony Sanctuary, *Rope, Twine and Net Making*, Princes Risborough, Buckinghamshire: Shire Publications Ltd, 1996.

J.C. Turner and P. van de Griend (eds.), *The History and Science of Knots*, Singapore: World Scientific, 1996.

Susan Wylly, *The Art and History of Weaving*, Georgia College and State University, 2003.

11.35 Infectious Messages (opening an email virus)

L.M. Adleman, 'An Abstract Theory of Computer Viruses', *Advances in Cryptology – Crypto '88*, LNCS 403, 1988, pp. 354–74.

ASC, Current Working Report, Anti-Spyware Coalition, Center for Democracy and Technology, 19 November 2007.

CERT/CC, 'Love Letter Worm', CERT® Advisory CA-2000-04, Carnegie Mellon University, 2000.

Graham Chapman, John Cleese, Eric Idle, Terry Jones and Michael Palin, 'Spam', final sketch of the 25th show of *Monty Python's Flying Circus*, broadcast 15 December 1970, BBC Television.

Fred Cohen, *Computer Viruses*, PhD Thesis, University of Southern California: ASP Press, 1988.

Jerry Felix and Chris Hauck, 'System Security: A Hacker's Perspective', *Interex Proceedings*, 1987, 1: 6.

Gunter Ollmann, 'The Phishing Guide: Understanding and Preventing Phishing Attacks', Network Security Library: Phishing, WindowSecurity.com, 2005.

David Streitfeld, 'History of Spam: Opening Pandora's In-Box', *Los Angeles Times*, Business, 11 May 2003.

Symantec, 'Internet Security Threat', Report Volume XII, Symantec Corporation, September 2007.

Zakiya M. Tamimi and Javed I. Khan, 'Model-based Analysis of Two Fighting Worms', IEEE/IIU *Proc. of ICCCE '06*, Kuala Lumpur, Malaysia, May 2006, vol. I, pp. 157–63.

Ken Thompson, 'Reflections on Trusting Trust', Turing Award Lecture, ACM, 1983.

H. Toyoizumi and A. Kara, 'Predators: Good Will Mobile Codes Combat against Computer Viruses', *Proc. of the 2002 New Security Paradigms Workshop*, 2002.

Various, *History of Malware*, Kaspersky Lab, 1996–2007.

A. Young and M. Yung, 'Cryptovirology: Extortion-based Security Threats and Countermeasures', IEEE Symposium on Security and Privacy, 1996, pp. 129–41.

13.00 Tight Squeeze (jammed)

Associated Press, 'Wal-Mart Worker Gets his Finger Stuck', 18 October 2007.

John J. Bergan (ed.), *The Vein Book*, London: Academic Press, 2006.

Gordon G. Giesbrecht, James A. Wilkerson and Andrea R. Gravatt, *Hypothermia, Frostbite and Other Cold Injuries: Prevention, Survival, Rescue and Treatment*, Mountaineers Books, 2006 (2nd edn.).

Vinay Kumar, Abul K. Abbas and Nelson Fausto, *Robbins and Cotran Pathologic Basis of Disease*, Philadelphia: W.B Saunders Co., 2004.

Jeffrey C. Leggit and Christian J. Meko, 'Acute Finger Injuries: Part I. Tendons and Ligaments', *American Family Physician*, 2006, vol. 73: 5.

Robert D. Olsen, *Scott's Fingerprint Mechanics*, Springfield, Il: Charles C. Thomas, 1978.

Pam Walker and Elaine Wood, *The Circulatory System (Understanding the Human Body)*, Lucent Books, 2003.

U. Wiedermann *et al.*, 'Vitamin A Deficiency Increases Inflammatory Responses', *Scand. J. Immunol.*, 1996, 44 (6): 578–84.

13.30 Fading Memories (computer hard disk failure)

Aris Christou, *Electromigration and Electronic Device Degradation*, John Wiley & Sons, 1994.

C. Evans-Pughe, 'Live Fast, Die Young', the Knowledge Network: Electronics, Institution of Engineering and Technology, 2007.

P.S. Ho, 'Basic Problems for Electromigration in VLSI Applications', *Proceedings of the IEEE*, 1982, IRPS: 288–91.

Charles M. Kozierok, 'Troubleshooting Hard Disk Drives', the PC Guide, 1997–2004.

Brien M. Posey, *Repairing Hard Disk Problems*, Posey Enterprises, 2002.

Ian R. Sinclair, *Hard Drives Made Simple*, Made Simple Books, 1995.

14.40 Shattered Hopes (broken finger)

A. Larry Arsenault and F. Peter Ottensmeyer, 'Visualization of Early Intra-membranous Ossification by Electron Microscopic and Spectroscopic Imaging', *Journal of Cell Biology*, 1984, vol. 98, pp. 911–21.

Barbara Bain, David M. Clark, Irvin A. Lampert and Bridget S. Wilkins, *Bone Marrow Pathology*, Blackwell Science Ltd, 2001 (3rd edn.).

J.M. Connor, *Soft Tissue Ossification*, Springer-Verlag, 1983.

Alan R. Gaby, *Preventing and Reversing Osteoporosis*, Prima Life, 1995.

Stephen Jay Gould and Elizabeth S. Vrba, 'Exaptation – A Missing Term in the Science of Form', *Paleobiology*, 1982, 8 (1): 4–15.

E.N. Marieb, *Human Anatomy & Physiology*, California: Benjamin/Cummings Science Publishing, 1998.

Frank H. Netter, *Musculoskeletal System: Anatomy, Physiology, and Metabolic Disorders*, New Jersey: Summit, Ciba-Geigy Corporation, 1987.

Beth W. Orenstein, 'Lost in Space: Bone Mass', *Radiology Today*, 2004, vol. 5, no. 16, p. 10.

St Andrew's Ambulance Association, St John Ambulance, British Red Cross, *First Aid Manual: The Authorised Manual of St. John Ambulance, St. Andrew's Ambulance Association and the British Red Cross*, London: Dorling Kindersley Ltd, 2006 (8th edn.).

G.J. Tortora, *Principles of Human Anatomy*, New York: Harper & Row Publishers, 1989 (5th edn.).

H.K. Väänänen, H. Zhao, M. Mulari and J.M. Halleen, 'The Cell Biology of Osteoclast Function', *J. Cell. Sci.*, 2000, 113, Pt 3, pp.377–81.

Xavier Wertz, Damien Schoëvaërt, Habibou Maitournam, Philippe Chassignet and Laurent Schwartz, 'The Effect of Hormones on Bone Growth is Mediated through Mechanical Stress', *Comptes Rendus Biologies*, 2006, vol. 329, issue 2, pp. 79–85.

B. Wopenka and J.D. Pasteris, 'A Mineralogical Perspective on the Apatite in Bone', *Materials Science and Engineering*, 2005, C. 25(2): 131.

17.50 That Sinking Feeling (dropping keys down drain)

Ugo Besson, 'How does Weight Depend on Mountain Altitude?', *European Journal of Physics*, 2006, 27, pp. 743–53.

R.P. Feynman, F.B. Morinigo, W.G. Wagner and B. Hatfield, *Feynman Lectures on Gravitation*, Addison-Wesley, 1995.

David J. Griffiths, *Introduction to Electrodynamics*, Prentice Hall, 1998 (3rd edn.).

David Halliday, Robert Resnick and Kenneth S. Krane, *Physics v. 1*, New York: John Wiley & Sons, 2001.

S.W. Hawking and W. Israel, *General Relativity: An Einstein Centenary Survey*, Cambridge University Press, 1979.

Brian May, Sir Patrick Moore and Chris Lintott, *Bang! The Complete History of the Universe*, Carlton Books Ltd, 2007.

Lisa Randall, *Warped Passages: Unraveling the Universe's Hidden Dimensions*, New York: HarperCollins, 2005.

Edward J. Rothwell and Michael J. Cloud, *Electromagnetics*, CRC Press, 2001.

Paul Tipler, *Physics for Scientists and Engineers: Vol. 2: Light, Electricity and Magnetism*, W.H. Freeman, 1998 (4th edn.).

Paul Tipler, *Physics for Scientists and Engineers: Mechanics, Oscillations and Waves, Thermodynamics*, W.H. Freeman, 2004 (5th edn.).

18.10 Feel the Burn (pulled muscle)

G.A. Brooks, T.D. Fahey and T.P. White, *Exercise Physiology: Human Bioenergetics and its Applications*, Mayfield Publishing Co. Holt, Rinehart & Winston, 1996 (2nd edn.).

C. Byrne and R.G. Eston, 'Exercise, Muscle Damage and Delayed Onset Muscle Soreness', *Sports Exercise and Injury*, 1998, 4, pp. 69–73.

E.B. Colliander and P.A. Tesch, 'Effects of Eccentric and Concentric Muscle Actions in Resistance Training', *Acta Physiol. Scand.*, 1990, 140 (1): 31–9.

David L. Costill and Jack H. Wilmore, *Physiology of Sport and Exercise*, Champaign, Illinois: Human Kinetics, 2004.

E.L. Fox, R.W. Bowers and M.L. Foss, *The Physiological Basis for Exercise and Sport*, Dubuque, IA: W.C. Brown, 1993 (5th edn.).

William F. Ganong, *Review of Medical Physiology* (Lange Basic Science), McGraw-Hill Medical, 2005 (22nd edn.).

R.J. Maughan, M. Gleeson and P.L. Greenhaff, *Biochemistry of Exercise and Training*, Oxford University Press, 1997.

Satoshi Ota and Naruya Saitou, 'Phylogenetic Relationship of Muscle Tissues Deduced from Superimposition of Gene Trees', *Mol. Biol. Evol.*, 1999, 16(6): 856–7.

George A. Ordway and Daniel J. Garry, 'Myoglobin: An Essential Hemoprotein in Striated Muscle', *Journal of Experimental Biology*, 2004, 207, pp. 3441–6.

U. Schlattner, M. Tokarska-Schlattner and T. Wallimann, 'Mitochondrial Creatine Kinase in Human Health and Disease', *Biochemica et Biophysica Acta*, 2005, 27.

18.20 Kitchen Fireworks (sparking microwaves)

Louis A. Bloomfield, *How Everything Works: Making Physics Out of the Ordinary*, New York: John Wiley & Sons, 2006.

J. Carlton Gallawa, *The Complete Microwave Oven Service Handbook – Operation, Maintenance, Troubleshooting and Repair*, CD-ROM, 2007.

Don Murray, 'Percy Spencer and His Itch to Know', *Readers Digest*, August 1958, p.114.

Tapan K. Sarkar, Robert Mailloux, Arthur A. Oliner, Magdalena SalazarPalma and Dipak L. Sengupta, *History of Wireless*, Wiley Series in Microwave and Optical Engineering, New York: John Wiley & Sons, 2006.

P.L. Spencer, Method for Treating Foodstuffs, US Patent number 2495429, 1950.

Paul Tipler, *Physics for Scientists and Engineers: Vol. 2: Light, Electricity and Magnetism*, W.H. Freeman, 1998 (4th edn.).

18.30 Finally Cracked (broken glass)

S.A. Baeurle, A. Hotta and A.A. Guse, 'On the Glassy State of Multiphase and Pure Polymer Materials', *Polymer*, 2006, 47: 6243–53.

Judy Bird, 'More than Just a Glassful!', *RB Magazine*, January 2007.

F. Celarie, S. Prades, D. Bonamy, L. Ferrero, E. Bouchaud, C. Guillot and C. Marliere, 'Glass Breaks like Metal, but at the Nanometer Scale', *Phys. Rev. Lett.*, 21 February 2003, 90, 075504.

Marcus Chown, 'Why do Teardrops Explode?', *New Scientist*, 11 February 1995.

Corning Museum of Glass, *Prince Rupert's Drop and Glass Stress*, New York: Corning Museum of Glass, 2002–2007.

William S. Ellis, *Glass*, New York: Avon Books Inc., 1988.

F.M. Ernsberger, in D.R. Uhlmann and N.J. Kreidle (eds.), *Glass: Science and Technology*, Vol. 5, New York: Academic Press, 1980.

Amir Fama and Sami Rizkalla, 'Structural Performance of Laminated and Unlaminated Tempered Glass under Monotonic Transverse Loading', *Construction and Building Materials*, 2006, vol. 20, issue 9, pp. 761–8.

D.G. Holloway, *The Physical Properties of Glass*, London: Wykeham, 1973.

D. Johannsmanna, 'The Glass Transition and Contact Mechanical Experiments on Polymer Surfaces', *Eur. Phys. J.E.*, 2002, 8, pp. 257–9.

C.A. Tolman and N.B. Jackson in W.T. Lippincott (ed.), *Essays in Physical Chemistry*, Washington, D.C.: American Chemical Society, 1988.

Masayuki Yamane and Yoshiyuki Asahara, *Glasses for Photonics*, Cambridge University Press, 2005.

18.40 A Black Mark (stains)

Susan Druding, 'Fiber Reactive Dyes and Cibacron F in particular', Textile Artists' Newsletter [TAN], 1982, vol. III, no. 3.

Dianne N. Epp, *The Chemistry of Vat Dyes*, Palette of Color Series, Middleton, Ohio: Terrific Science Press, 1995.

C.H. Giles, David G. Duff and Roy S. Sinclair, *Giles's Laboratory Course in Dyeing*, Society of Dyers & Colourists, 1989 (4th edn.).

R.W. Horobin and J.A. Kiernan (eds.), *Conn's Biological Stains: A Handbook of Dyes, Stains and Fluorochromes for Use in Biology and Medicine*, Bios Scientific Publishers Ltd, 2002 (10th edn.).

Victor B. Ivanov, *Reactive Dyes in Biology*, New York: Harwood Academic Publishers, 1987 (English translation).

Julie Johnson, 'Out, Out Damned Spot!', *New Scientist*, 24 December 1994.

John Shore (ed.), *Cellulosics Dyeing*, Yorkshire, UK: Society of Dyers and Colourists, 1995.

David R. Waring and Geoffrey Hallas (eds.), *The Chemistry and Application of Dyes*, Topics in Applied Chemistry, Kluwer Academic/Plenum Publishers, 1990.

19.00 Hot and Bothered (chilli pepper in eye)

AOAC, 'Official Method 995.03 Capsaicinoids in Capsicums and their Extractives, Liquid Chromatographic Method, First Action', *J. AOAC Int.*, 1995.

Catherine L. Barker, 'Hot Pod: World's Hottest Chillies', *National Geographic Magazine*, May 2007, p. 21.

Terry Berke, Proceedings of the 16th International Pepper Conference, Tampico, Tamaulipas, Mexico, 10–12 November 2002.

J. Billing and P.W. Sherman, 'Antimicrobial Functions of Spices: Why Some Like it Hot', *Quarterly Review of Biology*, 1998, 73 (1): 3–49.

A.M. Binshtok, B.P. Bean and C.J. Woolf, 'Inhibition of Nociceptors by TRPV1-mediated Entry of Impermanent Sodium Channel Blockers', *Nature*, 2007, 449 (7162): 607–10.

P. W Bosland, 'Capsicums: Innovative Uses of an Ancient Crop', in J. Janick (ed.), *Progress in New Crops*, Arlington, VA: ASHS Press, 1996.

Elizabeth Collingham, *Curry*, Oxford University Press, 2006.

Dave DeWitt, *The Chile Pepper Encyclopedia: Everything You'll Ever Need To Know About Hot Peppers*, Diane Publishing Co., 2003.

R. Mathur *et al.*, 'The Hottest Chili Variety in India', *Current Science*, 2000, 79 (3).

L. Perry *et al.*, 'Starch Fossils and the Domestication and Dispersal of Chili Peppers (*Capsicum* spp. L.) in the Americas', *Science*, 2007, 315: 986–8.

Paul Rozin1 and Deborah Schiller, 'The Nature and Acquisition of a Preference for Chili Pepper by Humans', *Motivation and Emotion*, 1980, 4 (1): 77–101.

C.G. Smith and W. Stopford, 'Health Hazards of Pepper Spray', *North Carolina Medical Journal*, 1999, 60: 268–74.

Donna R. Tainter and Anthony T. Grenis, *Spices and Seasonings*, New York: John Wiley & Sons, 2001.

Joshua J. Tewksbury and Gary P. Nabhan, 'Seed Dispersal: Directed Deterrence by Capsaicin in Chillies', *Nature*, 2001, 412, pp. 403–4.

A. Tiwari *et al.*, 'Adaptability and Production of Hottest Chili Variety under Gwalior Climatic Conditions', *Current Science*, 2005, 88 (10).

W.A. Watson, K.R. Stremel and E.J. Westdorp, 'Oleoresin Capsicum (cap-stun) Toxicity from Aerosol Exposures', *Ann Pharmacotherapy*, 1996, 30: 733–5.

19.15 Taking it All in (food on the floor)

Mark Feldman, Lawrence S. Friedman and Lawrence J. Brandt, *Sleisenger and Fordtran's Gastrointestinal and Liver Disease: Pathophysiology, Diagnosis, Management, 2-Volume Set*, New York: Elsevier, 2006 (8th edn.).

F. Guarner, G. Perdigon, G. Corthier, S. Salminen, B. Koletzko and L. Morelli, 'Should Yoghurt Cultures be Considered Probiotic?', *Br. J. Nutr.*, June 2005, 93(6): 783–6.

Arthur C. Guyton and John E. Hall, *Textbook of Medical Physiology*, New York: Elsevier, 2005 (11th edn.).

D. Kelly and J. Nadeau, 'Oral Rehydration Solution: A "Low-Tech" Oft Neglected Therapy', *Nutrition Issues in Gastroenterology*, 2004, 21: 51–62.

M. Salvatierra, A. Molina, M. Gamboa and M.L. Arias, 'Evaluation of the Effect of

Probiotic Cultures on Two Different Yogurt Brands over a Known Population of *Staphylococcus aureus* and the Production of Thermonuclease', *Arch. Latinoam Nutr.*, September 2004, 54(3): 298–302.

Alexander Swidsinski, Vera Loening-Baucke, Mario Vaneechoutte and Yvonne Doerffel, 'Active Crohn's Disease and Ulcerative Colitis can be Specifically Diagnosed and Monitored Based on the Biostructure of the Fecal Flora', *Inflamm. Bowel Dis.*, 29 November 2007.

Arthur J. Vander, James Sherman, Dorothy S. Luciano, Eric P. Widmaier (eds.), Hershel Raff (ed.) and Kevin T. Strang (ed.), *Human Physiology: The Mechanisms of Body Function*, New York: McGraw-Hill Education, 2003 (9th edn.).

19.40 Shocking (lightning kills the TV)

Charles K. Adams, *Nature's Electricity*, Pennsylvania: Tab Books, 1987.

Yoshihiro Baba and Vladimir A. Rakov, 'Voltages Induced on an Overhead Wire by Lightning Strikes to a Nearby Tall Grounded Object', *IEEE Transactions on Electromagnetic Compatibility*, 2006, vol. 48, no. 1.

D.J. Boccippio *et al.*, 'Sprites, ELF Transients, and Positive Ground Strokes', *Science*, 1995, 269: 1088–91.

D.W. Clifford, 'Aircraft Mishap Experience from Atmospheric Electricity Hazards', AGARD-LS-110, June 1980.

John D. Cutnell and Kenneth W. Johnson, *Physics*, New York: John Wiley & Sons, 1995 (3rd edn.).

F.A. Fisher and J.A. Plumer, 'Lightning Protection of Aircraft', NASA RP-1008, October 1977.

Alicia Frazier, *Theories of Lightning Formation*, Department of Atmospheric and Oceanic Sciences, University of Colorado, Boulder, 2005.

B.C. Gabrielson, *The Aerospace Engineers Handbook of Lightning Protection*, Gainesville, VA: Don White Publishing, 1986.

John Gookin, 'Backcountry Lightning Safety Guidelines', National Outdoor Leadership School, 2006.

P.H. Handel, 'Polarization Catastrophe Theory of Cloud Electricity Speculation on a New Mechanism for Thunderstorm Electrification', *Journal of Geophysical Research*, 20 June 1985, vol. 9, no. 03, pp. 5857–63.

Z.I. Kawasaki, T. Kanao, K. Matsuura, M. Nakano *et al.*, 'The Electric Field Changes and UHF Radiations Caused by the Lightning in Japan', Abstract, *Geophysical Research Letters*, 1991.

J.L. Knighten, 'An Overview of EMP Hardening Requirements', presented at the 1984 IEEE Regional Conference on EMC, San Diego, CA.

David R. Lide, *Handbook of Chemistry and Physics*, New York: CRC Press, 1996.

Zinnia Nair, K.M. Aparna, R.S. Khandagale and T.V. Gopalan, 'Failure of 220 kV Double Circuit Transmission Line Tower due to Lightning', *Journal of*

Performance of Constructed Facilities, 2005, vol. 19, no. 2.

V.A. Rakov and Martin A. Uman, *Lightning, Physics and Effects*, Cambridge University Press, 2003.

Mark Shrope, 'Lightning Research: The Bolt Catchers', *Nature*, 2004, 431: 120–21.

Martin A. Uman, *All About Lightning*, New York: Dover Publications, Inc., 1986.

US Department of Defense, The Militarily Critical Technologies List Part II: Weapons of Mass Destruction Technologies, Nuclear Weapons Effects Technology, 1998.

Lars Wåhlin, *Atmosphere electrostatics*, Forest Grove, Or: Research Studies Press, 1986.

20.15 Pus in Boots (burns and blisters)

Carol Allison, 'Hot Liquid Pleasure (The History of Tea, Coffee and Chocolate)', transcript of March 2004 meeting of the Keyworth and District Local History Society.

Chrissie Bosworth Bousfield, *Burn Trauma: Management and Nursing Care*, New York: John Wiley & Sons, 2001 (2nd edn.).

J. Martin Carlson, 'The Friction Factor', *OrthoKineticReview, Orthotics&Prosthetics*, November/December 2001.

Tammy Hanna and J. Martin Carlson, 'Freedom from Friction', *OrthoKineticReview*, March/April 2004.

Shehan Hettiaratchy, Remo Papini and Peter Dziewulski (eds.), *ABC of Burns*, BMJ Books, 2002.

J.J. Knapik, K.L. Reynolds, K.L. Duplantis and B.H. Jones, 'Friction Blisters: Pathophysiology, Prevention and Treatment', *Sports Medicine*, 1996, 20(3): 136–47.

Yu Lu and Francis Ross Carpenter, *The Classic of Tea: Origins and Rituals*, New York: Ecco Press, 1995.

Peter Schmid, 'Quantitation of Specific Proteins in Blister Fluid', *Journal of Investigative Dermatology*, 1970, vol 55: 4.

St Andrew's Ambulance Association, St John Ambulance, British Red Cross, *First Aid Manual: The Authorised Manual of St John Ambulance, St Andrew's Ambulance Association, and the British Red Cross*, London: Dorling Kindersley Ltd, 2006 (8th edn.).

A.H. Swain, B.S. Azadian, C.J. Wakeley and P.G. Shakespeare, 'Management of Blisters in Minor Burns', *British Medical Journal*, 1987, 295, p. 181.

Fukuya Yasuhiko, Takano Kunio, Fujimaki Ayako, Noguchi Norio, Ganno Hideaki and Miura Takako, 'Clinical Comparison on Blister-burns: Preservation of Blister Liquid vs. Aspiration', *Japan Journal of Burn Injuries*, 2002, vol. 28: 2, pp. 80–86.

20.45 Jumping Tunes (scratched CD)

Luc Baert, *Digital Audio and Compact Disc Technology*, Focal Press, 1995 (3rd edn.).

Tom Bishop, 'Is Music Safe on Compact Disc?', BBC News, 27 August 2004.

A. Earnshaw and Norman Greenwood, *Chemistry of the Elements*, London: Butterworth-Heinemann, 1997 (2nd edn.).

R. Gordon Gould, 'The LASER, Light Amplification by Stimulated Emission of Radiation', Ann Arbor Conference on Optical Pumping, June 1959.

Kenichi Iga, 'Surface-emitting Laser – Its Birth and Generation of New Opto-electronics Field, *IEEE Journal of Selected Topics in Quantum Electronics*, 2000, 6(6): 1201–15.

T. Kasparis and J. Lane, 'Adaptive Scratch Noise Filtering', *IEEE Transactions on Consumer Electronics*, 1993, Vol. 39, Issue 4, pp. 917–22.

OSTA, CD-R & CD-RW Questions and Answers, OSTA Optical Storage Association, OSTA-4, Revision 2.00, 15 July 1997.

James T. Russell, Photographic Record of Digital Information and Playback System Including Optical Scanner, United States Patent 3624284, 1971.

Bahaa E.A. Saleh and Malvin Carl Teich, *Fundamentals of Photonics*, New York: John Wiley & Sons, 1991.

Paul Tipler, *Physics for Scientists and Engineers: Vol. 2: Light, Electricity and Magnetism*, W.H. Freeman, 1998.

USByte, Compact Disk (CD), USByte. eMag Solutions LLC, 2006.

21.00 Chewing it Over (broken tooth)

Aetna Inc., *Oral & Dental Health Basics: Fractured and Broken Teeth*, Colgate World of Care, Aetna, Inc., 2005.

B.T. Amaechi and S.M. Higham, 'In Vitro Remineralisation of Eroded Enamel Lesions by Saliva', *Journal of Dentistry*, July 2001, Vol. 29, No. 5, pp. 371–6(6).

M. Ash and Stanley J. Nelson, *Wheeler's Dental Anatomy, Physiology, and Occlusion*, 2003 (8th edn.).

K.K. Cheng, Iain Chalmers and Trevor A. Sheldo, 'Adding Fluoride to Water Supplies', *British Medical Journal*, 2007, 335: 699–702.

William S. Cordua, *The Hardness of Minerals and Rocks*, Lapidary Digest, 1998.

M. Eisenburger, M. Addy, J.A. Hughes and R.P. Shellis, 'Effect of Time on the Remineralisation of Enamel by Synthetic Saliva after Citric Acid Erosion', *Caries Research*, 2001, 35: 211–15.

J.M. Hardie, 'The Microbiology of Dental Caries', *Dental Update*, 1982, 9, pp. 199–208.

P.J. Holloway, 'The Role of Sugar in the Etiology of Dental Caries', *Journal of Dentistry*, 1983, 11, 189–213.

C.R. McHenry, S. Wroe, P.D. Clausen, K. Moreno and E. Cunningham, 'Supermodeled Sabercat, Predatory Behaviour in *Smilodon fatalis* Revealed by High-resolution 3-D Computer Simulation', *PNAS*, 2007, 104: 10610–15.

B.W. Neville, D. Damm, C. Allen and J. Bouquot, *Oral & Maxillofacial Pathology*, New York: W.B. Saunders, 2002 (2nd edn.).

Karl-Erich, Schmittner and Pierre, Giresse, 1999. Micro-environmental Controls on Biomineralization: Superficial Processes of Apatite and Calcite Precipitation in Quaternary Soils, Roussillon, France', *Sedimentology*, 1999, 46/3: 463–76.

A.R. Ten Cate, *Oral Histology: Development, Structure, and Function*, Saint Louis: Mosby-Year Book, 1998 (5th edn.).

21.45 Patience and Pain (stubbing toe)

M.F. Bear, B.W. Connors and M.A. Paradiso, *Neuroscience: Exploring the Brain*, Baltimore: Lippincott, 2001.

J.R. Clay, 'Axonal Excitability Revisited', *Prog. Biophys. Mol. Biol.*, 2005, 88(1): 59–90.

Robbie Davis-Floyd and Joseph Dumit (eds.), *Cyborg Babies: From Techno-Sex to Techno-Tots*, New York and London: Routledge, 1998.

A.L. Hodgkin and A.F. Huxley, 'A Quantitative Description of Membrane Current and its Application to Conduction and Excitation in Nerve', *J. Physiol.*, 1952, 117(4): 500–44.

B. Feinstein, J. Langton, R. Jameson and F. Schiller, 'Experiments on Pain Referred from Deep Somatic Tissues', *J. Bone Joint Surg.*, 1954, 36-A(5): 981–97.

E.R. Kandel, J.H. Schwartz and T.M. Jessell, *Principles of Neural Science*, New York: McGraw-Hill, 2000 (4th edn.).

Don Ranney, 'Anatomy of Pain', Ontario Inter-Urban Pain Conference, Waterloo, 29 November 1996.

D.J. Taylor, N.P.O. Green and G.W. Stout, *Biological Sciences*, Cambridge University Press, 2003 (3rd edn.).

Ann Waugh and Allison Grant, *Anatomy and Physiology in Health and Illness*, Edinburgh: Churchill Livingstone, 2001.

M.G. Zhao, H. Toyoda, Y.S. Lee, L.J. Wu, S.W. Ko, X.H. Zhang, Y. Jia, F. Shum, H. Xu, B.M. Li, B.K. Kaang and M. Zhuo, 'Roles of NMDA NR2B Subtype Receptor in Prefrontal Long-term Potentiation and Contextual Fear Memory', *Neuron*, 2005, 47(6): 859–72.

20.00 Eureka! (overflowing bath)

B. Baldwin, 'The Date, Identity and Career of Vitruvius', *Latomus*, 1990, 49, 425–34.

David Biello, 'Fact or Fiction?: Archimedes Coined the Term "Eureka!" in the Bath', *Scientific American*, 8 December 2006.

Craig R. Carignan and David L. Akin, 'Actively Controlled Mockups for EVA Training in Neutral Buoyancy', IEEE International Conference on Systems, Man and Cybernetics, 1997.

Robert Jackson, *Liners, Tankers, Merchant Ships: 300 of the World's Greatest Commercial Vessels*, Expert Guide, Grange Books, 2002.

Mitch Leslie (ed.), 'The First Eureka Moment', *Science*, 2004, 305: 1219.

Paul Tipler, *Physics for Scientists and Engineers: Mechanics, Oscillations and Waves, Thermodynamics*, W.H. Freeman, 2004 (5th edn.).

J.S. Turner, *Buoyancy Effects in Fluids*, Cambridge University Press, 1979.

Acknowledgements

Thanks to: Gordon Wise and Kate Cooper for the deals and advice; my editor, Sophie Lazar, for her enthusiasm and constructive criticism for this book; Udi Schlessinger and Nguyet Ta for their feedback, proof-reading and fact-checking. Also to all the scientists and their efforts referenced in this book for their dedication and hard work in the quest for improving our understanding of the world around us. And to you, my reader, for your curiosity. Be careful what you believe and never stop asking, *why?*

And finally (as usual) I would like to thank the cruel and indifferent, yet astonishingly creative process of evolution for providing the inspiration for all of my work. Long may it continue to do so.

Science is an incremental process of improvement. If you spot something in this book you think is inaccurate, out of date or wrong, feel free to get in touch at <ithinkyourewrong@peterjbentley.com> and tell me about it. However, I'm afraid I will believe you only if you provide the evidence with a complete reference to the original source of your information, which should have been verified, preferably through peer-review (a web page address is not good enough, sorry). I can't promise to reply to all emails, but I will read them all! If you provide a valid amendment that is used in future editions, you will be acknowledged in the book.

Index